Popular Resistance in the French Wars

Also by Charles J. Esdaile

THE SPANISH ARMY IN THE PENINSULAR WAR

THE DUKE OF WELLINGTON AND THE COMMAND OF THE SPANISH ARMY

THE WARS OF NAPOLEON

SPAIN IN THE LIBERAL AGE: From Constitution to Civil War

THE FRENCH WARS

THE PENINSULAR WAR: A New History

FIGHTING NAPOLEON: Guerrillas, Bandits and Adventurers in Spain, 1808–1814

Popular Resistance in the French Wars

Patriots, Partisans and Land Pirates

Edited by

Charles J. Esdaile

To John with sincere worries about him not having better things to spend his money on!

palgrave
macmillan

First published 2005 by
PALGRAVE MACMILLAN
Houndmills, Basingstoke, Hampshire RG21 6XS and
175 Fifth Avenue, New York, N.Y. 10010
Companies and representatives throughout the world

PALGRAVE MACMILLAN is the global academic imprint of the Palgrave
Macmillan division of St. Martin's Press, LLC and of Palgrave Macmillan Ltd.
Macmillan® is a registered trademark in the United States, United Kingdom
and other countries. Palgrave is a registered trademark in the European
Union and other countries.

ISBN 978-1-4039-3826-8

This book is printed on paper suitable for recycling and made from fully
managed and sustained forest sources.

A catalogue record for this book is available from the British Library.

Library of Congress Cataloging-in-Publication Data
Popular resistance in the French wars : patriots, partisans and land pirates /
    edited by Charles J. Esdaile.
       p.   cm.
    "The papers contained in this volume of essays were originally presented
    at a symposium held in the School of History in the University of
    Liverpool in September 2003"—Pref.
    Includes bibliographical references and index.
    ISBN 978-1-4039-3826-8 (cloth)
    1. Wars of Liberation, 1813–1814.   2. Guerrilla warfare—Europe—
    History—19th century.   3. Napoleonic Wars, 1800–1815—Underground
    movements.   4. France—History, Military—1789–1815.
    5. Europe—History, Military—1789–1815.   6. Europe—Politics and
    government—1789–1815.   7. Nationalism—Europe—History—
    19th century.   I. University of Liverpool. School of History.
    DC236.P66 2004
    940.2'73—dc22   2004053529

10   9   8   7   6   5   4   3   2   1
14   13   12   11   10   09   08   07   06   05

This book is respectfully dedicated to the memory of the 192 citizens of Madrid who died in the terrorist attacks of 11 March 2004, and especially to that of Marion Subervieille, azafata *of the Biblióteca Nacional: the world is a sadder place without her smile*

This page intentionally left blank

Contents

List of Figures

Preface

The papers contained in this volume of essays were originally presented at a symposium held in the School of History in the University of Liverpool in September 2003. One of a series of bi-annual meetings of scholars working on the Napoleonic period, it was funded by the British Academy, the London branch of the Instituto de Cervantes and the University of Liverpool, and to all of these organizations I should like to extend my special thanks. To all the contributors, too, I am most grateful: they have been models of patience and hard work and have in a number of cases withstood the assaults of an all too heavy editorial hand with grace and good humour. If any of them are to be singled out, it should be my research assistant, Leonor Hernández Enviz, whose diligence, efficiency and sense of responsibility is the foundation of much that is contained within these pages. Behind the scenes, meanwhile, there stand my Head of School, Professor Pauline Stafford; our devoted School Administrator, Val Fry; and, at Palgrave Macmillan, Luciana O'Flaherty and Daniel Bunyard. Last but not least, there come my family: without their support and love none of this would have ever happened.

CHARLES ESDAILE

Liverpool

Acknowledgement

With regard to the jacket picture, which is here published for the first time, special thanks are due to the owner, Ilustrísimo Señor Don Antonio Gómez de Olea Nevada, Marqués de Velascó, who has kindly given his permission for its reproduction, and to the latter's nephew, Teniente Coronel Don José Pardo de Figueroa, of the Spanish army's Escuela de Guerra, whose good offices have throughout been of inestimable help in this connection. As so often before, then, the author is deeply indebted to Spanish generosity.

Notes on Contributors

Martin Boycott-Brown was for many years an English teacher in northern Italy. In 2002 he published *The Road to Rivoli: Napoleon's First Campaign*.

Emilie Delivré is a doctoral student at the European University Institute in Florence. She is working on the subject of political catechism in the Age of Revolution, and has presented papers at a number of international conferences.

Charles J. Esdaile is a Reader in History at the University of Liverpool. The author of numerous works on the Napoleonic period, including, most recently, *The Peninsular War: a New History* (2002), and *Fighting Napoleon: Guerrillas, Bandits and Adventurers in Spain, 1808–14* (2004), he is currently working on an international history of Napoleonic Europe.

Alan Forrest is a leading specialist on the French Revolution. He has a Chair in the Department of History at the University of York, and is the author of many works on the Revolution and its armies, including the seminal *Napoleon's Men: the Soldiers of the Revolution and Empire* (2002).

Janet Hartley has a personal chair in the Department of International History at the London School of Economics. Britain's leading expert on Russia in the Napoleonic period, she is the author of *Alexander I* (1994).

Leonor Hernández Enviz is a freelance researcher living in Madrid. She is the author of various conference papers on the Peninsular War, and is at present preparing a doctoral thesis at the Universidad Complutense.

Antonio Moliner Prada is a professor at the Universidad Autónoma de Barcelona. A leading specialist on Spain and, especially, Catalonia, in the Napoleonic period, his many publications include *La Catalunya Resistent a la Dominació Francesa, 1808–1812: la Junta Superior de Catalunya* (Edicions 62, 1989), *La Guerra del Francés a Mallorca, 1808–1814* (2000) and *La Guerrilla en la Guerra de la Independencia* (2004).

Michael Rowe was until the summer of 2004 a lecturer in History at Queen's University, Belfast. As this work was going to press, however, he was appointed to a lectureship at King's College, London. The editor of a collection of essays on Napoleonic Europe that was published by Palgrave Macmillan in 2003, in the same year he also published *From Reich to State: the Rhineland in the Revolutionary Age, 1780–1830* (2003).

Vittorio Scotti-Douglas is a senior fellow at the University of Trieste and is the editor of the historical journal, *Spagna Contemporanea*. An expert on the contents of the Archivo General de Simancas, he has published a variety of articles and conference papers on the Peninsular War.

This page intentionally left blank

1
Patriots, Partisans and Land Pirates in Retrospect

Charles J. Esdaile

Summarizing two days of lively academic debate is not an easy task, and is one that will not be attempted here. Suffice to say that the symposium on which this collection of essays was based was united in its recognition of the facts; first, that the subject of armed popular resistance in Napoleonic Europe is an area of which we still know surprisingly little that is worthy of further exploration, and, second, that its investigation on a continent-wide scale is not something that could ever be attempted by a single scholar working on his or her own. As in the case of the governance, organization, implantation and impact of the Napoleonic empire, the way is therefore open for a variety of collaborative research projects. Where individual scholars can make a difference lies rather in the study of individual states, territories, regions or districts, and in this respect the hope was duly expressed that the revolts in Spain, Portugal, Calabria, northern Italy, the Tyrol and Germany would all receive further attention. Other topics that were raised as possibilities, meanwhile, include outbreaks of guerrilla warfare beyond the confines on the Napoleonic empire – the obvious examples are Finland and Serbia – and the extent of popular participation in the climactic campaigns of 1812, 1813 and 1814. It was noted, however, that even the more limited approach inherent in country-by-country studies was not without its difficulties: if one thing is apparent in relation to the subject of 'people's war' in the age of Napoleon, it is that those who work in it must be polymaths who are capable of assimilating a wide variety of different approaches to their subject – who must, in short, be able to combine an understanding of, say, agrarian unrest with one of the origins and development of *la petite guerre*. Setting aside invitations to further study, however, what the Liverpool symposium chiefly provided

1

was an opportunity to review what we know of popular resistance and in the process to challenge a number of common suppositions.

In this respect the most obvious place to begin is the idea that armed resistance on the part of the common people was in all parts of the Continent a likely response to French invasion. As the historical record shows, this was simply not so, or not, at least, if what is meant is anything more than a more-or-less isolated and short-lived riot or village insurrection. Guerrilla warfare was in almost every case the result of large scale popular insurrections against the French and their surrogates, and, with some exceptions (of which more below), such events did not occur in places where there were large concentrations of enemy troops. As Michael Rowe tells us, in the Rhineland enormous numbers of French troops were constantly *in situe* in the 1790s when the area was very much in the frontline of the Republic's military campaigns, whilst even afterwards the fact that the area was the gateway to central Germany ensured that there was a constant to-ing and fro-ing of imperial bayonets. Thus, in 1805 it was a jumping off point for the campaign of Austerlitz; in 1808 large numbers of French troops marched back across it *en route* for the emperor's revenge in Spain; in 1809 it was a base for the campaign against Austria; in 1811 and 1813 it saw the passage of large contingents of conscripts bound for their deaths in Russia and Saxony; and in 1814 it was a bastion of Napoleonic resistance in the last ditch defence of France's frontiers. There was, in fact, some low-level resistance in the 1790s – resistance that was in reality little more than brigandage – but by the time of the empire Trier, Mainz and the other Rhenish towns and cities were quiet postings where the soldiers of Napoleon could take their ease in safety. Grumbling took place aplenty, in which respect one might quote the memoirs of Heinrich von Brandt, a German officer serving with Napoleon's auxiliary 'Legion of the Vistula'. Thus, marching from Metz to Mayence in April 1812, he noticed 'some unequivocal signs of discontent'; as he said, 'People were growing tired of the continual passage of troops despite the money that was thus being spread along the way.'[1] Nor is this surprising. Travelling the other way in 1808, the hussar officer, Rocca, remembered:

> After having passed the Elbe and the Weser, we reached the left bank of the Rhine and France... It was with deep sorrow and almost with tears in their eyes that our hussars quitted Germany... We traversed France as if it had been a land newly conquered and subjected to our arms... The soldiers of the grand army did not lose... the habit they had contracted in Germany of now and then maltreating the citizens... with whom they lodged.[2]

And yet, withal:

> The inhabitants of the towns and villages through which we passed
> suffered all patiently till the armed torrent was drained off.[3]

Why was this so? After all, the Rhineland's forest and hills offered at
least some potential for guerrilla operations, whilst, as Martin Boycott-
Brown shows, the case of northern Italy suggests that the mere presence
of large numbers of enemy troops was not in itself sufficient to guarantee
acquiescence. For explanation, one might point to historical experience:
in the seventeenth century the Rhineland had been repeatedly plagued,
and sometimes physically devastated, by the visitations of occupying
armies, and it may be that a habit of mind had been engendered that
accepted such misfortunes as acts of God that were no more avoidable
than bad harvests. To put the same point another way, experience may
also have shown that armed opposition was in the end counter-productive –
that it was literally easiest to choose the path of least resistance. Then,
too, we come to the issue of leadership. As the AHRB-British Academy
research project analysed in this study reveals, élite leadership was of
great importance in the emergence of large scale popular resistance to
the French. Indeed, this may have been even more the case than the
figures given by the author and his colleague, Leonor Hernández-Enviz,
suggest: recent discussions with a direct descendant of the guerrilla
commander, Francisco Longa – a man who has gone down in history as
by origin a simple blacksmith – have revealed that the family papers
show him to have been in reality the proprietor of a substantial iron
foundry![4] In the Rhineland, however, much of the élite seems to have
been happy to go along with the French, whilst, in those cases where
they were not, there was always the relatively easy option of emigration, as
witness the case of Cleves. But what of the people themselves, or, to be
more precise, the general populace? Under the empire the constant
passage of French troops made their situation very unpleasant, whilst,
as Rowe shows, the pressure of conscription was no more popular in,
say, Trier than it was in Trieste. Yet there was more to Napoleonic rule
than conscription and taxation. Much more work is needed on this
issue, but so far as can be ascertained the Rhineland appears to have
done slightly better out of the emperor than some other areas of the
French imperium. Whereas in some states – the Grand Duchy of Warsaw,
for example – the abolition of feudalism left the peasantry in many
respects even worse off than they were before, in the four Rhenish
departments the situation was rather different. Thus, the various judicial

reforms introduced by the French made the law courts more accessible and more trusted (as Rowe shows), whilst the sale of the lands of the Church was administered in such a way as to assuage the sensibilities of the largely Catholic populace and allow the peasants to acquire a share of the spoils. At the same time, a reasonably favourable settlement was reached with regard to the thorny question of precisely which dues were still owed by the peasantry in the wake of emancipation, whilst a series of decrees against the Jews, including one which effectively annulled many of the debts owed to money lenders by the peasantry, further eased the financial situation. And, last but not least, the Rhineland's agricultural products generally fetched high prices, and textiles and metallurgy developed apace, whilst even the behaviour of the soldiery was rendered somewhat more tolerable by the money that they paid for food, wine and other services. To quote Herbert Fisher, then:

> At the end of the Napoleonic period there were...complaints that the peasant had become over-prosperous, that he sat in the tap-room playing for gold stakes, and that no wine would content him but the best...It was not till 1813 that...an active spirit of discontent, mainly caused by military requisitions, manifested itself in the country. But the inhabitants had no burning desire to change their political allegiance, for upon the whole they had prospered under the rule of Napoleon.[5]

The mere density of enemy troops, then, does not in itself necessarily explain away an absence of popular resistance. Whilst it may have been a factor, in the Rhineland, at least, other issues were also important. And even then it has to be accepted that the passivity depicted by both Fisher and Rowe can be exaggerated. In the 1790s the whole region was swarming with bandits, of whom the most famous was the infamous Johann Bückler or 'Schinderhannes', whilst on a number of occasions angry inhabitants rioted or attacked French soldiers. Given the important role played by banditry in Spain as a focus for *la guerrilla*, insurrection was therefore at least a possibility, and in 1799 anti-French feeling in the Rhineland reached such a pitch that, had the initial run of success enjoyed by the British, Russians and Austrians in the War of the Second Coalition continued, it is more than possible that the region would have risen in revolt: such at least is the opinion of Tim Blanning.[6] Yet if we look, as Rowe asks us to do, at examples where revolts did break out, we can see that the latter has a point. Let us take the case of Spain and Portugal. Thus, when insurrection broke out in 1808 neither country had much more than a token French presence. The overall number of troops involved was quite impressive: there were 94 000 men in Spain and another 25 000 in Portugal. But the actual distribution of these forces reveals a different picture. In the former country the bulk of the French army – 56 000 men – was concentrated around Madrid, and apart from this the only substantial garrisons were to be found in Barcelona, Pamplona, San Sebastián, Burgos, Lerma, Vitoria and Figueras (to put this more graphically, the French zone of control consisted of no more than a long finger of territory extending from the French frontier at Hendaye along the line of the main road to Madrid, and a second such finger extending from the other end of the Pyrenees at Port-Bou to Barcelona). As for Portugal, meanwhile, 15 000 men held Lisbon and the mouth of the Tagus, whilst another 10 000 manned the border positions of Alcoutim, Elvas and Almeida. In large parts of the Iberian peninsula, then, there was literally not a Frenchman to be seen for hundreds of miles, whilst those French troops who had been seen were hardly such as to inspire much in the way of fear. Thus, the first 'Army of Spain' was very much a scratch force most of whose members were newly inducted conscripts who were so raw that they hardly knew how to load and fire their muskets. Organized in *ad hoc* provisional regiments and 'legions of reserve' and dressed in a motley collection of cast-off uniforms, they were not much of an advertisement for the Napoleonic military machine. Faced by even mildly difficult conditions, meanwhile, their bearing simply broke down under the strain: most of the troops dispatched to Lisbon in October 1807 fell out along the way, whilst those that managed to remain with the colours were reduced to such a state that they more resembled an army that had been thoroughly defeated than one that was engaged in a triumphal progress. Small wonder, then, that there appears to have been little awareness of what war against the emperor would entail, not to mention a credulous audience for patriotic writers whose stock-in-trade was a burlesque vision of a Napoleon gibbering with fear in his throne room at the thought of the heroism about to be unleashed on him.[7]

As in Iberia, so in the Tyrol. Taken from Austria after the battle of Austerlitz in 1805, this province had been given to Bavaria. French troops had been seen by the populace in all the campaigns of 1796–97, 1799 and 1805, but in all of these the traditional Tyrolian militia – the *landsturm* and the somewhat better equipped *schutzen* – had acquitted themselves well against the forces who invaded the area from Italy, Switzerland and Bavaria (a fact that undoubtedly engendered the same sort of over-confidence that was on show in the Peninsula). At the end of 1805, however, all of the French troops as such had been withdrawn. Eager to assimilate their new acquisition, the Bavarians duly sent a garrison in their place, but the Bavarian army was hardly the most impressive in Europe – French complaints of its indiscipline and lackadaisical attitude are legion – whilst the number of men in cornflower-blue who appeared was surprisingly small. Thus, in 1809 there were no more than 4500 Bavarian troops in the area, and possibly as few as 3400. Even these, meanwhile, were confined to just five posts, of which the most important were Innsbruck and Brixen. As such, each of these boasted precisely two battalions of infantry, one squadron of cavalry and two field pieces, whilst the insurgents could by contrast count on the support of around 10 500 Austrian regulars who were poised to cross the frontier on the outbreak of hostilities.[8] Outside help, then, was at hand, and it may be that this was a feature in provoking revolt whose importance has hitherto been overlooked. After all, as Martin Boycott-Brown tells us, there was a general expectation in Pavia that an Austrian army was in the vicinity, whilst in Calabria, too, the presence of British troops in Sicily may have encouraged the local inhabitants to believe that they could strike at the French with impunity. And in the Peninsula, of course, Patriot proclamations, newspapers and handbills were soon full of claims that the redcoats – a common enough sight in both Spain and Portugal in the eighteenth century – were on their way.

What, though, was the populace to do until help arrived? In Portugal, Piedmont – the *barbets* discussed by Boycott-Brown are a force that antedated the Revolutionary and Napoleonic Wars by many years, being irregular bands that were raised whenever war broke out with France to defend the passage of the Alps[9] – the Tyrol and parts of Spain – Catalonia, the Basque provinces and Galicia – the answer was to be found in popular institutions that had survived intact for hundreds of years in the form of local homeguards. Irregular militias in which all men of military age were theoretically liable for service in time of war, these provided a means of organizing the populace for action against a foreign enemy as well as a legacy of practical experience: in such regions guerrilla warfare did not in any sense have to be invented, but was something that was a tried and tested response to invasion and conquest and, more to the point, a weapon that was ultimately in the hands of the state (though in 1809 the Tyrol was a temporary exception in this respect). As we have already seen in the case of the Tyrol, moreover, these forces had in many cases seen action against the French in the recent past, a further example here being the Basque and Catalan militias, both of which had been heavily involved in the Franco-Spanish conflict of 1793–95. And, last but not least, the organization of the populace into such forces provided security in another sense, for men who were enrolled as *ordenanças, barbetti, schutzen, landsturm, somatenes, migueletes* or *alarmas* had some hope that combatants who fell into the hands of the enemy would not simply be executed as brigands. Also comforting was their association, at least on the whole, with regions that were extremely mountainous – above all, the Alps and the Pyrenees – that offered irregular combatants some degree of shelter and protection, or, to put it more starkly still, the hope of survival.

Was rebellion the fruit of rational calculation, then? By stressing issues such as the numerical strength of the occupying forces, the availability or otherwise of external help and the existence of traditional frameworks of organization and armament, we could easily come to such a conclusion. If we consider Italy, however, we can see that these arguments are not sufficient either. The French did not necessarily have a great many troops immediately to hand: in 1796 Napoleon only had 38 000 men with him when he invaded Piedmont, whilst ten years later the French officer put in charge of the occupation of Calabria, General Reynier, had a mere 10 000; equally, as Boycott-Brown tells us, rebellion broke out in Pavia after the main body of the French army had marched away. However, almost anywhere in Italy insurrection carried with it the threat of confrontation with the French troops. When the mountainous parts of the duchy of Piacenza rose in revolt in protest at the imposition of conscription towards the end of 1805, for example, they did so in the face of a French army of 50 000 men (though it is worth noting that the revolt coincided with the outbreak of the War of the Third Coalition, and, more particularly, the invasion of the neighbouring Kingdom of Italy by substantial Austrian forces headed by the renowned Archduke Charles).[10] Indeed, resistance frequently arose directly out of confrontations between soldiers and civilians. Such situations were unusual in the rest of Europe: practically the only instance in which unarmed civilians who were not already in a state of war flung themselves directly on a French garrison that comes to mind is the rising of the Dos de Mayo in Madrid. Even this example, meanwhile, is subject to heavy qualification: the incident began as a species of panic thanks, above all, to the spread of rumours that the soldiers of Marshal Murat, who included a number of Muslim mamelukes whom Napoleon had brought back from Egypt, had launched an unprovoked attack on the inhabitants; meanwhile, the city itself again contained very few troops, the bulk of Murat's men being encamped beyond its limits.[11] In Italy, however, it is a different story. To take the example given us from the area of Rivoli by Boycott-Brown, trouble broke out at the village of Gaon as a direct response to French marauding, whilst in Calabria the first major incident of the insurrection arose out of a fight that broke out on 22 March 1806 in the town of Soveria between a group of French soldiers out requisitioning horses and a crowd of inhabitants led by one Carmine Caliguri.[12]

What is striking about all these examples, however, is the complete absence of any political or military preparation. In Spain the insurrection of 1808 was preceded by a long period of radicalization in which the populace was prepared for revolt against the legitimate authorities – for in the absence of French troops this was what insurrection necessarily amounted to – by a torrent of propaganda against the hated royal favourite, Manuel de Godoy. Equally, in the Tyrol *anno neun* was the fruit of a plot that was hatched by a group of notables who had succeeded in gaining the support of elements of the court in Vienna. In Italy, however, there was no such political context: indeed, efforts to raise the *calabresi* in defence of the régime of Ferdinand IV and Maria Carolina as the French moved in at the beginning of 1806 had proved an abject failure: far from fighting for the Bourbons, the populace rather turned on the British, Russian and Neapolitan soldiers deployed in Calabria and pillaged their supply trains. On occasion, indeed, they even actively supported the French. In the words of Roger de Damas, the French *émigré* general who commanded the bulk of King Ferdinand's army:

> The people of the country, who had always been represented to the prince as ready to shed their last drop of blood for their sovereigns, had not furnished a single man to fight for them. In the hope of saving themselves from pillage by giving the French a good reception they hid all their provisions from us ... I had to occupy the town of Cosenza ... where I was absolutely obliged to give my troops twenty-four hours of rest. I found it necessary to protect myself from the inhabitants as much as from the enemy. The principal townsfolk came to assure me that if I should make any attempt at resistance under their walls, the people would join the French against me ... When I left the town ... the inhabitants carried out their threats and formed themselves into a body of infantry to support the enemy's advanced guard of cavalry in attacking my rearguard. [13]

It will be objected here that in 1799 Cardinal Ruffo had succeed in stirring up a great revolt in Calabria against the short-lived Parthenopaean Republic. But in reality this is a most problematic example. Ruffo landed at Reggio at the very time that the French, who were being hard pressed in the north by the Austrians, evacuated their Neapolitan conquests, and the result, as Damas observed, was that 'in all his peregrinations he never met a single Frenchman'.[14] As the general continued:

> When ... the gazettes reported that Cardinal Ruffo had reconquered the kingdom with the Calabrian masses, no sensible person, surely, accepted the story as anything but a newspaper tale. He began his expedition at a time when there was no enemy to oppose him except Jacobinism, the rallying word of unbridled pillage. Two poor villages accused a rich one of Jacobinism, whereupon the cardinal promised that the two should combine to pillage the third. Without seeing a single Frenchman he advanced from province to province till he was reinforced by detachments of English, Russians and Turks, who all landed from their ships. Thus supported, he reached Naples, whence the French had gone to oppose the advance of Suvorov, so he handed over the capital to be devastated by his acolytes.[15]

In this account there is, or so one suspects, both personal jealousy and the fear of the common people that was but natural in the mind of an aristocrat who had opposed the French Revolution from the very beginning. Nor was Damas the most perspicacious of men. The British officer, Henry Bunbury, describes him as 'a man of pretension and address, but not of abilities; gallant and gay in the proud alcoves of royalty, but without resources or judgement in difficulties'.[16] Yet British observers paint much the same picture, both Bunbury, who served as the Quartermaster General – effectively chief of staff – of the British army in Sicily, and Sir John Moore writing with repulsion of the insurgents they encountered on the mainland of southern Italy during the campaign of Maida as mere bandits who were interested only in pillage and never came forth except when the French were weak or in retreat. In the words of the latter, indeed, they were '*mafia* ... a lawless banditti, enemies to all governments whatever ... fit to plunder and murder, but much too dastardly to face an enemy'.[17] Not for nothing, then, did the Napoleonic Wars give us the word 'ruffian'.

If these views are stripped of their élitist language they provide us with another slant on popular resistance. We come here to the issue of social conflict. In Calabria collaboration was associated with the towns and the propertied classes, and resistance with the countryside and the poor, much the same distinctions being visible in Spain and Portugal.

In the Rhineland, Jews – a group who were perceived as having benefited both economically and politically from French conquest and furthermore were hated on account of their association with usury – were a favourite target of Bückler and his fellows. And, finally, in the Tyrol the revolt was very much a rural phenomenon, and one from which the burgers of Innsbruck and other towns suffered accordingly. Thus, when the capital was overrun by the rebels on 12 April 1809 it was systematically plundered and the more prosperous inhabitants subjected to a variety of indignities, other groups to suffer being officials – 'peasant skinners' in local parlance – and, once again, the Jews.[18] Given the fact that in the Po valley opposition was closely linked to peasant risings of a sort that had long been familiar across Europe, from all this it would seem to follow that popular resistance was at root a social movement in which peasants and day labourers sought both to redress long-standing grievances and to escape from short-term pressures. After all, brigandage, especially, was at one and the same time a traditional response to rural poverty, a means of survival for would-be deserters and draft-evaders and a framework that could accommodate the hordes of malcontents generated by assimilation into the Napoleonic empire. But this view of popular resistance as a phenomenon linked to social protests is somewhat undermined by evidence from Spain, and, more specifically, the province of Navarre. Divided into the wet and mountainous *montaña*, which borders on the Basque provinces and the Pyrenees, and the dry and undulating *ribera*, which borders on Aragón and Old Castile, this region is home to two very different systems of agriculture. Thus, the *montaña* is characterized by small farms worked by owner-occupiers and long-term tenants, and the *ribera* by great estates worked by day labourers. Of these two social groups the former was by Spanish standards reasonably prosperous and independent and the latter desperately poverty stricken and very much at the mercy of the landowners. Also very different was the position of the Church: in the *montaña* the dominant institution was the small village parish ministered to by local men of peasant stock, whereas in the *ribera* it was rather the great monastery, the contrast being that support was contrasted with oppression. If social strife is the key to popular resistance, then the bulk of Navarre's insurgents should logically have come from districts in the Ebro valley such as those of Tudela and Corella, but in reality the majority came from the north, the greatest centres of resistance being such areas as the isolated Pyrenean valleys of the Roncal and the Baztán.[19]

Very clearly, then, popular resistance – and in northern Navarre it is worth pointing out that what the French faced was not low-level brigandage but a full scale war waged with a mixture of skill, energy and devotion – was not just linked to poverty. Yet, that said, the example of the Navarrese *montaña* is exceptional: one of the few areas of the Iberian peninsula where the rural populace may be said to have been genuinely contented with its lot – where it had, in short, positive reasons to fight for the *ancien regime* – it may fairly be contrasted with areas such as the Serranía de Ronda where there was great poverty but also high levels of resistance, even if the latter was combined with strong elements of *jacquerie* and hostility to the military authorities.[20] Where, then, should this thought take us? Principally, it would seem, to the behaviour of the French themselves. Thus, in Navarre as much as in the Serranía de Ronda, in Piedmont as much as in Calabria, the catalyst that caused the French to come under attack from the civilian populace was the requisitioning and brutality engaged in by the French soldiers. To prove this point, let us examine it a little further. Thus, although both Spain and Naples were at war with Napoleon, and, in addition, engaged in an attempt to raise the entire populace against the invaders, in neither country did the authorities have much success so long as the French remained a distant threat. If we take the region of Galicia as an example, we find that in 1808 active support for the war was almost non-existent: the number of patriotic volunteers soon dwindled to a trickle, whilst the battle to impose conscription proved long and difficult. In January 1809, however, all this changed. Determined to capture the army of Sir John Moore, which was retreating on the port of La Coruña at full speed, the French poured across the frontier from León and proceeded to wreak havoc in the towns and villages through which they passed. As a result, within a matter of days large parts of the province – again, for the most part, those areas that were not actually occupied by the enemy – rose in revolt.[21]

It is worth noting here that the Galician revolt came as a response to occupation rather than invasion: when the French actually marched on Galicia, few of the inhabitants showed the slightest disposition to resist the oncoming enemy columns, whilst, in the same way, when the French moved into Andalucía in January 1810 attempts to meet them with an irregular *levée en masse* proved to be an embarrassing failure. Resistance, then, was to a certain extent linked to French policy. The business of requisitioning, for example, was certain to cause friction even if it was conducted with a modicum of restraint, and might even spark off a riot. But, to return to Boycott-Brown's chapter, the example of Gaon shows that such events did not have to produce a guerrilla war. On the contrary, through the exercise of common sense and compromise the local French commander was able to avoid bloodshed and bring the peasantry to accept the realities of occupation. Such prudence, however, was rare. As Alan Forrest has shown, the concept of brigandage was throughout the period 1792–1815 something that stirred strong feelings in the French mind. Those who engaged in acts of irregular resistance had *ipso facto* placed themselves beyond the pale of humanity not simply because of the savagery of which they were undoubtedly capable, but also because of their association with counter-revolution, or, to put it another way, their rejection of modern civilization. In Calabria and Spain alike, then, rebellion was met with a response so brutal as to destroy all hope of compromise, the speed and decision with which the French acted undoubtedly being accentuated by the Catholicism that charac-terized both these two parts of Europe. In the immediate wake of the outbreak of revolt in Calabria, for example, the town that had been the site of the first serious incident was sacked and burned down, whilst a military tribunal established in Cosenza executed 200 suspects within a month. Also destroyed, meanwhile, were the villages of Savelli, Cassino, Gerenza and Cachari, whilst the savagery contained without let-up thereafter: in the memoirs of Nicolas Desvernois, a French cavalry officer serving in the new Neapolitan army established by Joseph Bonaparte who was made governor of Amalfi, there is a proud account of how he executed 184 men belonging to the band of one Giusipello and exhibited their heads along the main coast road in iron cages.[22] And in Spain the firing squads that dealt with the insurgents who took part in the Dos de Mayo have been immortalized by Goya (though in fact the number of people they executed appears to have been no more than 114), whilst a number of towns whose inhabitants were accused of firing on the French – most notably, Medina de Río Seco and Chinchón – experienced appalling massacres.[23]

To describe this policy as genocide – a term that can certainly be applied in other contexts, most notably the Vendée – would be to go too far. Many French officers were, in fact, keenly aware that their aim had to be driving a wedge between the insurgents and the populace as a whole and struggled hard to keep their men under control, whilst further restraints were often exercized by the civilian officials who became involved in the various anti-bandit tribunals established by such rulers as Joseph Bonaparte. But the fact is that levels of repression were high and, on occasion, extreme, and that in the short term this exacerbated the problem. Thus, the population of entire villages might flee their homes and in consequence be left with no other means of survival than violence; equally, if some of the particular tales told in this respect are mere fables – among the Spanish guerrilla leaders who are falsely claimed to have lost wives or parents to enemy atrocities are El Empecinado and Julián Sánchez – there were undoubtedly cases in which the French generated an intense desire for revenge. Nor was the situation aided by other aspects of occupation policy. The chief culprit here was conscription. Though never introduced in Spain and Portugal, fear that it was coming was undoubtedly an underlying factor in the Iberian insurrections, whilst it played a major role in radicalizing the population of the Tyrol, this province having traditionally enjoyed exemption from service in the regular army under the Habsburgs. But its impact was at its most severe in Calabria. Thus, by the spring of 1809 three years of a mixture of ferocious repression and efforts to win over the populace had done a great deal to reduce the strength of the insurrection. At this point, however, Joachim Murat, who had replaced Joseph Bonaparte as King of Naples when the latter had been transferred to Spain, introduced conscription. The result was immediate: large numbers of fresh recruits fled to the bands, whilst the French lost control of many villages that had hitherto been quiet.[24]

In this particular respect, the French were forced to back off: Calabria was informed that its manpower would only have to serve in the civic guard that had been organized in its towns and villages, whilst no soldiers were ever actually levied in this fashion. On occasion, too, compromise was reached in Spain where a pattern of tit-for-tat executions eventually led Francisco Espoz y Mina and the French governor of Navarre to respect the lives of prisoners. In the midst of the most brutal warfare, then, there was generally sufficient flexibility on both sides to ensure that there was always some sort of 'golden bridge' that avoided full scale apocalypse. In rare exceptions, however, this was not the case, in which respect it behoves us to pay particular attention to the most obvious example, and all the more so as this has been regularly advanced as proof of the way in which the Napoleonic Wars generated new styles of warfare. We come here to the events that ravaged central Portugal between September 1810 and April 1811. In brief, faced by a French army of invasion commanded by Marshal Massena which he suspected he would not be able to check in the open field, Wellington fell back from his positions on the frontier of Beira in the direction of Lisbon, which he had protected by an impregnable zone of fortifications known as the Lines of Torres Vedras. As the French advanced, moreover, they were confronted by a scorched-earth policy that saw large numbers of the inhabitants driven from their homes and forced to migrate to *ad hoc* refugee camps created around the capital and such food stocks as could not be transported to Lisbon burned or spoiled. To these demands, however, there was much resistance: many people refused to leave their homes and either hid supplies of grain and other foodstuffs in caves, cellars or abandoned houses, or buried them beneath barnyard or threshing floor. Confronted by the Lines of Torres Vedras, the invaders – some 60 000 men – came to a dead halt, but, whilst Massena realised that trying to fight his way through the maze of inundations, abattis, escarpments and redoubts that Wellington had constructed was impossible, he refused to retreat, and therefore blockaded the Anglo-Portuguese forces in their positions in the hope that fresh troops might arrive from Spain. There followed one of the most dreadful episodes of the entire Napoleonic era. Assailed by ever growing hunger, the French turned on the inhabitants who had been left behind and set about extracting such food supplies as remained to them. Increasingly desperate, foraging parties resorted to torture and murder as a matter of course. Let us here quote Jean-Baptiste Lemonnier-Delafosse, an officer who was serving in a light-infantry regiment in the division of General Heudelet:

The French army entered Portugal with six days' worth of supplies in each soldier's haversack, and on top of that a few wagons. It was, therefore, without any proper magazines, and soon it found itself without food of any sort. Nevertheless, it was necessary to live. Once the initial resources had run out...a regular system of marauding was organized...Woe be to the peasant who was caught by such an expedition! The poor unfortunate was stripped of all he had and often...put to death by men whom hunger...had rendered cruel and savage. When the troops were operating in places they did not know, guides were needed. If no-one came forward at their call, someone would be seized at random. Having got such a person, he would be ordered to take them to a village...and, once he had got there, to point out where all the food had been hidden...The poor devil would not know where it was any more than those who were searching for it, and the confusion into which he was necessarily thrown was taken as proof of bad faith by the soldiers. Threats were then quickly followed by actions: a rope would be put round his neck, and the unfortunate man would hear the words, 'Up you go until you tell us where the grain is!' As he could give no answer, he would be strung up until he began to turn blue, whereupon he would be taken down and given another chance to speak. Alas! Worse than barbarous as they were, these atrocious means sometimes succeeded, but this was only when fate had pitched upon an inhabitant of the village that was being raided. Unless that was the case, such men could reveal nothing, and so the soldiers said to them in their ferocity, 'Oh, you don't want to tell us where the grain is, do you? You are a brigand: hanged you were and hanged you will remain!'[25]

Needless to say, the response of the population was to turn to wholesale resistance. In brief, there was nothing else left for them to do: it was literally a question of seizing food from the French or starving to death, and, still more bluntly, killing the invaders before they themselves were killed. As Lemonnier-Delafosse lamented, 'Once an affair of civilized peoples, our war had become a war to the death.'[26] Finding themselves assailed in this fashion, the French troops lost all vestige of humanity and engaged in a series of atrocities whose nature horrified the most hardened British soldiers when they reoccupied the area the following spring after Massena had finally given up the struggle and retreated to Spain. As one of Wellington's *aides de camp* wrote, 'The French have certainly made an inglorious campaign... To picture the infamous way in which they have left the country and the inhabitants is quite impossible: they have burned every village and town they went through, and murdered every peasant they could find.'[27]

The apocalyptic scenes witnessed in central Portugal in the winter of 1810–11 are no more typical of armed popular resistance in Napoleonic Europe than peasant risings and the formation of guerrilla bands are typical of the general response of the populace to the French imperium. Even in areas gripped by partisan warfare, it is fairly clear that the preferred option of a large part of the inhabitants was to stay out of harm's way and remain aloof from the struggle. To quote the British diplomat, Thomas Sydenham:

> The feelings of all the provinces through which I have passed are decidedly inimical to the French and favourable to the common cause... At the same time... the patriotic feelings of the lower classes are of little use to their country. It is a passive feeling which murmurs under the oppression and tyranny which it suffers without exerting itself to remove or diminish what it complains of. The people pay their contributions and deliver up their mules, grain and provisions whenever they are demanded... by the enemy. Of course they complain of these exactions and are happy to see the English... But... it does the enemy no harm nor us any good.[28]

In general, then, what we see is a situation in which, even in the relatively areas few areas where it was an issue, popular resistance was a phenomenon that for the most part affected only a minority of the population. At the same time, it was something that was likely to take root only in certain very specific circumstances. Only very rarely could the common people be relied on to fight for the Old Order on social or economic grounds. Sensing this, a number of propagandists anxious to stir up people's war against the French attempted to reach out to them, and, in particular, to air the political issues involved in the conflict in a style that was accessible to a mass audience. Hence the use, as outlined for us by Emilie Delivré, of political catechisms (though it should be noted that these were not the only form of propaganda to be made use of in this respect: in Spain, at least, we only see the employment of the literary style known as *costumbrismo* in which characters featured in pamphlets and manifestos were made to engage in dialogue couched in the language of the streets). But in the absence of the conditions that made revolt a reality the publication of such documents remained an empty gesture. There is little evidence that the efforts of Arndt, Von Kleist and Von Hormayr had much effect on the situation in Germany: only one popular insurrection – that seen in Hamburg – occurred in the campaign of 1813, and this not only took place after the French had evacuated the city; but also seems to have been the work of the ruling oligarchy, the chief aim of this group being to maintain order and ensure that their homes and businesses were not sacked by the Cossacks who appeared hot on the heels of the French.[29] What is even more striking, meanwhile, is the very small number of examples of political catechism that Delivré has been able to uncover, not to mention the clear preference that can be seen in the documents which she examines for keeping popular action under the control of the state.

In Germany, then, it can safely be said that there was little real enthusiasm for independent action on the part of the people. Nor was this only the case in Prussia, Austria and the states of the Confederation of the Rhine: In Spain, too, there was real ambivalence about the issue of guerrilla warfare. Here the political élites were rather more enthusiastic: aside from offering them a means of both preferment and self-glorification, the formation of partisan bands could be represented as being much more of a military necessity. In consequence, the Patriot authorities were besieged by *pretendientes* anxious to secure a commission as a *cabecilla*. Yet, whether implicitly or explicitly, there was constantly a sense of dicing with the devil: the people, might, or so it was argued, hate the French, but they were also brutal, ignorant, irrational and ungovernable. Even when formed into organized militias, in fact, the *populacho* – literally, the rabble – could not be relied upon. As Antonio Moliner shows us in his paper on Catalonia, the *somatens* and *miquelets* of that province were always prone to riot, desertion and pillage, and could not always be trusted to put up much of a fight. Hence the emergence of the corpus of regulation analysed by Vittorio Scotti-Douglas: the formation of guerrilla bands and even 'land piracy' were to be encouraged, certainly, but the phenomenon was also to be kept under control and directed into safe channels. As was implicitly recognised, in fact, to the extent that it existed at all, the desire to take up arms reflected not devotion to the *patria*, but rather an attempt to find a solution to some of the problems that beset the populace: the *partidas*, as we have seen, offered food, pay, plunder, freedom from service in the regular army and the chance to make an end of hated social superiors. In short, the French were right: apart from in certain very particular instances, left to itself, in so far as guerrilla warfare was concerned, genuine popular resistance – in other words, the action of irregular bands of armed civilians as opposed to that of detachments of regular troops sent into 'the bush' to harass the enemy – *was* brigandage, and only ceased to be brigandage to the extent that members of the élites or ambitious adventurers of vision and foresight succeeded in subjecting the phenomenon to military discipline. Even the worst brigands, of course, could still inflict harm on the enemy on occasion, but little was to be expected from such privateering. To quote a letter written by an officer of the Third Foot Guards named William Stothert in December 1811:

> At present the only troops in Spain which carry on a successful warfare against the French are the guerrillas, or armed peasants, and it may fairly be presumed that they are incited to attack the enemy's convoys and straggling parties as much by the hope of plunder as from patriotism. This cannot be supposed to influence the minds of their gallant chiefs [a belief in which Stothert was sadly mistaken], but the peasant, when compelled by the ravages of war to abandon the scenes of peaceful industry, becomes of necessity a soldier... as the only means of supporting his existence... It is not surprising ... that such a body... should carry terror and dismay... into the ranks of the French soldiery... But it is perfectly evident that the deliverance of Spain can never be achieved by the efforts of a force so rudely constituted, however... successful as it has often proved against small parties of the enemy.[30]

In so far as possible, then, wherever we look we see that the people continued to be assimilated into the structures of the state. This leads us on, however, to the very interesting question broached by Janet Hartley. Whatever the established order's views on guerrilla warfare and popular revolt may have been, it cannot be denied that from Madrid to Moscow enemies of the French made greater use than ever before of language and methods that were designed to reach out to the people and persuade them that the overthrow of Napoleon was an enterprise in which they both had a stake and should sacrifice themselves and give their all. Did this encourage the mass armies that everywhere had perforce to be fielded against the French to fight harder and show greater willingness to accept their lot? As Hartley shows, in the case of Russia at least this cannot be proved: the officers were in many instances enthused by a new spirit that had as one of its consequences the Decemberist revolt of 1825, but it is difficult to argue the case one way or the other with regard to the common soldiers. Certainly, the Orthodox religion was made use of to stimulate loyalty and devotion, and certainly, too, at Borodino and other battles the Russian forces fought with desperate heroism. But had anything really changed? Russian soldiers were notorious for their fighting capacity and staying power: prior to the campaign of 1812 Napoleon's worst experience on the battlefield had come at the hands of General Bennigsen at the battle of Eylau, whilst in the Seven Years' War Frederick the Great had repeatedly been very roughly handled by the green-coated soldiers of the Empress Elizabeth, gaining an extremely pyrrhic victory over them at Zorndorf in 1758 and going down to ignominious defeat at Kunersdorf in 1759. Other Russian victories from the same war numbered Gross-Jägersdorf and Kay, whilst in 1799 General Suvorov's invasion of Switzerland had seen Russian troops gain a series of dramatic successes: on 1 October, for example, 5000 troops under General Rosenberg had utterly defeated a column of more than twice as many Frenchmen under no less a figure than André Masséna, a general who is always rated as one of Napoleon's greatest commanders. In all this the self-same factors generally identified as the mainspring of Russian patriotism in 1812 had made an appearance. Thus, throughout the eighteenth century commanders such as Rumiantsev and Suvorov had made every effort to play on the devotion of the soldiery to the Orthodox faith and to instill love of the tsar. In this respect it is the opinion of some historians that they appear to have had at least some success.[31] Let us here quote Sir Robert Wilson's account of the Russian army that fought at Eylau and Friedland in 1807: 'The Russian, nurtured from earliest infancy to consider Russia as the supreme nation of the world, always regards himself as an important component part of the irresistible mass . . . Amidst the Russian qualities, the love of country is also pre-eminent, and inseparable from the Russian soldier. This feeling is paramount, and in the very last hour his gaze is directed towards its nearest confines.'[32] But, even supposing that this is so – and it should be noted that Wilson's claims fit in with a long line of distinctly uncritical western writings on the subject of Russia that stressed the devotion of the common people to the 'Little Father' and the Motherland – the net result must be to suggest that what happened at such battles as Smolensk, Borodino, Maloyaroslavets and Polotsk was not representative of anything out of the ordinary. Indeed, it could even be argued that the Russian armed forces were actually less patriotic in 1812 than they had been in, say, 1762. Thus, as Hartley rightly points out, there were many non-Russian conscripts, most notably Ukrainians, in the army of Alexander II. What she neglects to say, however, is that conscription had only been extended beyond the frontiers of Great Russia in the reign of Paul I, and that a number of contemporary writers had been expressing fears that this would dilute the morale and fighting power of the soldiery.[33]

For all the determined efforts of the régime to whip up popular patriotism in 1812, then, there is little concrete evidence that these made much difference in so far as the motivation of the common soldier was concerned: the Russian soldier fought in much the same style as he had for the past century. Why, then, was he able to give the French, the Prussian and the Turks such a tough time? One explanation that is sometimes put forward is that the conscripted serfs who fought for the Romanovs were so brutalized, so stupid and so devoid of initiative that they simply did not understand the concept of running away. The Polish leader, Kosciuszko, said that Russian soldiers fought as fanatics and ignored enemy fire so long as they had officers left to lead them, whilst, to quote Christopher Duffy, 'It was not enough simply to kill Rusians: you had to knock them down as well.'[34] However, this piece of type-casting does not work any better than that of the Russian soldier as the holy warrior of tsar and motherland. In the late eighteenth century, the Russian army had evolved a tactical doctrine that stressed initiative, flexibility and speed of movement, and, whilst Paul I did make some reforms, the fact is that he really only altered the emphasis of the regulations: firepower was now to be more important than the bayonet, but the same offensive spirit was still very much in evidence; simultan-eusly, meanwhile, the tsar initiated the practice of awarding medals to common soldiers. At the same time, under Alexander I there was a renewed move away from the Prussian models that had been favoured by Paul I and, at the time of the Seven Years' War, the Empress

Elizabeth: ever more emphasis was placed on the use of skirmishers, whilst the infantry adopted the same mixture of line and column visible in other armies. At Eylau, Friedland and Borodino the Russians certainly fought in dense masses, but this was not the result of bovine stupidity: rather, the position of the army was in each case very cramped with the result that there was little option but to form the troops in column and no means for them to change their position or take shelter. From this it follows that the performance of the Russian army was in the end determined by military factors. In the first place, it was plentifully supplied with artillery and therefore able to inflict terrible damage on its opponents, who were generally less well served in this respect: at Kay 28 000 Prussians and fifty-six guns faced 40 000 Russians and 186 guns, whilst at Kunersdorf 51 000 Prussians and 140 guns faced 41 000 Russians and 200 guns; moreover, both the organization and the armament of this arm of service were greatly improved under Paul I and Alexander I. The benefits of this situation continued to pertain in 1812 – at Borodino the Russian guns were both more numerous and heavier than their French opponents and even at the very end of the day they were still able to impose their superiority. Thus, according to the Russian commander, Kutuzov, 'A ferocious artillery duel lasted until it was completely dark. Our artillery caused immense damage with its roundshot and compelled the enemy batteries to fall silent, after which all the French infantry and cavalry withdrew.'[35] Beyond this, meanwhile, Russian troops were frequently surprisingly well trained. Thus, the eighteenth-century reformer, Rumiantsev, the towering genius, Suvorov, and the victor of Borodino, Kutuzov, had all placed great emphasis on realistic battle drills, the fact being that the Russian army was therefore a very tough nut to crack.

The issue of the extent to which patriotism became a force amongst the soldiers of the mass armies that eventually overthrew Napoleon is one that needs to be explored much further. If one has room to doubt the extent to which it was a factor of much importance in Russia, in the Prussian forces there is some evidence that there was a sea-change in the feelings of the soldiery. At Jena and Auerstädt the Prussian army had fought adequately, but its performance had hardly been heroic. At Leipzig and Waterloo, by contrast, it is claimed that a very different vision was on show. Let us here quote Gunther Rothenberg:

In 1806 the typical Prussian soldier had been a mercenary or a reluctant conscript; now he was animated both by patriotism and by a deep and even savage hatred of the French. The first expressed itself, as it had in the days of Frederick, by religion. As the Prussian infantry saw the French retreating the evening of Waterloo, the fusiliers began to sing the old Lutheran hymn, 'A mighty fortress is our God'...Hatred of the French expressed itself in bitter fighting and in the ability to rally after initial defeat.[36]

Well, perhaps. The Prussian army certainly fought very bravely in the campaigns of 1813–15, but the reality is that, as in the case of its Russian counterpart, we simply do not know enough about its *mentalités* to be able to make such a judgement. Such primary evidence as we have of enthusiasm for the war amongst the rank and file comes from the writings of confirmed German nationalists who were convinced that they were indeed engaged in a *befreiungskrieg* and were desperate to convey the impression that the struggle was genuinely a people's crusade. But all the evidence suggests that conscription was hated, desertion rife and volunteers both few in number and for the most part confined to the same groups that had always provided German rulers with the bulk of the men who had chosen to enter their service without compulsion. Before we can take on board the notion of a Prussian army enthused by a positive desire to smash the foe, a great deal more work is therefore necessary both on the means that were used to excite the feelings of the troops and the feelings of the men themselves, in which latter respect one can only hope that some Germanist will uncover the same sort of treasure trove as that revealed by Alan Forrest in his seminal *Napoleon's Men*. Only through the examination of such bundles of private letters will we ever be able to test the claims put forward by Rothenberg, and until that task has been carried out it is probably wise to remain at least a little sceptical.

With this remark, we return to our point of departure, which was to reassert the need for greater attention to be paid to the subject of popular resistance. In this respect the Liverpool symposium undoubtedly provided a useful forum for debate, but at the same time it revealed just how little we know about this issue. For many years to come, then, the patriots, partisans and land-pirates whom we have discussed in these pages will, or so it is hoped, continue to occupy the attention of the historical community. One might even voice the hope, indeed, that they might attract the attention of more of the historical community than has hitherto been the case. Spain has, perhaps, now been dealt with adequately, but Italy, the Tyrol and Portugal all offer opportunities for truly ground-breaking monographs that would add enormously to our understanding of the subject whilst at the same time testing out some of the conclusions reached in this collection of essays. In brief, these are five-fold. In the first place the popular will to take up arms was relatively limited even in those areas of Europe – a clear minority – which did experience armed resistance on the part of the populace. In the second, outbreaks of armed resistance were rarely ideological: whilst the masses were frequently worked on by members of the establishment, they do not seem to have been much moved by anti-French propaganda *per se*, but rather by their experience of enemy occupation and the extent of their ability to feed themselves and their families and to carry on some semblance of normal life. In the third, except in the cases of spontaneous riots and revolts such as those that gripped Pavia and Gaon – instances of violence that were on the whole very short-lived – the organization of effective popular resistance in many cases clearly depended on the state and its collaborators rather than springing from the populace itself. In the fourth, in those cases where popular resistance did spring from below, it was generally ineffectual and in the end prone to slide into mere banditry. And in the fifth it is clear that the subject cannot be studied effectively without a readiness to grapple with traditional military history: as the current author has shown in these pages, the motivation of the Russian army in 1812 needs to be discussed with the aid of some knowledge of its organization and war record; equally, in *Fighting Napoleon: Guerrillas and Bandits in Spain, 1808–1814* he has established that the *partidas* will never properly be understood if the role played in them by the Spanish regular army is not accorded its full weight. So where, then, does all this leave us? With a subject of great complexity, certainly: the successful historian of popular resistance must necessarily be able to draw on a variety of different sub-disciplines, identify and manipulate sources that are frequently as obscure as they are fragmentary and have an eye for events not just in his or her own area of study but in Napoleonic Europe as a whole. That said, however, it is also a subject of great potential: a rich orchard whose fruits await only the hands that should be stretched out to pluck them. Let us, then, conclude, with a quote from the gospel of Saint Matthew: 'The harvest is plentiful, but the labourers are few; therefore, ask the Lord of the Harvest to send out labourers into His harvest.'[37]

Notes

1. H. von Brandt, *In the Legions of Napoleon: the Memoirs of a Polish Officer in Spain and Russia, 1808–1813*, ed. J. North (London, 1999), p. 186.
2. A.J.M. de Rocca, *Memoirs of the War of the French in Spain* (London, 1815), pp. 24–5.
3. *Ibid.*, p. 25.

4. I owe this information to my esteemed friend Lieutenant Colonel José Pardo de Santayana of the Spanish army.

5. H. Fisher, *Napoleonic Statesmanship: Germany* (Oxford, 1903), pp. 370–2. For a very helpful, discussion of the economic impact of French rule on the Rhineland, cf. M. Rowe, *From Reich to State: the Rhineland in the Revolutionary Age, 1780–1830* (Cambridge, 2003), pp. 193–210. His conclusion confirms the impression given by Fisher, *viz.* 'The Rhineland was economically stronger at the end of the Napoleonic period than at the beginning.' *Ibid.*, p. 209.

6. For the banditry and unrest that gripped the Rhineland in the 1790s, cf. T.C.W. Blanning, *The French Revolution in Germany: Occupation and Resistance in the Rhineland, 1792–1802* (Oxford, 1983), pp. 286–316.

7. For a discussion of the military situation in Spain and Portugal at the beginning of the Peninsular War, cf. C.J. Esdaile, *The Peninsular War: a New History* (London, 2002), pp. 46–64 *passim*.

8. F.G. Eyck, *Loyal Rebels: Andreas Hofer and the Tyrolean Uprising of 1809* (New York, 1986), pp. 59–60.

9. For some details of the *barbetti*, as they were called in Piedmont, cf. M. Broers, *Napoleonic Imperialism and the Savoyard Monarchy, 1773–1821: State Building in Piedmont* (New York, 1997), pp. 134–5.

10. For the revolt in Piacenza, cf. M. Broers, *Europe under Napoleon, 1799–1815* (London, 1996), p. 104.

11. The Dos de Mayo has yet to receive the scholarly analysis which it deserves. However, for a relatively recent Spanish account, cf. J.C. Montón, *La revolución armada del Dos de Mayo en Madrid* (Madrid, 1983).

12. M. Finley, *The Most Monstrous of Wars: the Napoleonic Guerrilla War in Southern Italy, 1806–1811* (Columbia, South Carolina, 1994), p. 26.

13. R. de Damas, *Memoirs of the Comte Roger de Damas, 1787–1806*, ed. J. Rambaud (London 1913), pp. 398–9.

14. *Ibid.*, p. 279.

15. *Ibid.*, pp. 400–1.

16. H. Bunbury, *Narratives of some Passages in the Great War with France from 1799 to 1810* (London, 1854), p. 222.

17. For a digest of these views, cf. C.J. Esdaile, *The Wars of Napoleon* (London, 1995), pp. 119–20.

18. Eyck, *Loyal Rebels*, pp. 69–70.

19. For all this, cf. J.L. Tone, *The Fatal Knot: the Guerrilla War in Navarre and the Defeat of Napoleon in Spain* (Chapel Hill, North Carolina, 1994), pp. 9–41, 162–71 *passim*.

20. An excellent eye-witness account of the guerrilla war in the Serranía de Ronda may be found in Rocca, *Memoirs*, pp. 122–63; for a critical discussion, meanwhile, cf. C.J. Esdaile, *Fighting Napoleon*, pp. 124–5.

21. For events in Galicia in 1808–09, cf. C.J. Esdaile, 'Rebeldía, reticencia y resistencia: el caso gallego de 1808', *Trienio*, no. 35 (May, 2000), pp. 57–80.

22. Finley, *Most Monstrous of Wars*, pp. 28–30; E. Bousson de Mairet (ed.), *Souvenirs Militaires du Baron Desvernois, Ancien Général au Service de Joachim Murat, Roi de Napoles, Commandeur de la Légion d'Honneur et de l'Ordre Real de Deux Siciles* (Paris, 1858), pp. 103–4.

23. The incident that took place at Chinchón is commemorated in some of the gorier scenes in Goya's famous *Desastres de la Guerra*.

24. Finley, *Most Monstruous of Wars*, p. 116.
25. C. Bourachot (ed.), *Souvenirs Militaires du Capitaine Jean-Baptiste Lemonnier-Delafosse* (Paris, 2002), pp. 57–8.
26. *Ibid.*, p. 59.
27. R. Muir (ed.), *At Wellington's Right Hand: the Letters of Lieutenant-Colonel Sir Alexander Gordon, 1808–1815* (London, 2003), p. 174. The full story of what went on behind Massena's lines in the winter of 1810–11 has never been documented. However, for a most thoughtful and well-researched fictional version, cf. C.S. Forester, *Death to the French* (London, 1932).
28. T. Sydenham to H. Wellesley, 12 September 1812, University of Southampton, Wellington Papers, 1/361.
29. For the Hamburg insurrection, cf. Esdaile, *Wars of Napoleon*, p. 266.
30. W. Stothert, *A Narrative of the Principal Events of the Campaigns of 1809, 1810 and 1811 in Spain and Portugal* (London, 1812), pp. 274–6.
31. E.g. B. Menning, 'The imperial Russian army, 1725–1796', in F. Kagan and R. Higham, *The Military History of Tsarist Russia* (London, 2002), p. 70.
32. R. Wilson, *Brief Remarks on the Character and Composition of the Russian Army and a Sketch of the Campaigns in Poland in the Years 1806 and 1807* (London, 1810), pp. 4–5.
33. A. and Y. Zhmodikov, *Tactics of the Russian Army in the Napoleonic Wars* (Westchester, Ohio, 2003), I, p. 5.
34. C. Duffy, *Borodino and the War of 1812* (London, 1973), p. 39. For Kosciuszko's views, cf. Zhomodikov, *Tactics of the Russian Army*, p. 3.
35. Duffy, *Borodino*, pp. 134–5.
36. G. Rothenberg, *The Art of War in the Age of Napoleon* (London, 1977), p. 195.
37. Matthew 9, 37–8. The text is from the New RSV.

2
The Ubiquitous Brigand: The Politics and Language of Repression

Alan Forrest

Brigands were familiar figures on the eighteenth-century landscape – only too familiar for traders and travellers between major cities if the reports of the local police and the story lines of early novels are to be taken as a guide. Thieves gathered in *bandes* to attack mail coaches and rob passing traders, often secure in the knowledge that, as local men, they could expect to enjoy a degree of protection from their own communities against the attentions of the law. They congregated on frontiers, mingling with bands of smugglers and *contrebandiers* who were assured rich pickings in the sand dunes around Dunkerque or the mountain pastures of the Pyrenees, areas where only they knew the hidden paths that led across into Spain or the Austrian Netherlands. Or they simply formed themselves into casual bands when famine threatened, groups of local men who had fallen on hard times and hoped, like so many others, to inspire sufficient trepidation within their community to deter informers and thwart the efforts of the *maréchaussée*. Often, it would seem, they succeeded only too well, since policing in many parts of France was ineptly organized and seriously underfunded, as Iain Cameron's account of the police of the eighteenth-century Auvergne makes clear. Here the attentions of the *maréchaussée* were focussed almost entirely on capturing vagabonds and army deserters along the principal highways – the latter being a particular priority in times of warfare such as the American War of Independence. The only successful repression of a *bande* of thieves recorded over a seventy-year period revealed a few neighbours supplementing their income with occasional moonlight sorties, not at all the sort of banditry that spread fear and panic through the French countryside.[1]

The bandits of legend – those who terrorised whole provinces and who inspired a folklore all of their own – were on a different scale entirely, bands who lived *en marge de la société*, moving under cover of darkness from clearing to clearing, seeking refuge in shepherds' huts on the slopes above isolated villages, robbing only those who were outsiders to the local community, celebrating their successes over noisy meals in wayside inns, and casually disarming any gendarmes sent to hunt them down. Some, like the notorious *bande d'Orgères* in the Beauce, survived in this way for decades, robbing travellers on the highly lucrative turnpike between Paris and Orleans, and maintaining a fluctuating membership of men, women and children, all enjoying a degree of local protection while stubbornly living as outlaws, beyond the protection of civil society. They may have been feared by local people, and respected for their power and their defiance of the authorities, but there is no evidence that they were hated, especially since, like all the best bandit gangs, they served a useful and much-appreciated function in redistributing wealth, artificially injecting money stolen from merchants and other travellers into a hard-pressed local economy.[2] Eric Hobsbawm is surely right when he presents some of the great bandits of history as men of the people, commemorated in folk-song and in popular prints, and lionized by those from whose roots they had sprung.[3] When they were finally caught and brought to trial men like Mandrin and Cartouche inspired awe as much as fear. They belonged to the same popular class as the mass of the people, yet they had turned their backs on poverty and cocked an almighty snook at the dual authority of Church and State. And in their way they were heroes to the mass of the people: even the more obscure among them were built into mighty figures of legend, their criminal exploits praised in folk-song and in luridly-coloured *images d'Epinal*. Even unexceptional robbers like Poulailler, by the time of the Revolution, were being featured in popular prints, distributed by peddlars at village fairs and in the popular quarters of Paris. Their crimes were talked of with awe, the danger they presented to the public unscrupulously exaggerated to inspire fear – there was talk of 'the famous Poulailler, captain of a band of more than 500 robbers distributed between various provinces'.[4] The trials of such brigands became the subject of intense interest both amongst the educated public and in the pages of chapbooks and the *bibliothèque bleue*; while many of the thousands who turned out to watch their executions were there not to gloat at their downfall but to secure a last, secret glimpse of their folk-heroes. As Richard Cobb rightly observed, the Criminal Hero would easily outlast the Revolutionary Martyr. 'Cartouche, Mandrin, Hulin remained far more popular, reassuring heroes than the newly established boys and girls who perished, holding the bridge, pierced with a thousand lances, or standing on burning decks'.[5]

The popular image of the brigand was thus tinged with a certain romanticism, an admiration for his daring, an empathy with his contempt for authority. Behind every bandit leader there was just a vestige of Robin Hood. Yet we should not be deceived. Not all bandits could aspire to be local heroes, just as not all had the swagger and the anarchic style needed to appeal to the popular imagination. The average brigand's existence was generally more prosaic, his exploits born of simple desperation rather than of an anarchic temperament, while his rapport with the local population was far from assured. Bands of outlaws were often formed from those with little or no stake in local society – *vagabonds* who had come into the area from elsewhere, from communes that could not give them sustenance, and were desperate for food and lodging, however they might come by it. They drew on a criminal underclass of men who had been released from jail after serving their sentence, *gens sans aveu* for whom no one would vouch and who had no escape from destitution; and deserters from the armies, their number swollen after each campaign, fearful of arrest and condemned to a life on the move, often, of course, armed, a prey to any temptation that might come along. Indeed, the mingling of deserters and draft dodgers with hardened criminals and smugglers served only to strengthen the equation that already existed in many people's minds between soldiers and violent crime, the belief – shared by, among others, Voltaire – that the line armies of Europe were drawn from the dregs of society, the human detritus from prisons and poorhouses who, when they no longer had enemy armies to attack, would turn their violence and their weapons against peaceful civilians. It had, it seemed, always been so. Both the *grandes compagnies* of the fourteenth century and the *écorcheurs* who replaced them in the fifteenth belonged to that tradition, as did the Mandrins who ravaged much of rural France in the eighteenth. So, too, it was bands of soldiers, turning to crime when they were paid off after the end of the Italian Wars, who murdered and tortured their way across France until Francis I, in a bid to end what the whole country saw as a fearful scourge, turned state terror against its perpetrators, importing from Germany the terrible punishment of breaking on the wheel as a final deterrent for highway robbery. There was nothing romantic about this, a final act of savagery to add to the savage catalogue of crimes which the brigands had committed. But the popular prints of the day tell a slightly different story. The sheer horror of the wheel, and the torment in which many of the most notorious brigands died, added an extra *frisson* to the public's undoubted fascination with violent criminals.[6]

The connection between brigandage and the soldiery was one that would have required no explanation to an eighteenth-century audience. They were used to the violence and debauchery of the armies that criss-crossed the continent during the long wars of the century, many of them foreign mercenaries, and would have had little cause to draw any significant distinction between those fighting for the French monarchy and those against whom they fought. Soldiers were reviled as being drunken, violent and – particularly when on foreign soil – gratuitously dangerous. Nor did they necessarily improve their behaviour when they ceased to be employed in the armed service of one or other of the European monarchs. The entry on 'brigands' in the *Encyclopédie* quite specifically makes a direct connection between soldiers and banditry. A brigand, it declares, is a 'vagabond who makes use of military campaigns to plunder and rob travellers. The name is sometimes given to undisciplined soldiers who devastate the countries in which they are fighting and never stay around to fight the enemy'. Hence, the article continues, rather delicately stepping over contemporary examples in favour of the security of the exotic, 'the Tartar hordes, and the gangs of Arabs who insult travellers in the Levant'. As for the origins of the term, there the encyclopaedists admit to a degree of uncertainty. It could come from the name of Burgand, who laid waste much of Guienne in the time of Nicholas I. Or again, they suggest, rising to their theme, it might stem from the reputation of a company of soldiers raised by the city of Paris back in 1356, and fitted out with *brigandines* to defend them against enemy archers. So heinous was their reputation with local people, and so serious the destruction that they caused, that they were referred to as *brigands*, and so, it was implied, the word had entered the language. In either case (and the article went on to propose other, similar explanations), the existence of a link between brigandage as a serious crime – 'robbery openly carried out by force, such highway robbery and other such acts' – a crime, moreover, that carried the death penalty in most European societies, and brigandage as the normal conduct of violent and lecherous soldiers, had been firmly established in the minds of their readers.[7]

That link was still understood by those who lived through the Revolutionary and Napoleonic Wars, since the huge armies that were recruited by all the main belligerents inevitably contained their quota of criminals and ne'er-do-wells, raised from among those who sought out army life to escape family squabbles at home, or had been given the option of enlistment or the gallows; this in turn fostered violence and produced a predictable explosion in crime. Soldiers billeted far from home felt few of the social constraints that helped moderate their conduct in their home villages, while debt, hunger, drink and sheer desperation all contributed to an increase in violent behaviour. There was the usual flurry of thefts from lonely farmhouses, stabbings in wayside bars and murders committed under the influence of drink, all of which were regarded as customary when armies passed through a rural community. Revolutionary and Napoleonic soldiers were no worse than those from previous eras; indeed, at certain times the laws against looting and pillage were so severe that standards of behaviour probably improved. But, more alarmingly for the authorities, there was an upsurge in highway robberies during these years, most particularly during the Directory. Soldiers were again turning to armed attacks and *brigandage*, though it was less a crime of serving soldiers than of those who sought to avoid service in the battalions, whether through desertion or by avoiding the draft, living a semi-clandestine existence in a *demi-monde* of vagrants and criminals. Such was the case with the infamous *bande de Salembier*, which ravaged much of the Nord and Pas-de-Calais during Years III and IV, with army deserters merging into a band of ordinary criminals, sixty strong, complete with their women and their family groups. In the Sarthe eye-witnesses spoke of up to forty deserters grouped in bands and spreading terror through the countryside; in the Ardèche the government's *commissaire* reported that 'the bands of brigands who devastate us' consisted principally of 'conscripts and draftees' who must be incorporated into their units without delay as a measure of public safety.[8] The link between soldiers and brigands was so clearly drawn in people's minds that highway robbers around Nyons in the Drôme were even reported to be passing themselves off as army deserters in order to allay public suspicion and gain a certain anonymity.[9]

So-called brigands were to be found everywhere – in the Pyrenees ambushing French soldiers on their way to Spain, in the Alps and the Apennines, swarthy mountain-dwellers using their native cunning and their knowledge of the countryside to outwit the revolutionary forces, as well as in the lawless periphery of France itself, towards the delta of the Rhône, for instance, or in the badlands of the Drôme or the Vaucluse. They were, it might appear, a rather indiscriminate bunch. Some were simple criminals, outlaws who lived in the woods or on the edge of remote villages, robbing strangers and merchants on the highways or – particularly during the Directory – concealing their criminal intentions behind vaguely royalist names and concentrating their thieving on mail coaches and other property of the French state. Others appeared to be committed to the counter-revolutionary cause, in the Vendée, for instance, or among the *chouans* in Brittany, men and women who had chosen a deliberate political path and who, by so doing, had placed themselves beyond the protection of the law. They had made a conscious choice not to be citizens, and had in consequence forfeited the rights which citizenship bestowed. They had slipped, seemingly effortlessly, from their place among the generality of Frenchmen – those who lived within the law and who could be presumed to be good and civically-motivated – into that grey area inhabited by those who fell beyond the pale of revolutionary orthodoxy to become the victims of what Sophie Wahnich has termed 'the logic of revolutionary exclusion'.[10] And though the level of threat that they posed to the authorities was never again to reach the proportions of the full scale civil war that was the Vendée during the spring and summer of 1793, brigandage would achieve its greatest geographical extent during the later 1790s, in the years of the Directory and Consulate.

The problem of brigandage during these years was one of public order, of course, and it is as such that it is generally treated in prefects' reports and other administrative despatches. For the authorities it was a 'social scourge' or a 'frightful plague', something that could only be overcome through a policy of severe repression, and if the Directory never succeeded in stamping it out, Napoleon came rather closer to restoring public order by attacking the brigands with all the armed might of the state. But the rise in the incidence of brigandage in this period, especially in some of the more peripheral areas of the country – *barbets* in the Alps, for instance, and *chauffeurs* in the Nord – alarmed the authorities and posed a severe threat to the governability of these regions, while the targets they selected for attack and the presence in their ranks of large numbers of army deserters alerted the government to their political as well as criminal intent. They focussed their attacks on merchants and other outsiders so as not to alienate local people. Systematically, too, they attacked symbols of governmental prestige and authority, like mail coaches and liberty trees, while the presence in their ranks – in the South-east particularly – of priests and refractory clergy gave a clear indication to the communities where they were staked out of a Catholic and counter-revolutionary ideology.[11] Their numbers were swollen by draft dodgers and by those who fell out with the revolutionary authorities, but – as the Directory itself recognized – the explosion in the scale of banditry in these years cannot be explained without reference to revolutionary politics. To take one example from just outside the *hexagone*, if the introduction of the conscription law caused the initial outburst of violence in Ghent in 1798, it cannot explain the so-called *guerre des paysans* which followed and which engulfed the Belgian departments:

> Conscription appears only to have been the pretext. [The revolt] was the result of British intrigue and of fanaticism. The motors of the rebellion are men attached either to the government of the erstwhile Belgian state or to the party of the *stathouder*; and the rebels themselves priests, monks, vagabonds and foreigners.[12]

Brigandage, in other words, was a complex construction which blended both the anti-revolutionary and the anti-social. Some of those denounced as brigands, like the *barbets* along the Italian frontier, appeared to start out with rather idealistic goals and were driven by a political agenda, but they fell into ordinary crime to keep themselves alive and were, by the end of a twenty-five year campaign of violence in the department of Alpes-Maritimes, indistinguishable from any other band of thieves and bandits.[13] Others were simple criminals, who skulked in the outskirts of southern cities to waylay passing mail coaches, often using royalist or anti-republican slogans to give themselves some pretence of legitimacy. In either case the effect was to dislocate local government and to deflect the military from their true vocation. The brigands sapped the strength and manpower of the Republic, targeting the very soldiers and gendarmes who were sent out to confront them, to the point where, in Stephen Clay's words, 'the roads leading to and from the Army of Italy were strewn with the corpses of soldiers who had been ambushed by brigands'.[14] Troops were tied down for months on end in an unsuccessful campaign to root them out, an aspect of Directorial policing which *émigrés* and counter-revolutionaries remarked upon with ill-concealed satisfaction, since it provided the proof they needed that public order had collapsed and that committed Catholics had been driven into clandestinity and a prolonged campaign of violence against the authorities. Like the various crimes on which they reported in France and the countries France occupied, the spread of brigandage was taken by the *émigré* press to demonstrate the social and moral degradation that resulted from the Revolution's 'new morality'.[15]

But how far should the definition of 'brigandage' extend? Did it have to involve armed robbery, or could it be used in a more generic way, to cover all those who by their actions placed themselves outside society,

unprotected by the law? For the Napoleonic régime, both inside France
and in occupied Europe, popular resistance was customarily explained
away as a criminal activity, as the work of bandits and outlaws who
sheltered among the people and cowed them into silence, rather than
of some national or popular movement that might be accorded a degree
of legitimacy. Napoleonic officials, both civil and military, sought to
deny their opponents any vestige of dignity, to strip them of the kind of
honourable feelings which only soldiers could be expected to display,
in short to reduce them to the level of common criminals who abused
popular trust in their quest for gain and local power. They could not,
obviously, condemn foreign armies in these terms; men who fought
against the French in the recognized military units of their states were
accorded the meagre respect due to enemy soldiers, while their officers
might expect to be treated with a respect appropriate to their rank.
Brigands were men who were not soldiers – irregulars, freedom-fighters,
guerrillas, militiamen, all might be wrapped up in the same term of
condescension, and be criminalized in the event of a French victory.
They were men who did not fight cleanly and did not accept the rules
of war, men who laid ambushes for the French, sought concealment
amongst the local civilian population, or otherwise resorted to tactics
unworthy of fighting men. It was not a precise term in the way that
'guerrilla' was to become, and it was used, apparently randomly and
indiscriminately, to describe those whose activity was deemed improper,
or underhand, or otherwise shameful. Napoleon did not hesitate, for
instance, to suggest that the men who burned Moscow to drive back his
advancing troops were themselves 'brigands'. Though they had acted
under the orders of General Rostopchin, he implied that they were no
better than common criminals, and in his bulletin from Moscow on
17 September 1812 he would say as much. 'On the 16th,' he reported,
'three to four hundred brigands set fire to the city in five hundred
places at once', and, fanned by fierce winds, their fires destroyed an
entire capital. The loss was incalculable. 'Churches, there were 1600 of
them; palaces, more than 1000; immense magazines; almost everything
has been consumed.' And who was responsible for the destruction of
such wealth and magnificence? 'Brigands', according to Napoleon,
'felons liberated from the prisons', the lowest of men; the sorts of men
who were not proper combatants and who therefore – as in the Peninsula
or the Vendée – could not expect to be treated as soldiers if they fell
into enemy hands. When the French captured them, they briefly interrogated them to establish that they had acted under orders; then, in
their hundreds, they were summarily shot.[16]

This use of the term 'brigand' had by 1812 become a commonplace of French imperial usage, a means of distinguishing between the proper and honourable French way of doing things and the underhand stratagems that were resorted to by their opponents. It was widely used during the Italian campaign to describe those who took advantage of the Alpine weather and of their intimate knowledge of the local topography to embarrass the French forces – the variously-named *barbets* and *chasseurs de montagne* who were such a significant fighting force in the passes and valleys of the *pré-Alpes*. Italy was the first campaign where the French felt they were fighting brigands rather than soldiers, and where their efforts were undermined both by a local population that was always prone to revolt and by an army of part-timers and irregulars whom they were unable to repress. They could never be sure whom they were fighting, or who their real enemy was. Each day, it seemed, villagers joined with escaped prisoners-of-war to attack the French; it was not like fighting an army, for the enemy was constantly changing and rarely identified itself as a military unit. Each day, as one desperate French soldier expressed it, 'We hunt down those villains who are set on murdering us, and when we do take prisoners we have no choice but to have them shot on the spot.'[17] Why? Because the nature of the fighting and of the terrain made it impossible to keep prisoners – a factor that would have led to a lot of shootings even in more conventional warfare – but also because, as armed civilians, often indistinguishable by any form of uniform, they were 'brigands', men to whom the normal rules of war simply did not apply. 'In the little town where I am stationed', wrote Claude Lavit to his father in 1809, 'the troops have their work cut out. The brigands are causing us a lot of trouble; for we are shooting large numbers of them, and we are the only ones to hunt them down, day and night.'[18] The imagery here is significant. Lavit is not talking of fighting or armed combat, man to man, as he would when describing engagements with the Austrians or Prussians. Rather it is the language of the hunter closing in on his prey. The 'brigands' are playing the role of wild animals, skulking in their dens, dehumanized, there to be killed before they could sink their fangs into the flesh of the troops themselves.

If the Italians were brigands, so, too, were the Spaniards and the Portuguese. Indeed, in the brigandage stakes, the Italian campaign faded into relative insignificance; the Iberian peninsula was, without doubt, the main feature. Here the term was almost automatically transferred to the villagers and guerrilla fighters who, without being incorporated into any regular force, demonstrated a natural genius for war on their own terrain, ambushing French units and critically holding up the armies' advance. Local people connived with them, sheltered them and offered them protection, standing lookout for them and warning them of any French approach. They gave them food when they refused to sell anything to the French. They treated them as their own, as kith and kin, which they probably were in many cases, though the French had no means of knowing and little means of distinguishing between fighter and protector, soldier and civilian. It was this that made the troops in the Peninsula so mistrustful of everyone they met, male and female, old and young. All were potential enemies, secretly and stealthily, turning their villages into armed encampments where any French soldier risked being treated with legendary cruelty. All might be allied against the invader in a war without rules, where killing was the major goal of soldier and civilian alike. The entire population had become indistinguishable, merging into one vast and incoherent viper's nest, a nation of 'brigands' who obeyed no laws and were governed by none.

If this was the language of official proclamations and military communiqués, how much more was it that of the troops themselves, constantly apprehensive and unwilling to trust anyone in a society they saw as unparalleled in its duplicity.[19] Napoleonic soldiers seem to have shared a horror of fighting there, especially after experience of other theatres of war, like Germany and Central Europe. Spain and Portugal were widely believed to be savage and inhospitable countries where French soldiers were left to die by callous villagers set on vengeance, where local people refused to sell them foodstuffs, and where they were virtually prisoners in their camps because of the activity of local 'brigands'.[20] The Peninsula was a miserable place for a soldier; as Jean Chapuy explained from Valladolid in 1809, the food and the climate conspired to make them ill, while the local people could then be counted upon to take advantage of their weakened state to attack them. 'We are in a country where one is in danger of falling ill', he wrote to his parents, 'and where one is also at risk of being assassinated by the peasants who are in revolt in every part of Spain.'[21] Few of his comrades would have disagreed with his pithy verdict. Even in hospital beds they were not safe, since in Iberia public morals were such, they believed, that no form of brutality or deception, however contemptible, could be ruled out. Joseph Vachin, a soldier from Mende in the Lozère, complained that an extended spell in hospital had reduced him to penury, since the orderlies stole from their patients while they were weak or delirious.[22] And the course of the war was so terribly unpredictable, they had no idea where the danger would appear from next. Letters spoke of troops being stoned and ambushed by civilians, of prisoners being brutally massacred, even of soldiers being burned alive. In words carefully chosen for posterity, Jean Marnier recalled that in Spain French troops faced a quite different sort of war. One of 'constant ambushes, murders and extermination', it was not like the ones that they had become accustomed to fighting elsewhere in Europe:

> There were not any battles to compare with Eylau or Friedland, but fighting on a daily basis against invisible assailants, spread out in their thousands behind bushes, at the bottom of ravines, hidden at the corner of every wall; we never enjoyed a truce or any rest, and treason was a constant risk, day and night, whether at the other side of the road or at the head of one's bed. Everyone was to be feared, even those seemingly hospitable people who took you into their homes.[23]

Since in Spain and Portugal the rules of civilized warfare were not respected, it followed that any form of retaliation was justified. The soldiers accepted that, since they were dealing with bandits, they could not afford to treat the enemy with the respect which the rules of war demanded. The Iberian front, the French were convinced, was one like no other, where no prisoners were taken and all – soldiers and civilians – could expect to be butchered without mercy. Any reprisals, however brutal, seemed justified as guerrilla warfare disintegrated into random tit-for-tat killings, with the French forced to accept the methods of the guerrillas and often tempted to ignore their own military discipline:

> Our light infantry picked up all those who had taken to flight and had hidden in the rocks. Not a single prisoner was taken. As thirty-five dragoons had been murdered by the inhabitants of this area, all the villages were burned and their inhabitants put to the sword. On the following day the same routine was repeated.[24]

All this might sound barbaric in any other context other than the Peninsula, where torture and massacre went unpunished and brutality bred brutality. The French torched the Portuguese town of Amarantes, for instance, after a number of men of the 17th Regiment had been seized and thrown on to a fire of live coals. The fire had been lit explicitly for the purpose, with an almost sadistic deliberation, and the soldiers had been quite callously left to burn painfully to death.[25] Like any act of terrorism, it was intended to infuriate the invader, to goad the French into losing their own discipline, and in this it undoubtedly succeeded. It is easy to see why the French loathed fighting in the Peninsula, and how deeply they came to hate Spain and Portugal and their people. 'The only thing that's any good in this country [i.e. Spain]', grumbled Vachin, 'is the bread, the wine and the meat; without them it would be the end of the world.'[26]

For many soldiers the issue at stake was the nature of the war itself. They were prepared to treat other armies with decency because they shared the same conception of warfare, exposing themselves to the same dangers, admiring the same qualities of courage and military science. But guerrillas were different. They detested fighting against them, or responding to tactics which only too often were intended to goad regular troops into anger and outrages that would, in turn, help to unite local people against them. The troops found it very hard to resist turning their fury on the local population; they were tired, constrained by military discipline, and revolted by what they saw; and often their tolerance had been pushed beyond endurance. Chevalier cites this lurid but very typical instance from the war in Calabria, but it could just as easily have taken place in Spain or Portugal. The French had reached a little town called Lauria, perched on a rock over the plain, and their general had sent an officer to negotiate with its citizens and to ask for food to provision the army. Their response was abrupt:

> As soon as the officer entered the town, he was murdered by the inhabitants, who brutally cut his body into pieces, put them in a basket and got French prisoners to return them to us with the message: 'This is the ration of food which the inhabitants of Lauria send to the French, the only one that can suit them'. Then our enraged soldiers scrambled up the rocks and, despite the desperate defence mounted by the inhabitants and a hail of bullets fired against them, they stormed the village. Everything was then sacrificed to pitiless vengeance. The old men, women and children fired on us from their windows or threw stones at us; it was just like Zaragoza. We were forced to set fire to every quarter of the town. A horrible scene then unfolded, as women, children and old men rushed from their blazing houses and threw themselves at the feet of the victors, only to be massacred by the enraged and furious troops.[27]

Even the rawest conscript had little difficulty in distinguishing such behaviour from war. War had rules, and – as it was learned in the eighteenth-century regiment – it was played out according to certain principles of honour and chivalry. What they experienced in Spain could not therefore be encompassed within the normal vocabulary of warfare. It was unregulated barbarism which the soldiers regarded as criminal rather than military, base and demeaning behaviour which was best seen as a particularly nasty form of brigandage.

The language of brigandage was not new to the First Empire; it had, indeed, been a favoured term during the French Revolution and throughout most of the eighteenth century to describe, belittle and demonize resistance to the authorities. Indeed, in revolutionary discourse about their opponents it is hard to escape references to 'brigands', or to avoid the feeling that 'brigand' had become by the mid-1790s a universally accepted term of abuse for political opponents, indeed for anyone who dared to reject the libertarian message that was handed down from Paris. And if for the Napoleonic armies the quintessential home of brigandage was the Iberian Peninsula, for the revolutionaries it was inside France itself, in a shadowy world inhabited by refractory priests and returned *émigrés*, monarchists and federalists and men bribed by the gold of Pitt and Albion. Most particularly, brigands were assumed to infest the six departments of the West that constituted the *Vendée militaire* and to stir up popular dissent amongst the peasantry. Local Jacobins in the cities of the West had reviled the peasant insurgents since the very first vestiges of revolt, long before the Convention or the Paris Jacobins joined in, denouncing the insurrectionists, quite predict-ably, as outlaws and murderers, and as 'brigands' who had chosen to betray their country and deny their membership of the French nation. For the authorities it was a natural term of abuse – as we shall see by examining the ways in which the rhetoric was used. The rebels, on the other hand, might adopt it with pride as a part of their collective identity, rather as the *sans-culottes* had done in Paris. Thus the more radical Patriots in Avignon showed little reluctance to be identified as *bons brigands* whilst they led their attack on the authorities, still glorying in the name after they had seized control of the Club and the National Guard in 1791.[28] Nor did the Belgian peasants in 1798 feel any embarrassment at adopting the language of brigandage, again the defiance of the *bons*, in their case against the iniquities of both revolution and occupation. It was a way of underlining their illegal status inside the French republic, and it was suggestive of the patriotism and the proto-nationalism they preached. Just as the *Vendée* would be remembered as a region defined by its politics, and by the intransigence of its opposition to the republic, so the peasants of 1798 would enter Belgian history as heroes – as 'brigands' – led by national heroes like the *capitaine des chauffeurs*,

Moneuse.[29] In popular movements brigands had something rather heroic about them which radiated a more general appeal. It is no accident, as Xavier Rousseaux reminds us, that by the twentieth century the words 'Brigand' and 'Moneuse' would be familiar in a rather different context, as widely appreciated brands of Belgian beer.[30]

The revolutionary response to the Vendée was not intended to evoke images of heroism, however, but to discredit any political or social movement that offered a different view of the world. To such people the Revolution could offer no quarter; they were therefore dismissed as outlaws, as 'brigands', as common criminals who should be hunted down and slaughtered as such. Attempts to distinguish between leaders and followers were soon abandoned, since at a time when republican soldiers were being killed and tortured by the rebels any desire to distinguish between degrees of responsibility soon faded. The entire population of the West was demonized as people in a state of rebellion, men and women led into sedition by their nobles and priests – especially by their priests in a countryside where all were assumed to be pawns of a refractory and deeply reactionary clergy. The Vendean is not just *séditieux*; he is *fanatisé*, deaf to reasoned argument and a dupe to the local clergy, his credulity and child-like faith making him putty in the hands of the local nobility and of British agents. He was perceived as the other, the epitome of all that was antipathetic to the Revolution and to republican France. On the battlefield he appeared to delight in acts of unspeakable cruelty. In Turreau's words, 'They are less concerned here with fighting than with taking us by surprise and massacring us. The leaders of the rebels kidnap our soldiers and make them die in the most indescribable torment'.[31] Because, as in the Iberian peninsula, the French faced an enemy who elected to fight through ambushes and guerrilla tactics, leaning heavily on the support of villagers and of their womenfolk, there was little reason to count them as soldiers, or to treat with honour people who responded with cunning and savagery, the language of denunciation became stronger, the representation more cruelly distorting. The Vendean was condemned as a criminal, a bandit, an outlaw, out to undermine the republic and destroy public order – in short, he was a brigand. But he was also so much more.

As this was a civil war in which hatreds ran much deeper, it was not sufficient merely to categorize the Vendean as a brigand. Brigands, after all, might be criminal in their use of violence against the republic, and might, if caught, deserve the death penalty for their crimes; but they remained human beings, capable of rational – if at times deeply flawed – choices. Of course they were not rational or enlightened human beings: that was self-evident. They were primitive peasants who belonged to what the revolutionaries saw as an alien and superstitious culture, one where men sought the blessing of their priests before battle and the promise that, should they have the honour of dying for Christ and King, they would return from the dead within three days.[32] But was it possible that men who committed such atrocities in cold blood could retain even the palest remnants of human sensibility? Were they really men at all? In the language of urban *commissaires* and of deputies on mission to the West it is noticeable how systematically the terms of abuse that were heaped on the rebels sought to dehumanize them, and to suggest that their behaviour was akin to that of wild beasts rather than of men. The same language occurred again and again in reports and memoirs, words like 'beasts', 'monsters', 'vermin', or 'ferocious animals who seek to devour the republic' – words which were used with cold deliberation to devalue the lives of the enemy. They had, it was inferred, a taste for blood and a love of killing that more properly belong to wild animals, and, like refractory priests and *émigré* nobles, their savagery was reserved for supporters of the new political order. This impression was made more vivid when it was observed that they lived like beasts, skulking behind hedges, leaping out from bushes, retiring to lick their wounds in a clearing in the scrub or dragging their unfortunate victims back to their lairs (*tanières*).[33] The propaganda effect of this language was considerable, especially in the capital and the republican strongholds of the interior, and also in the army, where soldiers soon learned that these were not honourable opponents whom they should treat with respect. They obeyed no rules of war, nor had they any understanding of honour in the way the revolutionary soldiers understood it. Indeed, it was their animal instincts which best explained their successes in engaging the republican army. As one cavalryman from the Gironde wrote of his experience in the Vendée, 'if they had not acted like wild beasts and sought refuge in the woods', they would surely have been wiped out.[34]

There was nothing haphazard about this representation. As in more recent wars, the government was dehumanizing its opponents and spreading atrocity stories with a clear awareness of the effects their propaganda would have in angering civilian opinion and spurring their soldiers to new efforts.[35] This was a war in which public opinion mattered, and where words carried a special weight. Once dehumanized in this way, once stripped of those characteristics which others shared with him and depicted as a beast of the fields, the Vendean became an easier target for vengeance. French civilians would be less likely to shelter him, while revolutionary soldiers would have fewer qualms about order- ing him before a firing squad. It is easy to see why. Wolves and wild dogs pose an obvious threat to human beings, and no French peasant would hesitate to gun them down. Vermin must be trapped or poisoned so that others can enjoy good health; they have to be wiped out, eradicated in the interests of survival. The language that was used to revile the Vendeans went a long way to remove any lingering sense of the sanctity of human life, leaving them vulnerable to republican revenge. It is the language of extermination, the extermination of a corrupt community, an act of killing that evoked few moral qualms or repugnance, and no danger of fellow-feeling. Killing became a cleansing exercise, *épuration* in the fullest sense of the term. The Vendean was a wild beast, unworthy of life; and, like a wild beast, his continued existence would put the French and their republic at risk. The Revolution had moved on from depictions of brigandage and criminalization to portrayals of the enemy as an inferior species, a systematic resort to dehumanization that has encouraged historians of the right, like Pierre Chaunu, to talk of the Republic's record in the West as genocide, and to compare it to more infamous genocides of the twentieth century, in Germany, Rwanda, Cambodia, and elsewhere.[36]

This should, I suggest, be seen as a more extreme instance of the same process – the use of images and propaganda to belittle and demean the opponents of the régime, be it Revolutionary or Napoleonic. It had its effect on civilian opinion, and so, as in Spain, it affected the way French troops fought and the light in which they regarded the enemy. Just as they would do in Spain, French soldiers who were sent to fight in the Vendée learned from the propaganda of their generals and refused to see the Vendeans as combatants to whom the honours of war were due. And that in turn changed the character of the war.[37] The French troops expressed their horror at the atrocities they witnessed, their comrades betrayed and ambushed before being left hacked to pieces with bayonets on the highway. They expressed contempt for the superstitious naivety – as they saw it – of the Vendeans, and for the gross excesses to which this gave rise. For Savary, for instance, everything came down to religion, since the Vendean believed anything, however absurd, that was whispered to him by his priest, to the extent that he became 'the instrument and the victim of the forces that set him in motion'.[38] That helped explain his ruthlessness, his wanton cruelty, his lack of scruples; and it also explained the eager savagery of the French response. Faced with a population that was *fanatisée* and with potential enemies in every village and behind every hedgerow, the French could not afford the luxury of clemency. As Boissé, a municipal officer from Bordeaux serving in the West, wrote home in 1793, 'In the Vendée the idea of forgiving an enemy is unthinkable.'[39] Prisoners were therefore butchered – after the fall of Noirmoutier they shot them in batches of fifteen hundred – and the priests figured in the front line of their imagined foes. For Jean-Charles Bouquet, the son of an ironmonger from Reims and a committed republican, the society of the West was riddled with priests, and hence with the basest treachery; he had no sympathy for those who fell into republican hands and delighted in watching them drown in the Loire:

> The priests who had dared to resist the General Will were put on board a boat which already held a number of refractory priests, but, thanks – who knows? – to the workings of the Republican genius, a rotten plank got loose. With water pouring in on all sides, the vessel sank with all its equally rotten priestly cargo.[40]

This is one take on the *noyades* of Nantes which caused such outrage in Paris after Thermidor, when every detail was pored over during the public show trial of Carrier as France tried to purge itself of its collective guilt. It is an approach that suggests a terrible cruelty on the part of the republican troops, a cruelty that comes close to bloodlust. But the soldiers were the same men who had fought in Belgium, on the Rhine and along the Moselle, and who in these ordinary contexts had never thought in such terms. They were not naturally savage or inhumane. Rather they had been accustomed by relentless propaganda before they left for the West, and subsequently by evidence of how a guerrilla war was fought, to regard the enemy as less than honourable, as 'brigands', ultimately as wild beasts of the fields and woods. They were *Untermenschen*, unworthy of the name of humanity. That propaganda should be seen as an essential part of the French armoury in both the Vendée and, later, in the Peninsula. It was part of the nation's defence against guerrillas and irregular forces, against whom regular battalions experienced considerable difficulties in the field. Its predictable outcome was a war conducted with a total lack of fellow-feeling or mutual understanding, with no hint of *considération* between the warring sides. To that degree the war against 'brigands' was also a victory for political rhetoric, for one discourse over another, a victory by revolutionary and Napoleonic *spinmeisters* which effectively complemented that of the nation's military battalions in the field.

Notes

1. I.A. Cameron, *Crime and Repression in the Auvergne and Guienne, 1720–1790* (Cambridge, 1981), pp. 189–90.
2. R. Cobb, *Reactions to the French Revolution* (Oxford, 1972), pp. 128–79.
3. E. Hobsbawm, *Bandits* (London, 1967) provides an excellent overview of the place of bandits and brigands in history.
4. Cobb, *Reactions to the French Revolution*, frontispiece, and notes, pp. 272–5.
5. *Ibid.*, p. 138.
6. M. Marion, *Le brigandage pendant la Révolution* (Paris, 1934), pp. i–iv.
7. D. Diderot and J. d'Alembert (eds) *L'Encyclopédie, ou Dictionnaire raisonné des sciences, des arts et des métiers*, (Paris, 1751), II, p. 420. The word 'brigandine' was also used in the English language from mediaeval times onwards. However, a more common alternative was 'jack'. Aside from giving us the expression 'every man-jack', this term survives as a another term for the knave in a pack of cards. Again, then, we see the instinctive linkage between the soldier and crime.
8. A. Forrest, *Conscripts and Deserters: the Army and French Society during the Revolution and Empire* (New York, 1989), p. 124.
9. An excellent account of brigandage in this department is to be found in R. Maltby, 'Le brigandage dans la Drôme, 1795–1803', *Bulletin d'archéologie et de statistique de la Drôme*, LXXIX, no. 390 (1973), pp. 117–34.
10. S. Wahnich, 'La logique de l'exclusion révolutionnaire', in J.C. Martin (ed.), *La guerre civile entre histoire et mémoire* (Nantes, 1995), p. 65.
11. G. Lewis, 'Political brigandage and popular disaffection in the South-east of France, 1795–1804', in G. Lewis and C. Lucas (eds), *Beyond the Terror: Essays in French Regional and Social History, 1794–1815* (Cambridge, 1983), pp. 195–231.
12. F. Stevens, 'La résistance au Directoire dans les départements réunis: la "guerre des paysans" (octobre–novembre 1798)', in P. Bourdin and B. Gainot (eds), *La République directoriale* (Clermont-Ferrand, 1998), II, pp. 1025–6.
13. M.A. Iafelice, 'Les "barbets" des Alpes-Maritimes: origines et caractérisation du barbétisme', in F. Lebrun and R. Dupuy (eds), *Les résistances à la Révolution* (Paris, 1987), pp. 126–32.
14. S. Clay, 'Le brigandage en Provence du Directoire au Consulat, 1795–1802', in J.P. Jessenne (ed.), *Du Directoire au Consulat (3): Brumaire dans l'histoire du lien politique et de l'Etat-Nation* (Rouen, 2001), pp. 70–1.
15. S. Burrows, *French Exile Journalism and European Politics, 1792–1814* (London, 2000), p. 209.
16. Twentieth and Twenty-first *Bulletins de la Grande Armée*, Moscow,17 and 20 September 1812, J.D. Markham, *Imperial Glory. The Bulletins of Napoleon's Grande Armée, 1805–1814* (London, pp. 298–300.
17. A. Palluel-Guillard, 'Correpondance et mentalité des soldats savoyards de l'armée napoléonienne', in *Soldats et armées en Savoie: actes du 28e Congrès des Sociétés Savantes de Savoie* (Chambéry, 1981), p. 206.
18. Archives Départementales (hereafter AD), Savoie, L1137: letter from C. Lavit, Legnano, 5 August 1809.
19. The discussion that follows of soldiers' views of fighting in Spain is taken from my recent book, *Napoleon's Men: the Soldiers of the Revolution and Empire* (London, 2002), pp. 124–7.

20. AD Oise, series R (unclassified): letters of imperial soldiers to their families, an VIII – 1823.
21. AD Haute-Loire, R5973: letter from Jean Chapuy to his parents in Saint-Julien-Chapteuil, 1 August 1809.
22. AD Lozère, F424: letter from Joseph Vachin to his uncle in Mende, 1 September 1808.
23. J. Marnier, *Souvenirs de guerre en temps de paix* (Paris, 1867), p. 36.
24. AD Finistère, 35J11: letter from François Avril to his parents from Zamora, 26 July 1809.
25. *Ibid.*
26. AD Lozère, F424: letter from Joseph Vachin to his uncle, from Burgos, 10 April 1808.
27. J.M. Chevalier, *Souvenirs des guerres napoléoniennes* (Paris, 1970), p. 74.
28. R. Moulinas, *Histoire de la Révolution d'Avignon* (Avignon, 1986), pp. 175–9.
29. For a typically heroic view, cf. A. Gallez, *Un émule de Cartouche sous le Directoire: le brigand Moneuse, capitaine des 'chauffeurs du Nord'* (Brussels, 1959).
30. X. Rousseaux, 'Brigandage, gendarmerie et justice: l'ordre républicain dans les départements du nord de la France et les départements réunis (Belgique, Rhénanie) entre Directoire et Consulat (1795–1804)', in Jessenne, *Brumaire*, p. 94.
31. M. Chatry (ed.), *Turreau en Vendée: Mémoires et correspondance* (Cholet, 1992), p. 270.
32. P. Tyson, 'The Role of Republican and *Patriote* Discourse in the Insurrection of the Vendée' (MA dissertation, University of York, 1994), p. 98.
33. *Ibid.*, pp. 96–7.
34. G. Pages, 'Lettres de requis et volontaires de Coutras en Vendée et en Bretagne', *Revue historique et archéologique du Libournais*, CXC (1983), p. 155.
35. Cf., by way of example, J. Horne and A. Kramer, *German Atrocities, 1914: A History of Denial* (New Haven, 2001).
36. R. Secher, *Le génocide franco-français: la Vendée-vengé* (Paris, 1986), *passim*. The idea that the Vendée is best understood as genocide is proposed in the *préface* by Jean Meyer, who compares the repression of the region with that of German Jews in the Holocaust (p. 15), and in the *avant-propos* by Pierre Chaunu, who writes that 'the sadistic imagination of Turreau's columns equals that of the SS, the gulags and the Khmers Rouges' (p. 22).
37. A. Forrest, 'La Guerre de l'Ouest vue par les soldats républicains', in J.C. Martin (ed.), *La guerre civile entre histoire et mémoire* (Nantes, 1995), pp. 91–9.
38. J.J. Savary, *Guerres de Vendée et des Chouans contre la République Française* (Paris, 1824), I, p. 29.
39. A.D. Gironde, 12L1: letter from Boissé to the President of the Club National in Bordeaux, 24 September 1793.
40. F. Coutansais, 'La Guerre des Géants vue par les bleus', *Revue du Bas-Poitou*, LXXIV (1963), p. 432.

This page intentionally left blank

3
Guerrilla Warfare *avant la lettre*: Northern Italy, 1792–97

Martin Boycott-Brown

According to *The Oxford English Dictionary*, the term 'guerrilla' first appeared in the English language in 1809. However, it is fairly obvious that the concept of the guerrilla, and the type of warfare associated with it, are much older than that. If we look at the definition of the phenomenon provided by *The Shorter Oxford English Dictionary*, which states that it is 'an irregular war carried on by small bodies of men acting independently' and that a guerrilla is 'one engaged in such warfare', we can see similarities with the type of military action that eighteenth-century military men often refer to as *la petite guerre* or *klein Krieg*, which was characterized by sporadic skirmishes, ambushes, and raids by small groups of lightly armed troops. However, this kind of fighting was normally carried out by men who were, at least technically speaking, soldiers. (In the case of the earliest Hungarian hussars and the first of the Austrian army's Croats, there is at least some doubt whether they can properly be classed as 'soldiers'.) Although the dictionary definition quoted above says nothing about the composition of guerrilla bands, it is probable that most people nowadays would not think of them as being made up of soldiers, but rather as consisting mostly of armed civilians, perhaps with a sprinkling of uniformed men.

Such groups of armed civilians certainly existed in northern Italy in the 1790s, though in most cases they were not highly organized or long-lived, nor did they always have a truly military purpose. It should be noted that the dictionary definition implies that in order for a group of people to qualify for the name 'guerrilla' they have to be involved in war, not in some other violent activity, such as banditry, but there are times when it is difficult to know where one such activity ends and the other begins. However, arriving at a precise definition of the meaning of the terms 'guerrilla' and 'guerrilla warfare', and deciding whether the armed civilians of northern Italy were 'proper' guerrillas, is not what this chapter is about. Rather, the main intention is to look at a few specific cases of popular resistance (in the mountains of the Riviera, in the Po valley, and around Rivoli), and the sometimes surprising French reaction to them. In other words, we will look, if only superficially, at the relationship between the civilians and the military, concentrating more on individuals than on relations at the level of leaders and institutions, and see what kinds of relations existed between them at different times and places. At this point it should be made clear that this chapter is based on published sources, so it owes a large debt to others, particularly some Italian local historians, who have found and published much interesting material relating to the subjects we shall be looking at. But as their work remains largely unknown to those who have no Italian, it is to be hoped that it will still add something to the debate. In passing, it might also be observed that this chapter touches on an aspect of war that is too often neglected by military historians, who rarely have anything to say about civilians and often write about warfare as if it took place in the middle of the ocean, in areas where nobody lives. Yet civilians suffer dreadfully from the effects of war, and every single campaign and battle – with rare exceptions – takes place in somebody's cornfield, in somebody's orchard, or in somebody's village.

We shall begin by examining the Riviera, and, in common with the other areas we shall be discussing, it is important to look first at its geography. Put very simply, much of the area would seem to have been ideal terrain for brigands or guerrillas. Not only is it hilly or mountainous, but much of it is, and was, covered with fairly dense woods. There were few good roads, but many, many, mule tracks winding over the broken terrain, giving any number of escape routes, or places where ambushes could be made. It was also an extremely poor area, little suited to agriculture, and had a sparse population. Politically speaking, most of the coastal strip belonged to the Republic of Genoa, and was neutral in the War of the First Coalition, but only a few miles inland the territory belonged to Piedmont, which was at war with the French. The latter first moved into the Riviera in September 1792, when they captured Nice, which at that time was a Piedmontese possession. They then occupied various parts of the Riviera until Napoleon Bonaparte's offensive of April 1796 took the main sphere of military operations inland to Lombardy.

The French had not been in the Riviera long before they began to encounter hostile armed civilians (sometimes alone, and sometimes in bands) whom they called *barbets*. To return to terminology for a moment, *barbet* was a local dialect word of obscure origins that had once been applied to the Waldensians, who had been persecuted by the Piedmontese government because of their religion, and had taken refuge in the mountains. The *barbets* of the 1790s who ambushed French soldiers and raided some of their positions might be called brigands or guerrillas, though it is difficult to say which title is more appropriate. In referring to them, the French seem habitually to have used the word *barbets*, rather than 'brigands', but this may just have been the result of soldiers adopting the terminology used by local people in the area where they were serving, as happened in Spain from 1809, when the English began to use the word 'guerrilla'. We should also probably not read too much into the fact that there are occasional references to the *barbets'* mode of dress marking them out. When the body of a man with a musket beside him was found in the mountains near a village, for example, the local mayor commented that 'It is probable that this body is that of a *barbet*, to judge from the clothes'.[1] Yet we have no way of knowing if this is a reference to clothes that were suitable to a life of fighting, or merely to a state of raggedness indicative of living rough. More to the point, perhaps, it seems impossible to prove that *barbets* ambushed passing French soldiers for military reasons, rather than reasons of theft, which makes it impossible to state categorically that they were involved in warfare rather than acts of brigandage. Indeed, it seems probable that these bands were not formed in response to the French invasion, but were originally groups of robbers who preyed on the many travellers who used the road from Nice to Turin, which passed over Colle di Tenda and was one of the most important routes from the Mediterranean into northern Italy. The character of these bands no doubt changed with the French invasion of Nice. Deserters from both the French and Piedmontese armies would have provided a useful flow of recruits, who would have brought their own weapons with them, and would have been familiar with the military methods of both sides, as well as being used to a dangerous and violent life. But the arrival of deserters from opposing camps must surely have made it much less likely that the bands would engage in the kind of patriotic struggle in defence of an invaded homeland that is commonly associated with guerrilla activity.

Whatever the reasons for their activities, the French soon found the *barbets* enough of a nuisance to mount organized operations against them. One of the earlier descriptions of such an operation dates from the spring of 1793, and formed part of a letter that Barthélemy-Catherine

Joubert (later one of the most successful generals of the 1796 campaign) wrote to his father. He says:

At the end of April [1793] I was given the mission of chasing from their rocks and caves some *barbets* who were murdering our orderly dragoons. With fifty grenadiers I pursued them for a day and a night, in the most abominable places. One could only reach their rocks by having risked breaking one's neck a hundred times. Often one had to drag oneself on one's belly. Many times I found myself with one or two grenadiers at most. We killed a *barbet* and took eight of them.[2]

The fact that a force of fifty men had been sent to deal with this band suggests that their activities must have been causing some annoyance, though we may infer that they did not pose a serious military threat. Indeed, after giving us this very brief description of the *barbets*, the rest of Joubert's letter, which is a long one, deals with a conventional military operation against a Piedmontese outpost in the mountains. This gives us some idea of the relative importance of the two types of operation, at least in the mind of Joubert. Nevertheless, the County of Nice continued to be a most dangerous area for the French, and attacks on them showed no sign of ceasing. Indeed, they became so serious that Bonaparte mentioned them at the end of one of his letters to the French government, written from Milan on 25 August 1796:

The King of Sardinia having disbanded his provincial regiments, the *barbets* have increased in number. A wagon carrying silver has been pillaged. General Dujard, while going to Nice, has been killed. I have organized a mobile column with a tribunal against the *barbets* to mete out justice to them.[3]

A mobile column of 4000 men under General Casabianca had been duly formed, and the commander of the French garrisons in Piedmont, General Macquart, was ordered to cooperate with his task as much as possible. It does not seem to have been wholly successful, and in September Bonaparte invited the Piedmontese government to position their own troops in the areas of Limone, Demonte, Cuneo and Barcelonette, to oppose the *barbets* and protect the French convoys.[4]

In other parts of the Riviera, armed resistance was undoubtedly directly linked to outrages committed by the French.[5] According to Leonello Oliveri, a historian who has made a special study of the wars in the Val Bormida (where the French first arrived in September 1794),

'To begin with, the local population did not welcome the French troops badly, but rather they watched their battles with the Austrians almost like neutral spectators...and the greatest worries were about the damage to the crops.'[6] But the French offensive of April 1796 brought a different set of circumstances, when French troops were pushed to the limit, and soon outdistanced their meagre and inefficient supply trains, having to go for days without rations. Moreover, the military situation was fluid and confused, and the rapid movement created conditions that many soldiers were able to exploit by absenting themselves to look for loot. The locals therefore found themselves inundated by hordes of desperate men looking for food, or money and valuables. Their reaction was as violent as the treatment they had been subjected to. A fairly graphic description of the fate of the area around Dego in April 1796 is given by a local minor noble, Count Moretti. He was avowedly pro-Austrian and anti-French, which may lend colour to his story, but there seems little reason to doubt the overall outline of his account:

> Now from these two battles [of Dego] begins the painful story of these villages of ours, Rocchetta, Dego, Giusvalla, Piana (our house is the one that suffered more than any other), Brovida, Santa Giulia, and La Scaletta were barbarously sacked without any restraint for eight days together...cattle, grain, wine, everything was taken, the furniture was taken away or burnt, people tortured with the most barbarous methods to get them to give up their money...the women were treated with the ultimate indignities, after first stripping them of whatever valuables they had...I will not speak of the churches and sacred objects, which are things that horrify. The last two days, however, the villagers recovering a little from the shock, especially those of the nearby *langhe*,[7] and fear having changed to desperation, they united in armed bands, and moving day and night through the nearby hills and roads, they began to kill whatever enemies fell into their hands without quarter, and firing on those who came out to sack, blunting their pride somewhat, keeping them away from many villages, so that all the *langa* of La Rocha, Serole, Gorio, Olmo, Perleto and Cagna were exempt from robberies. The villagers also continued this practice in the days after the truce [the armistice of Cherasco], attacking and despoiling entire convoys of French.[8]

Moretti was not the only eye-witness to comment on the formation of bands of armed civilians. Another such was a lawyer from Millesimo, called Fassino, who observed that civilian resistance continued after the end of the war with Piedmont in April 1796, and that 'the French army was split up by the various bands of armed country people, who killed all those who remained behind, and the small squads that were trying to reach their units.'[9]

This does not seem like mere banditry, because the bands seem to have been formed to take revenge on the French for their excesses, rather than for motives of theft, but it is perhaps too much to attribute a truly military intention to their activities. As Oliveri remarks, 'Information relative to the Val Bormida is fragmentary and does not permit us to know if there was organised resistance or mere episodes that did not come out of an agreed plan of combat.'[10] Elsewhere he is more definite, stating: 'This is not a guerrilla movement according to modern canons, but a spontaneous armed resistance which manifests itself here and there. Where the peasants have to pay the price of the invasion they do not welcome the French troops with that enthusiasm that was manifested in many intellectual coteries.'[11] Yet for all that he may not have been a guerrilla, the Piedmontese peasant, faced with the devastation of his home and the likelihood of death from starvation, put up a ferocious resistance. It was a reaction that was feared by at least some French generals. Joubert, for one, expressed his disquiet in a letter, saying:

> Everything would go very well if the soldiers did not abandon themselves to pillage: not a day passes without some pillagers being shot. Despite this severity the mania does not stop: the country people are arming themselves.[12]

As Bonaparte himself had written before the beginning of the campaign, 'The poverty [of the troops] has authorised indiscipline, and without discipline, [there can be] no glory.'[13] It therefore seems likely that several threatening orders that were issued to the troops had as much the intention of maintaining the cohesion of the army as that of protecting civilians.

To summarize, the French came up against determined, though limited, resistance from armed civilians along the Riviera, but though it caused annoyance it never became a serious threat to military operations. Some of this resistance may well have been put up by pre-existing bands of brigands who were probably more interested in loot than in defeating a French invader, while other instances of resistance were born out of a struggle for survival or a desire for revenge, and involved groups of peasants taking up arms against isolated groups of soldiers. In this case there is an element of wishing to defeat an invader, but whether it can be called guerrilla warfare is highly debatable. As to the French reaction, it is somewhat surprising that the civilian sources quoted here make no mention of reprisals. One might have expected the heavy hand of repression, but Count Moretti, for example, says only that the French began to avail themselves of Piedmontese troops to protect their convoys, and gives not the slightest hint of any repressive measures being taken. Yet we know that when there were major insurrections in the Val Bormida three years later, the French shot more than a few insurgents when they captured them. It seems improbable that the French did not do their best to hunt down the armed peasants in the Langhe, particularly when they took such large measures against the *barbets* further west, but it would seem that they did not capture many.

Let us now look at events in the Po valley, where the French were to spend nine months fighting the Austrians between the beginning of May 1796 and February 1797. As before, it is important to say something about the geography, which could hardly provide a greater contrast with the Riviera. While the latter is mountainous and forested, the Po valley is a wide, flat, open plain with only low hills in a few areas. The land has been intensively cultivated for centuries and there is almost no forest. Unlike the mountains of the Riviera, where a few peasants scratched out a living from the thin soil and there were no large towns, the Po valley was fertile and populous and home to wealthy cities like Milan. In other words, it was terrain that seemed to offer little to favour the guerrilla fighter. There were few, if any, natural refuges in which to conceal a band of men, and flat terrain makes cavalry and artillery both more usable and less dispensable. These are both arms in which guerrilla bands tend to be lacking, which puts them at a disadvantage against a conventional army in flat lands. It is not surprising, therefore, that the most serious instances of armed resistance to the French in the Po valley took the form of insurrections, rather than the raids and ambushes that characterized civilian action in the mountains. Most of these insurrections occurred in Lombardy (a province that had once been ruled by Spain and had then passed under Austrian control) and Emilia Romagna, which belonged to the Papal States.

When the French launched themselves into Lombardy, it was with a lightning movement that gave rise to a situation that was every bit as confused and fluid as that which had existed during their attack through the mountains of the Riviera the previous month. As before, in rural areas the soldiers found opportunities to commit all sorts of abuses. The parish priest of Ombriano, a village not far from Crema, tells us that on 11 May, the day after the battle of Lodi, the French advance guard reached his village at about eight in the morning. It was a traumatic event:

> The troops...broken with fatigue, hungry, despoiled all the houses, the parishioners having fled to other villages and into the marshes... I was with Sig Francesco Donati, and was assailed by a picket of twelve French hussars, who robbed us of everything, with sabres and with muskets at our chests.[14]

Terrified, the priest and his companion hid in a nearby mill, from which they could only watch in anguish as his house was broken into and his church desecrated, the soldiers taking away all the church vestments and sacred objects. This was not an isolated case, nor were the French the only culprits, as we may gather from the testimony of an engineer called Massari, who lived in Crema:

> We had only just entered the Ombriano Gate [of Crema] when we saw the country people come running panting into the town from the nearby villages, saying that the few Germans [i.e. Austrians] who were retiring had begun to steal, at first only at isolated farmhouses, and then in some of the villages, and the first small groups of French who pursued them had begun to do the same as well. At the very same instant that this news spread through the town, with the addition that the French themselves were arriving at any moment, you could see all the houses and shops and also even the gate of the town shut with precipitate speed, so that it seemed that the end of the world had come.[15]

According to Massari, the panicky reaction of the people of Crema was due to 'the very great fear that they had of the French...a fear that had taken hold of almost all the inhabitants of Italy because of the great vendetta and tyranny that was attributed to them both by the public newspapers and gazettes as well as by all those who could not even hear speak of them, such was the hate and aversion that was generally felt towards the French in Italy.'[16]

Whether or not the views of most Italians were as Massari says, the French hardly conducted themselves in a manner that was conducive to good relations. Not only was there small scale pillaging of houses and churches by individuals and groups of soldiers, there was also official – or apparently official – looting on a grand scale. In addition, the French made exorbitant demands for supplies, and began to rearrange the government of Lombardy. Lodi provides a fairly good example of what happened in the province. First it had to provide a large number of rations for the Austrian army as it moved through in its retreat, then it had to do the same for the French army when it arrived. On 10 May it was ordered to provide 40 000 rations of food, and the same number for each of the following two days.[17] For a town that counted 12 000 inhabitants, this kind of demand meant using up practically all the reserves of staple foods, with the result that the local population would not have enough to last until the next harvest. Lodi was lucky in that it was able to obtain extra food from Milan, but the strain on local resources was enormous. The next misfortune that befell Lodi concerned its Monte di Pietà, a credit institution of a kind that was very common in Italy. They were run under the auspices of the church, and their function was to advance small loans to less affluent people at low rates of interest, in exchange for items deposited as securities. They therefore held numerous precious articles of every sort and description, as well as less valuable items. The total value of the cash and objects deposited with the Monte in Lodi at that time came to about 235 000 lire, which made it a tempting target. On 11 May its offices were visited by a French commissary, Collot, who sequestered all the valuables, though in a show of Republican egalitarianism, poor people were allowed to reclaim non-valuable items free of charge. The tickets attached to the precious objects were ripped off, so that their owners could not be identified, after which the objects themselves quickly disappeared. What happened to them does not seem to be recorded, so we do not know if they went into the army's coffers, or Collot's.[18]

It was much the same story in other parts of Lombardy, which the French seemed to regard as a kind of gold mine to be exploited without restraint. On 17 May, Bonaparte wrote to the French government saying, 'We shall obtain twenty millions in contributions from this country. It is one of the richest in the universe' though he completely undermined this justification by adding, 'but [it is] entirely exhausted after five years of war'.[19] Further bizarre contradictions followed hard on the heels of this. Apparently oblivious to the irony in what he was saying, Bonaparte issued an order the same day stating that French soldiers 'must respect and protect the inhabitants of the lands [they] have conquered' on the grounds that 'the General in Chief has too lively a desire to maintain the honour of the army to suffer any individual to violate property'.[20] He also dictated various letters that day and the next concerning vast sums of money and paintings to be taken from Parma, Modena, and Milan to be sent to Paris. Then in a proclamation to the people of Lombardy issued on 19 May he unveiled to them the huge amount of money he expected them to hand over to the army, presenting it as a fair price for liberation from the Austrians, and 'a very small contribution for countries so fertile'.[21] Yet Pietro Verri, who was involved in the administration of the province, commented that the sum was equivalent to four years' direct taxation, and that it would take many years 'perhaps even a generation'[22] to recover from the effects.

Not only had the economy been thrown out of equilibrium by the arrival of the French, but so had the political organization of Lombardy. The Austrian governor (the Archduke Ferdinand) had left hurriedly, consigning power to a group of local notables. Not only was this arrangement rapidly dismantled by the French, but a large number of local revolutionaries and French sympathisers, who had previously kept a low profile, began to throw their weight around, secure in the protection of the 'liberating' army. Trees of liberty began to be erected in town squares and symbols of real or supposed tyranny were destroyed by excited 'Jacobins'. One particular act of this kind was to be a large contributing factor in the gravest outbreak of civilian violence against the French. The events provide an interesting contrast with the kind of resistance that had sprung up in the mountains of the Riviera, where the occasional ambush seems to have been the norm. On 16 May a tree of liberty had been put up in the town square of Pavia. Unfortunately, the square was also the site of an ancient equestrian statue, known as the Regisole, which represented a Roman Emperor. The local people were proud of it, and it was regarded as something of a symbol of the city – but the Jacobins who had put up the tree of liberty decided that it must be the statue of a tyrant, and that it should not be allowed to share the same space as the new symbol of the people's freedom. They therefore clamoured to smash it down. The French commanders in the town, generals Augereau and Rusca, seem to have been reluctant to sanction this act of vandalism, but eventually gave way. While the French did not directly take a hand in destroying the statue, it was only the presence of squads of soldiers in the square that made it possible for the Jacobins to carry out their work without being lynched.

It seems worth commenting that what had been destroyed here was a powerful symbol of local identity and tradition. The attack on the local people's sense of identity, though not directly carried out by the French, can only have increased the sense of alienation and enmity felt towards them. Although there was no immediate large reaction by the local civilians, there were clear signs of unrest in the country around Pavia in the days that followed. On 17 May a local man called Fenini, who was going to Milan on official business, noticed groups of up to 100 peasants armed with agricultural implements at almost every village along the road.[23] The local authorities were sufficiently worried that they sent Fenini and two others to a couple of villages to try and restore calm. A letter from the bishop of Pavia, also appealing for calm, was read to the parish priests. For a while at least, a major outbreak of violence was avoided. It was a different story when the bulk of the French army began to move away in the direction of Mantua, where the Austrians had taken refuge. On the morning of 23 May, two days after Augereau's division marched off, leaving a small garrison in Pavia, people began to gather in the square near the tree of liberty. Fenini recognised some of the people, whom he described as being 'of humble origins'[24] and names half a dozen of them. The angry crowd tore down the tree of liberty, then the French soldiers guarding the gates were overpowered. Alarm bells were rung from the town hall and the churches, which attracted people armed with all sorts of weapons from the nearest villages. As the day progressed, the multitude grew, isolated French soldiers were attacked and some were killed. The Marchese Belcredi, a local diarist, wrote an arresting description of these events, in which he expressed a patrician distaste for the 'lower orders' who were at the forefront of the troubles, but also made some revealing comments regarding the behaviour of the civilians towards the soldiery, noting that: 'It is remarkable that the common townsman is always more respectful and generous in his attitude towards the soldiers, but not so the rude and ferocious peasant.'[25]

This difference could no doubt be partly traced to the different treatment that town and country dwellers received from the soldiers. Isolated houses or small hamlets were easier targets for pillagers, though they rarely contained much of value, so country districts suffered most from pillaging. Conversely, there was little scope for looting in the towns under normal circumstances, there being too many people who could prevent it, but towns tended to be where pillagers sold their ill-gotten valuables and spent the money they made from them, which meant a welcome increase in business for some of the townspeople. Unfortunately this had knock-on effects, and so many soldiers were selling items in Lodi that the local authorities had to prohibit townspeople from buying anything from them, in case it encouraged further looting.[26] Although town and country people saw soldiers differently, however,

Belcredi observed that: 'They were united in thought... in hunting the Jacobins, who were hated equally by everybody, and as many as they could herd together they took away as prisoners.'[27] As things got further out of hand, the French garrison barricaded itself in the castle. General Haquin, who was on his way to join the army, happened to enter the city and was promptly made prisoner. Four small ornamental cannons that had decorated the front of the palace of Prince Alberigo in Belgioioso were brought to the castle where they were loaded with scrap, as there was no proper ammunition for them. The day closed in a stand-off between the insurgents and the occupiers of the castle.

Although the demolition of the Regisole and the revenge attack on the symbol of French identity, the tree of liberty, seem to have sparked off the revolt, there were clearly other causes as well. Belcredi gave three apart from the demolition of the Regisole, which he called an act of 'mere spite... on the part of the Jacobins which greatly irritated the people'. These were: the edict restoring the tax on salt and tobacco 'which seemed tyrannical to the plebeians and the peasants'; the fact that 'the small number of French soldiers left to garrison Pavia awoke arrogance and boldness in the rabble who, ever cowardly as they are, seek the opportunity to bully and avenge themselves with unequal numbers'; and lastly the invitation put out by the Jacobins to 'whoever wishes to live as the tranquil possessor of his goods' to join them.[28]

He might have added that the local peasantry had been subjected to countless acts of pillaging by the French soldiers, and like the peasants of the Riviera had seized the opportunity for revenge, though not in the manner of isolated ambushes, but in the much more risky manner of an insurrection and the attempted capture of a whole town. The consequences of such a strategy cannot have been understood by most of those who took part in the rebellion, which seems to have been spontaneous and without a guiding organization. A sober analysis by the most ordinary military mind would have concluded that there was no chance of the insurgents holding out against the French army, and there was certainly no place that such a band of insurgents could go and hide to avoid the retribution that was bound to come when French senior commanders realised what was happening. But to judge from Belcredi's account of the events of 25 May, it seems likely that the insurgents were encouraged by the unfounded belief that the French had suffered a reverse, and that they were therefore safe from reprisals.

It was not just the people in the area of Pavia who were driven to revolt, however, for Como saw an insurrection at the same time, so did Varese, and there were serious disturbances in Milan on the morning of

24 May. A courier with news of the trouble was hurriedly sent off to Bonaparte, who had only left the city that morning on his way to start the next offensive in the direction of Mantua. Before long, news of what was happening in Pavia and other places began to filter through, forcing Bonaparte to turn back with a brigade of grenadiers commanded by Jean Lannes, some cavalry and artillery. This force made towards Pavia, but was halted in the afternoon at Binasco, half-way between Pavia and Milan, by a large body of insurgents. This has been variously estimated at between 700 and 1000 men. There was a short, unequal fight that drove the rebels to flight, after which the French sacked the village, then burnt it, destroying about half the houses.

While this had been happening the situation in Pavia had continued to be chaotic. Belcredi tells us that:

> On the morning of Tuesday 24 . . . they negotiated for the surrender [of the castle] but did not agree on the conditions. The bold peasants demanded bread, wine and cheese from the Municipality . . . The peasants, not content with the food supplied to them, demanded contributions of food and wine from all the citizens and the monasteries, which caused great worry among those who foresaw the consequences. After lunch, the negotiations for the surrender of the castle were begun again through the forced mediation of the captured general [Haquin], and it was concluded that at eight o'clock on the following morning [Wednesday] the garrison would give itself up as prisoners, if the citizens guaranteed that they would accompany the soldiers and defend them from the insults of the peasantry.[29]

The last sentence suggests that the French were well aware that they were in greater danger from the peasants than the townspeople, whom they must have known had suffered less from the depredations of the marauders. Haquin also noted that the town officials had protected him when the mob had dragged him out of the safety of the Town Hall, 'covering me with their bodies' and making 'every effort to contain the people'.[30]

We may also note from Belcredi's comments that the insurgents had begun to demand 'contributions', or rations, not unlike a real army. This may have been nothing more complicated than a desire to profit from the power that the insurgents wielded at that moment, but it may, perhaps, give some indication of how they viewed themselves, and of their over-confident mood. Further proof of the latter was the continuing growth of the rebel force, and according to Belcredi, 'On Wednesday

25 our streets swarmed even more with armed peasants.'[31] They also gained a notable victory with the surrender of the castle, the garrison, as had been requested, being taken away under the protection of the townspeople and given a meal. The surrender agreement was careful to stipulate that the Municipality had done everything in its power to protect the soldiers.

Had there been any proper military scheme or leadership among the insurgents they might have garrisoned the castle, but according to Belcredi their behaviour was anything but prudent or disciplined:

> Almost as puffed up and drunk with exultation as if they had gained a vast empire, and even more because of the rumour that was spread by some evil-doers that the Germans [Austrians] were near, even that there were Croats...on the road to Milan and also uhlans at Santa Cristina, the armed rebels caused anguish among the good citizens who had an interest in keeping them quiet. They ordered the bells to begin ringing again, and wildly toured the city drinking, requisitioning things from the families, and many were already heated and fuming because of the excess of wine they had drunk.[32]

Unfortunately for the insurgents and the townspeople of Pavia it was the French, not the Austrians, who were approaching. Ahead of them came the Archbishop of Milan and two other prelates to appeal to the insurgents to lay down their arms, but their pleas were in vain, the mob becoming even more heated at their words. Even so, Belcredi felt that if the clerics had been given twenty-four hours to exercise their powers of persuasion, the situation could have been defused. But Bonaparte was not prepared to wait:

> Perhaps not even two hours had passed when the French were already investing the city from two sides...with cannons loaded with ball and grape, they bombarded it fiercely...Then the populace dispersed like a slight cloud at the puff of a north wind...and in the blink of an eye those squares and streets that had earlier swarmed with violent armed people were deserted.[33]

The French troops were given licence to sack the town for a number of hours, though precautions were taken to protect some of the more illustrious inhabitants, such as the scientist, Alessandro Volta. The town was expertly pillaged, and French soldiers were later seen in Lodi trying to sell the most varied items, including the bishop's mitre.

The sad sequel to the troubles was predictable: courts martial were set up, various ringleaders were shot, and hostages were taken. Despite these reprisals, there were more insurrections in other areas within weeks. There was a rebellion in the Imperial fief of Arquata Scrivia on 5 June, which was followed towards the end of the month by numerous revolts in Emilia Romagna. On 19 June it was the turn of Bologna, then Ferrara on the 23rd, Forlì on the 24th, various villages around Lugo on the 27th, Cesena on the 29th, and finally Rimini and Lugo on the 30th. Yet more rebellions were to occur later, though it is noteworthy that the French difficulties at the end of July, when they had to abandon the siege of Mantua and retreat to Brescia, do not seem to have been accompanied by uprisings of any size or danger in Lombardy. By then, it would seem, the local civilians were coming to expect and fear French reprisals.

It is striking that armed civilian resistance in the Po valley should have mostly taken the form of mass uprisings, usually focused on towns or villages, and leading to something that had vague similarities with conventional warfare (the capture of strong-points, use of artillery, action *en masse*) rather than the methodology of ambushes and raids favoured in the mountains of the Riviera, and it seems likely that terrain was the most important factor in this. It is also noteworthy that politics and religion seem to have had rather more importance than they had in the Riviera (at least in the examples we have looked at) and that the threat to a sense of local identity should also have played a part in driving the people to revolt.

We now move on to the area around Rivoli. This is not only interesting for the battle which took place there, but also for a quite remarkable contemporary account of the French occupation of that area. It was written by a local priest called Giovanni Battista Alberghini, who was very roughly the same age as Napoleon, and it gives some unusual insights into relations between locals and soldiers. Because of this, it seems worth quoting long passages from it, though the good priest was no stylist, and his ponderous prose is not the easiest to read. The area described in Alberghini's story lies right at the foot of the mountains that stand between Lake Garda and the River Adige. There is a marked contrast of terrain, with a fertile plain and low hills on one side, and high mountains fringed by woodland on the other. The mountains, which lie to the north, are quite suited to guerrilla warfare, and were actually used by partisans during the Second World War. The area was of great strategic importance in the eighteenth century, being the site of some of the best defensive positions on the main route from Innsbruck to Mantua, the principal Austrian military base in northern Italy. For that reason, the French were eager to occupy Rivoli, though it belonged to the Republic of Venice, which was neutral.

The French advanced into the area at the end of May 1796, and their arrival, not surprisingly, was accompanied by the same sort of ruthless plundering that had been visited on other areas, in this case mostly perpetrated by cavalrymen. Eventually this torment came to a stop, but was replaced by excessive requisitions for food. The French stayed for two months, after which they were forced to retreat because of an Austrian offensive that succeeded in relieving Mantua. The Austrian soldiers that passed through the area were no more angelic than the French, and another bout of looting and even murder resulted, all of which Alberghini recorded in some detail and in the most horrified tones. The Austrians were defeated shortly afterwards at the battle of Castiglione, and forced to retire, permitting the French to return to their old positions. With them came new disorders and sufferings for the villagers. Having just endured depredations at the hands the Austrians, they were less inclined to sit back and do nothing, as Alberghini tells us:

The passing of the days brought no respite from the robberies and invasions of the houses by the soldiers, because, with the pretext of searching for food, there was no piece of furniture or small animal that was safe from their hands. Thus the villagers, tired and angry at seeing themselves slowly stripped of their possessions, decided to put up a violent defence, and having got together in their respective villages they put their resolute resistance to the test, even at the peril of their lives. The village of Gaon was the first to give signs of intrepid resolution, and also served as an example to the other villages, its inhabitants having decided to die rather than put up with slow and silent destruction. They gave the first proofs of their courage on the 18th day of August, when, some soldiers having gone there on horseback to steal, as they had done other times, they were put to flight by those few intrepid villagers. At this unexpected reception the soldiers shouted with anger and declared that they would revenge themselves and would come back with the others and knock down everything. Nor did they forget their promise, and two days after, that is to say on the 20th of the same month, about forty-eight of them came back, all on horseback and armed with sabres and firearms, with the intention of sacking the houses in revenge for the affront they had received. But the villagers, having been warned of this by the sound of the bells of their church, armed themselves with sticks, pitchforks, and some of them even with firearms and edged weapons, soon assembled, drove the soldiers from the houses where they had begun their plundering, and routed them merely by loosing on them a storm of stones. Scattered here and there because of the need to run from the blows of the sticks and the stones that rained on their shoulders and courageously followed by the aforesaid villagers, some Frenchmen lost weapons, some their hats, and some even their horses (from which they had dismounted since the animals could not gallop due to the badness of the roads). The dismay and fear of the aforesaid soldiers was so great that they did not even have the courage to put a hand to their weapons and defend themselves in some way. If one of them took a weapon in his hand he was soon forced to put it down again on seeing a pitchfork aimed at his chest, or on being threatened with being knocked from his horse with a long pole. Only one had the daring to fire a musket shot at the villagers, but at that very moment a villager replied with a similar shot. With this solemnity the above-mentioned robbers were accompanied and chased by the courageous people of Gaon as far as the villa at Caiar, where the villagers themselves turned back towards their homes.[34]

We should note a few things about this assault on the soldiers. First, it was not an offensive act, like an ambush on stragglers or a supply train, but a reaction to an invasion and violation of property. Since the defence took place in the village itself it was very obvious who had been involved in it and where they came from – in other words, it was not a clandestine act of the kind commonly associated with guerrilla warfare. There were obviously considerable risks in such an overt display of defiance. It should also be pointed out that none of the French soldiers are reported as being killed or wounded, so there had evidently been some restraint on the part of the villagers, who had merely tried to scare off the marauders. It did not look as if things were going to end there, however, and the villagers began to take more serious measures, as Alberghini relates:

But fear, which is the follower of doubtful enterprises, awoke serious reflections in the minds of the aforementioned people of Gaon, and they suspected they would have to face a bigger attack. Because of this, not seeing any other means of protection, they took the extreme decision to resist to the death. Therefore, having gathered in the square they decided on the best method to defend themselves, and in orderly fashion divided among themselves the tasks and the places to be occupied. They all soon found themselves weapons, and moulded lead bullets in the square in public to demonstrate their firm willingness to defend themselves at any cost. They also readied great quantities of stones that were suitable for throwing by hand, in certain places from where it was possible to bombard the roads without being seen, because the latter, since they climb almost continuously and have many bends, can easily be guarded from a few high points, and defended simply by throwing stones. They also placed small bodies of guards and a few sentinels on certain heights so they might see if the French could be observed from afar while making their way up there. Lastly, they ordered the women and children, and those who were not fit for the trial, to retire to the crest of the mountain which stands above the said village to the north, and to take their animals and movable goods with them. The women, animated by the same resolution, were determined to roll great boulders at the enemy, and defend themselves if they were attacked. This example of daring was a spur to the nearby villages, so the inhabitants of these also set out to defend themselves from the incursions of the thieves. Indeed, many of them joined in alliance and gave help to each other. The resolution of the villagers soon made the French soldiers desist from the thieving they had started, and they feared a general rebellion.[35]

The striking thing here is the remarkable level of organization and planning that was put into the defensive measures, even extending to cooperation with other villages. Affairs seemed to have reached a critical point, and it is not difficult to see how the violence could have escalated, perhaps resulting in groups of men taking to the mountains and the woods and engaging in guerrilla warfare against the French. But there must have been at least one extremely wise head among the villagers, and they were not blind to the dangers of their situation:

However, the villagers themselves having thought better of their decision, which could have turned out to their harm and final destruction because of the desire imprudently to take offence with an army, they sent some people to General of Brigade Rampon, who commanded the troops camped in this area, to give him news of what had happened and also to beg him to use his authority to remedy these disorders. And he promised that he would stop them, adding that if the villagers were disturbed in the future by marauding soldiers, they should defend themselves with stones, poles, and other similar weapons, but they should not use muskets.[36]

At first sight, the last sentence seems extraordinary, and one is moved to wonder how many generals might have given a group of civilians authority to use various weapons to defend themselves against the soldiery. But as well as being an honest man,[37] Rampon was clearly aware of the advantages that might flow from assisting the villagers, not to mention the dangers that attended ignoring the abuses they suffered at the hands of the troops. Other perceptive soldiers knew very well what these were, as we may gather from the memoirs of Captain Laugier, who had found himself surrounded by the enemy on the other side of Lake Garda only three weeks before, and recounts how a friendly approach to the locals could make a crucial difference:

> I persuaded a farmer to sell us [some food] which I paid for generously. The man was so pleased that he promised to go to the town on the morrow and find out what was happening there and bring us food. He did this, and reported that the enemy had committed outrages in the town, and that the inhabitants were so indignant that they seemed ready to rise up if we had the least advantage...Towards evening the farmer informed me of the enemy's dispositions, that the main attack would be directed against the heights above us, and that it would take place on the morrow at the break of day, as duly happened. Such is the advantage that is obtained by respecting the inhabitants, that one is informed of everything, accurately and in good time.[38]

It was fortunate for both soldiers and civilians that the French army had its share of men like Laugier and Rampon. The latter's conciliatory attitude soon had greatly beneficial effects for Alberghini and his flock, as the priest punctiliously set down, despite his many reservations about the French:

> The...general kept his promise: indeed, to remedy the disorders better, he had a picket of about forty soldiers with their respective officers detached from the camp at Preelle every day, and sent to the *pieve* of Caprino where they stayed all day. From this picket some patrols were sent out to go round the villages to prevent any disorder that might take place. Nor did the village of Caprino omit to recognize this service, and every morning some portions of bread were given to

each soldier in the picket by the parish, and the officers were also given a ration of wine. The soldiers appreciated such recompense, though small, and were ready to show their gratitude towards the parish and the whole town, of which they gave particular proof when it was necessary to give communion to a sick person, and [the Holy Sacrament was going to have to be carried past the place] where the picket was, and it was feared that some irreverence might be shown, as had unfortunately happened in other similar cases. One of the officers having been asked to make his soldiers respect the Holy Sacrament, he replied that everything would be as it should.[39]

Here we can see important steps being taken in the normalization of relations between the two sides. The local French commander institutes very visible and effective measures to solve the problem the villagers have complained about. The villagers show their gratitude in tangible form, and soldiery respond by showing respect towards a religious procession. The process continued even further:

Every disorder having thus been remedied, and plundering and robbery prevented, the commissaries of the troops camped in the area did not, however, desist from troubling the communities with their arrogant demands, requesting, among other things, wood to bake bread. But the Councillors, made wise by experience, replied that they did not have wood to give them, and so, if they wanted it, they should go to the woods and cut it themselves. The French commissaries made no further resistance to this decision, but contenting themselves with this agreement they sent some villagers to cut it on Monte Gazo, where a section of woodland was assigned to them, and they paid the workmen every day in cash, also giving them a ration of bread and other things as had been agreed.[40]

As we can see, once the two sides had opted for cooperation rather than enmity, it became possible to develop a working relationship that permitted them to live in relative harmony. Intransigence on one side would only have bred intransigence on the other, with painful consequences for both. It is a pity that the sensible behaviour of the village elders and the French commander was not more widely imitated.

In conclusion, we may say that while there was a great deal of armed civilian resistance to the French in northern Italy between 1792 and 1797, not much of it conformed to modern notions of guerrilla warfare. The outbreaks of armed resistance that had the greatest effect on French operations (in Lombardy and Emilia Romagna) seem more like a clumsy attempt to engage in conventional warfare than the hit-and-run tactics more usually associated with guerrilla activity. The area where there was something like guerrilla warfare (the Riviera) had terrain that was ideally suited to it, and it seems to have developed out of pre-existing brigandage. But despite the annoyance it caused to the French it had no major effect on their operations. In another place where it could easily have developed (near Rivoli) the situation was defused because of the willingness of both locals and French to find solutions to the problems of co-existence, and to arrive at a modus vivendi. Protecting local property, respecting local traditions and leaving local institutions untouched were crucial in this. Had this lesson been learnt and applied by others perhaps it is even possible that the word 'guerrilla' would not exist in the English language.

Notes

1. F. Maurandi, *Les Annales de Levens*, (Nice, 1931), p. 118.
2. E. Chevrier, *Le général Joubert d'après sa correspondance* (Paris, 1884), p. 8.
3. Napoleon. *Correspondance de Napoléon Ier publiée par ordre de l'empereur Napoléon III* (Paris, 1858–69), no. 925 (hereafter CN).
4. See J.B. Schels, 'Die zweite Einschließung Mantuas, im August 1796, und gleichzeitige Ereignisse bei dem k. k. Heere unter dem FM Grafen Wurmser in Tirol und Vorarlberg', *Oesterreichische Militärische Zeitschrift*, Bd. 4 (1831), p. 279.
5. They were not the only ones to commit them. There are enough eye-witness accounts to prove that the Austrian soldiers could be just as keen for loot and as brutal in obtaining it.
6. L. Oliveri, 'L'insorgenza antifrancese in Val Bormida durante il periodo napoleonico (1794–1815)', *Bollettino della Società per gli Studi Storici, Archeologici ed Artistici della Provincia di Cuneo*, no. 91 (July 1984), p. 229.
7. *Langa* (plural *Langhe*) refers to the hilly country districts around the Belbo and the Bormida.
8. G. Conterno, 'Una cronaca inedita di età napoleonica in val Bormida', *Atti e Memorie della Società Savonese di Storia Patria*, XIX (1985), pp. 123–4.
9. L. Oliveri, 'Una comunità nella tempesta: la val Bormida durante l'invasione napoleonica 1792–1800', *Bollettino della Società per gli Studi Storici, Archeologici ed Artistici della Provincia di Cuneo*, no. 82 (January 1980), p. 136.
10. Cf. Oliveri, 'L'insorgenza antifrancese', p. 230.
11. Cf. Oliveri, 'Una comunità nella tempesta', p. 136.
12. Cf. Chevrier, *Le général Joubert d'après sa correspondance*, p. 36.
13. Cf. CN, no. 121.
14. M. Benvenuti, 'Curioso documento', *Archivio storico lombardo*, no. 9 (1882): 145–8, p. 147.
15. G. Agnelli, 'La battaglia al ponte di Lodi e l'inizio della settimana napoleonica lodigiana', *Archivio storico lombardo*, no. 60 (1933), pp. 58–9.
16. *Ibid.*, p. 60.

17. *Ibid.*, p. 49.
18. *Ibid.*, p. 54.
19. Cf. CN, no. 437.
20. *Ibid.*, no. 442.
21. *Ibid.*, no. 453.
22. P. Verri, *Lettere e scritti inediti di Pietro e Alessandro Verri* (Milan, 1881), IV, p. 215.
23. F. Bouvier, 'La révolte de Pavie (23–26 mai 1796)' *Revue historique de la Révolution française*, III, no. 2 (1911–12), p. 75.
24. *Ibid.*, p. 77.
25. C. Capra, *L'età rivoluzionaria e napoleonica in Italia, 1796–1815* (Turin, 1978), p. 111.
26. Cf. Agnelli, 'La battaglia al ponte di Lodi', pp. 45, 60.
27. Cf. Capra, *L'età rivoluzionaria*, p. 111.
28. *Ibid.*, pp. 110–11.
29. *Ibid.*, pp. 111–2.
30. Napoleon, *Correspondance inédite officielle et confidentielle de Napoléon Bonaparte: avec les cours étrangères, les princes, les ministres et les généraux français et étrangers, en Italie, en Allemagne, et en Egypte* (Paris, 1809), I, pp. 207–9.
31. Cf. Capra, *L'età rivoluzionaria*, p. 112.
32. *Ibid.*, p. 113.
33. *Ibid.*, p. 113.
34. G.B. Alberghini, *Gli austro-galli in val di Caprino (1796–1801) memoria storica* (Verona, 1880), pp. 39–40.
35. *Ibid.*, pp. 40–2.
36. *Ibid.*, p. 42.
37. The brief description of Rampon written by General Desaix, himself a very upright man, includes the telling words 'not a thief'. L. Desaix, *Journal de voyage du général Desaix, Suisse et Italie (1797)* (Paris, 1907), p. 138.
38. J. Laugier, *Les cahiers du capitaine Laugier* (Aix, 1893), pp. 93–4.
39. Cf. Alberghini, pp. 42–3.
40. *Ibid.*, p. 43.

4
Resistance, Collaboration or Third Way? Responses to Napoleonic Rule in Germany

Michael Rowe

The terms 'resistance' and 'collaboration' are evocative, and are generally applied to Nazi-occupied Europe. The characteristics of the collaborator are uniformly negative: somebody motivated by cowardice, malice or even ideological affiliation with the invader who betrays his country and fellow citizens. The resister is a hero, courageous, patriotic, fighting against the odds. These are the popular images. Of course, theorists of 'collaboration' and 'resistance', be they political scientists, sociologists or historians, are dissatisfied with such a simple dichotomy. Stephen Gilliatt, in his recent exploration of the dynamics of the phenomenon, notes that the term *collaborazionistas*, when it first appeared in an Italian dictionary in 1922 as a descriptor for socialists wanting to work with the bourgeois government, initially carried with it no negative connotations.[1] However, it quickly gained these even before World War II, when its current emotive meaning became widespread. Works of scholarly detachment, in contrast, view 'collaboration' as a political strategy, not pathological behaviour: it is a possible way of managing conflicting interests, as indeed is resistance. Beyond that, they fail to agree on any definitions, but tend to recognise that both 'collaboration' and 'resistance' are blanket terms covering various forms of behaviour and motivation. Typical is the following, from Peter Davies's recent book on wartime France: '... an act of resistance was, basically, anything that, in the mind of the person or group executing the act, *felt* like an act of resistance'.[2] Such an act might range from full-scale military action to accidentally-on-purpose bumping into a German on the street. The act of resistance, or indeed, collaboration, according to such a definition, might not be recognizable as such by the occupying forces, the rest of the occupied community, or indeed the later historian. Conversely, something perceived as 'resistance' or 'collaboration' by the occupation authorities or community might well be motivated by other considerations, and simply represent an unintended outcome or secondary result. Some label this as 'functional' resistance or, presumably, 'functional' collaboration.[3] Clearly, collaboration and resistance are not as simple as they might first appear.

Despite this, an attempt will be made in this chapter to apply these difficult concepts not to German-occupied France, but French-occupied Germany: more specifically, the German-speaking region to the west of the Rhine in the generation following the outbreak of the Revolutionary Wars in 1792. However, it is impossible to proceed without briefly considering the state of affairs in this region on the eve of occupation. The Rhineland lay in the far west of that loose collection of territories clustered within the 1000-year-old Holy Roman Empire.[4] It was one of the *Reich*'s most territorially fragmented regions, its 1.5–1.6 million inhabitants divided amongst over 100 (depending, in part, on definition) sovereignties that recognized no higher temporal authority other than the Emperor. Some of these were very small indeed, representing no more than glorified villages with populations in the hundreds, and ruled over by a colourful collection of imperial counts (including the Metternichs), imperial knights, imperial abbesses and abbots, and other minor princelings.[5] For their subjects, rule was personal; the allegiance they owed was to an authority that was near, and tangible. The pocket states, in which a significant minority of Rhinelanders had resided for centuries, did not face the same challenge of 'acculturizing' their subjects as was the case in Europe's larger territorial states. Hence the concepts of 'resistance' and 'collaboration', which are bound up with notions of legitimacy, patriotism and nationalism, hardly apply in these micro-states, or if so, in a form fundamentally different from larger territorial units.

Most Rhinelanders, however, lived within one of the larger entities: under one of the three archbishop electors – Cologne, Mainz, Trier – or under the sceptre of a distant Hohenzollern or Wittelsbach prince, who governed substantial Rhenish territories from Berlin and Munich respectively. What is significant about both these categories of territory – the ecclesiastical electorates, and the so-called *Nebenländer* ruled by the Hohenzollerns and Wittelsbachs – is that, through their nature, they failed to establish the kind of dynastic ties that existed elsewhere between princes and peoples. The monarchies of the ecclesiastical electorates could not, obviously, be hereditary; instead, their sovereigns were elected by the cathedral chapters. Certainly, some of them were monopolized by particular families for decades, if not centuries – as was the case with the Wittelsbachs in the Electorate of Cologne for much of the seventeenth and eighteenth centuries, for example – but they nonetheless failed to instil in their inhabitants the same kind of loyalty that the Wittelsbachs, Wettins, Habsburgs or Hohenzollerns managed in their core provinces. This same lack of devotion to dynasty was also apparent in the Rhenish possessions of German princes whose core territories lay far to the east. As already stated, their Rhenish territories are often referred to as *Nebenländer* – literally, lands 'beside from' or 'apart from' the core of the dynastic state. This term is accurate. Geographically, these territories were separated from the dynastic centres by intervening principalities. However, the detachment was not simply geographical. Not surprisingly, the Wittelsbach and Hohenzollern monarchies focused their reforming zeal in the eighteenth century on their central provinces, not on vulnerable and possibly expendable peripheral territories. In consequence, Rhinelanders escaped the kind of absolutism that much of central and eastern Europe experienced. They had not been 'broken in' by a generation or two of living under the likes of King Frederick William I of Prussia before the French arrived on the scene in the early 1790s. The crucial point here, though, is that their ruling dynasties, like absentee landlords in Ireland, remained distant, remote figures, whose own destinies were obviously not too much bound up with those of their Rhenish subjects.

So, given that the vast majority of Rhinelanders lacked a dynastic focus, what were they loyal to? There are several candidates here, and none of them are mutually exclusive. There was of course the Church. For the majority – a million out of the 1.5–1.6 million – this meant the Roman Catholic Church. For the rest, the church of Calvin or Luther, or, for perhaps 20 000, the synagogue. It goes without saying that religion, including the religious calendar, governed the lives of the vast majority, and that any power disruptive of this should be viewed with hostility.[6] Apart from the church, there was another power with universalistic pretensions (at least, originally), though one of a temporal rather than spiritual nature: the Holy Roman Empire. This institution has undergone much rehabilitation of late, and is now viewed as an at times surprisingly effective conflict resolution mechanism.[7] This in part, arguably, explains the support it received from Rhinelanders: ultimately, it protected their rights against princely absolutism. Beyond that, its military structure provided some form of mechanism that potentially shielded the region from French attack, as it had done in the days of Louis XIV.[8] Furthermore, the reforming zeal of Emperor Joseph II held out some hope for those dissatisfied simply with the preservation of the status quo.

What else might ordinary Rhinelanders owe their allegiance to? The answer is to either their city, or what in German is referred to as *Land*. Cities in old-régime Germany can be categorized according to the degree of independence they enjoyed from the territorial princes. Those with the greatest independence, and hence those whose citizenry generally invested the greatest pride in them, were the imperial cities. There were four in the Rhineland, the largest two being Aachen and Cologne. Cologne, founded in the days of Rome, had an especially well-developed sense of its own importance, something its burghers might share in.[9] More modest home towns, with smaller populations, less exalted histories, and less independence, could nonetheless engender similar loyalties.

The Rhineland was relatively urbanized in comparison with Europe's other regions, but nonetheless, most of its inhabitants were rural. They owed their allegiance not to a city, but to their *Land*. This word has no English equivalent. Historically, a *Land* was more than a mere territorial unit or administrative sub-division. Rather, it was defined by its peculiar and supposedly ancient customs and laws. Importantly, the ill-defined boundaries of the *Länder* did not match those of the dynastically defined territories into which the *Reich* was divided: larger dynastic conglomerations, like the Habsburg and Hohenzollern monarchies, contained many *Länder*. In territorially fragmented regions like the Rhineland, in contrast, individual *Länder* might be divided into many petty sovereignties. However, what is crucial is that loyalty towards the *Land* – *Landespatriotismus* – was not synonymous with loyalty towards the dynastic state – *Staatspatriotismus*. Indeed, the two might very well be conflicting. Loyalty towards the *Reich*, in contrast – *Reichspatriotismus* – would in all probability be compatible with *Landespatriotismus* (or loyalty to a city, in the case of urbanites), as the rights and privileges of *Länder* (and imperial cities) survived encroachment by the dynastic states thanks to the protection afforded by the Empire's legal cocoon.[10]

In addition to the list above, was there anything else that attracted Rhinelanders' allegiance? In particular, was there any sense of German nationalism? This is a controversial area. For much of the nineteenth and early twentieth centuries, the Rhine represented a national bone of contention between the French and Germans. Many a textbook on nineteenth-century Germany evokes the Rhine crisis of 1840 – the crisis that spawned Nikolaus Becker's immensely successful poem, *Der deutsche Rhein* – as the first spontaneous eruption of popular German nationalism.[11] The disputed status of the Rhineland in the immediate aftermath of

World War I aroused similar passions, on both sides. Given this, it is hardly surprising that historians from both traditions writing about the Napoleonic period tended to view that era through nationalist spectacles. Since the 1960s, however, and within the climate of Franco-German reconciliation, the tendency has been to deny the existence of German nationalism in this period. That is why the degree of popular opposition to French domination has often been played down, or else portrayed as something else, such as the hatred of ordinary people for the intrusion by the state into their everyday lives.

The late eighteenth century witnessed a growing sense of German national consciousness, if not nationalism. In part this derived from a common pride, amongst Germany's élite at least, at German achievements on the cultural front. The proportion of books published in German as opposed to Latin was increasing. The public sphere, and especially the political newspaper press, was also expanding rapidly; contemporaries often complained of *Lesesucht* – the addiction to reading news – that extended beyond the élite to commoners, something boosted by the Seven Years War, the American War of Independence, and the French Revolution.[12] The victories of Frederick the Great in the first of these struggles were also seen by many Germans less in terms of a contribution to an ongoing German civil war between Austria and Prussia, but as specifically German victories over the Russians and above all the French.[13] Incongruously (given that Frederick was also at war with the *Reich* as well as with the Continental Great Powers – the army defeated at Rossbach was, after all, a joint Franco-Imperial force), the cult of Frederick the Great that transcended Prussia's boundaries did not result in any diminution of *Reichspatriotismus* in the final decades of the century. The precise relationship between an early German national consciousness based upon culture, and a more politically orientated sense of affinity towards the Empire, is currently the subject of much scholarly debate.[14] Certainly, the two cannot be assumed to be synonymous: the one could be had without the other. For example, in parts of northern Italy where – it is not generally known – a residue of imperial rights and jurisdiction survived into the eighteenth century, a degree of *Reichspatriotismus* likewise subsisted. Yet obviously, no one here believed themselves part of a German *Kulturnation*.[15] On the other hand, this is perhaps an obscure exception that proves the rule: the vast majority of the *Reich*'s inhabitants were German speakers; after all, the Empire's full name was *Heilige Römische Reich deutscher Nation*. And whilst *Reichspatriotismus* was not synonymous with a German cultural nationalism, it could, nonetheless, reinforce it: just as cultural nationalism could be set up against French courtliness, so *Reichspatriotismus* might highlight the distinction between Bourbon despotism and German freedom. These ingredients, together with the aforementioned cult of Frederick the Great and the Francophobia based upon previous perceived injustices (such as Louis XIV's devastation of the Palatinate, the centenary of which fortuitously coincided with the French Revolution), helped shape Rhenish attitudes to the *Reich*, to what it meant to be German, to the French, and to the Revolution.

This chapter will now skip over the Revolutionary decade as quickly as possible, in order to focus on the Napoleonic period.[16] The period 1789 to 1799 can be split into two phases so far as the Rhineland is concerned. In the first phase, from 1789 to 1792 (the outbreak of the War of the First Coalition) Rhinelanders were spectators to events unfolding in France. These were viewed with interest by a broad cross section of society, which avidly read the sensationalist reporting of atrocities and violence.[17] A minority of intellectuals were sympathetic in their interpretation of events. One common position, which many Rhinelanders held, was that revolution was required in France to over-throw centuries of despotism, but that it was not needed in Germany thanks to enlightened princes and the conflict resolution mechanisms provided by imperial law.

Smug detachment turned into direct Rhenish involvement in the affairs of the French Revolution with the outbreak of the Revolutionary Wars. Due to its geographical position, the region became the major theatre of operations. It was occupied briefly by French forces in 1792, but these were pushed out by the Coalition the following year. French armies re-occupied the region in 1794, and this time they stayed. What can be said about the French military occupation? What is initially striking is its scale: 136 000 to 187 000 troops stationed in the region from 1794–97.[18] This represented about one-in-ten of the population. This needs to be borne in mind when contrasting the relative passivity of Rhinelanders compared with Vendéens in the 1790s, or Spaniards after 1808, or Tyroleans in 1809. Would, for example, the Spanish have been so successful in creating trouble for Napoleon had he been able to deploy a force equivalent to a tenth of the population of Spain – an army of perhaps 1.3 million – to the Iberian peninsula? Consideration of why people collaborate or resist cannot lose sight of perhaps the most important variable: the sheer extent of the occupier's power, and the concomitant chances of successful resistance.

The presence of a massive French force in the region created great hardship for civilians: requisitioning on a huge scale, forced billeting, hostage-taking, simple brutality by ill-disciplined soldiers against a sullenly resentful population, anti-clerical outrages including the desecration of churches, the looting of cultural treasures, and sporadic attempts to impose hated revolutionary symbols and political practices, such as planting liberty trees and introducing the revolutionary calendar.

How did Rhinelanders respond? Did they collaborate or resist? Armed resistance was out of the question, given French military power. However, there were plenty of other ways of registering hostility to the French and their revolution. These were largely of a symbolic or religious nature, and included vandalising liberty trees and other revolutionary symbols, ostentatiously taking part in religious processions, or – and in many respects, this is also a contemporary phenomenon – wearing rosettes or ribbons denoting allegiance to a power hostile to France. Of course, a popular and often effective means of resisting occupation was and remains the boycott: non-participation in revolutionary festivities, ignoring the new revolutionary calendar by donning one's Sunday best and demonstratively sweeping the porch the evening before, and so on and so forth; a hundred possible small individual actions denoting, publicly, opposition to the new order of things. At times, the French tried to counter such acts by, for example, inflicting collective punishment such as forced billeting on villages and towns whose liberty trees had been chopped down, or by banning public religious manifestations, or forbidding rosettes. However, as other authorities in a similar position have discovered before and since, attempting to enforce such restrictions is extremely costly, and ultimately futile: as soon as one form of popular manifestation is suppressed, a new method of symbolising opposition is discovered.

We have considered resistance. What about collaboration? It might be thought that this represented an easier option for Rhinelanders, but arguably it was the more difficult. The Rhineland might have been occupied by the French in the 1790s, but in terms of international law it remained part of the Holy Roman Empire. Both the Empire and the individual princes made it clear, in a number of decrees and proclamations from 1792 onwards, that ideological adhesion to the French cause would be viewed as treason, and punishable as such. Of course, these decrees and proclamations did not use the word 'collaboration', but they were referring to behaviour that today would be labelled as such. The decrees issued by Emperor Francis II in December 1792 and April 1793 referred to 'persons lacking German [*sic*] spirit and heart...who have volunteered or allowed themselves to be used as tools for seducing the people', and to 'criminals against us, the German *Reich* and their Fatherland'.[19] The explicit and deliberate references to Germany, or German characteristics, in these proclamations, suggests that the Habsburg government at least felt that there did indeed exist a sense of national solidarity amongst the peoples of the *Reich* that was worth playing upon.

What is also interesting in these proclamations is the distinction made by the Emperor and the individual princes between committed ideological adhesion to the French, which was naturally deemed unacceptable and treasonable, and collaboration that took the form of local officials simply continuing to fulfil their public responsibilities under occupation. Collaboration of the latter sort was not merely tolerated, but actually encouraged. Indeed, the Palatine government in Düsseldorf actually threatened to punish officials who deserted their posts during the French occupation.[20] Typical was the reasoning of the elector of neighbouring Cologne: 'It is far better [that the administration] should be in the hands of old established families than *sansculottes*.'[21] Not surprisingly, representatives of old established families in Cologne, and throughout the region, agreed, and used such arguments to justify working with the French occupation authorities.

Within this context, it is worth leaping ahead two decades to the years immediately after 1814, following Napoleon's defeat. During this period (the so-called Restoration), the Prussians, to whom most of the Rhineland was awarded by the Congress of Vienna, produced their own survey on the Rhenish administration they inherited. As part of this survey, they drew up reports on individual officials whom they categorized according to the extent to which they had collaborated with the French. These reports also sought to distinguish those who had engaged in disinterested public service from those besmirched by ideological commitment. Indeed, they split all those surveyed into three classes: class one consisted of those who had remained 'German' [*sic*] in their self-perception during French rule; class two included professionally competent individuals who had nonetheless soiled themselves through acceptance of a French honour, like the *Légion d'Honneur*. Class three, finally, contained unreformed Bonapartists who were deemed 'completely French' in their outlook.[22] These distinctions resemble those identified in Gilliatt's theoretical book, between what he calls 'collaborators', who are basically intermediaries between occupier and the occupied, and 'collaborationists', defined as ideological allies who genuinely believe in the political agenda of the occupying power.[23]

Of course, difficulties inevitably arise over trying to distinguish between disinterested, apolitical service in order to mitigate the worst effects of occupation and full ideological commitment. However, arguably this had not been the case in earlier periods, but was a result of the ideological divisions created by the French Revolution. During previous occupations in Europe – for example, during the Franco-Austrian occupation of the Prussian Rhineland during the Seven Years War – it was easy for public servants dispassionately to exercise their functions in an apolitical way: after all, no ideological gulf separated the occupying powers from the occupied enemy. This changed after 1789, and there was no escaping politics under French occupation in the 1790s. The first wave of revolutionaries were proselytisers, seeking to spread their principles across Europe. Obviously, they viewed local officials as being crucial in furthering their agenda through, for example, the enforcement of the revolutionary calendar, the erection of liberty trees, imposition of police restrictions on public religious practices, and so on.

Very quickly, therefore, Rhinelanders under French occupation in the 1790s, and especially those shouldering public responsibilities, found themselves in a quandary. On the one side, they faced the French occupation. Quite apart from treating them more like conquered subjects than liberated brothers, and extracting vast resources from them, these authorities demanded public displays of ideological adherence to the Revolution. On the other side, the princes, who had fled across the Rhine in the face of the French invasion, joined with the Holy Roman Emperor in issuing threats against collaboration. How did Rhinelanders respond to these conflicting pressures?

With respect to the princes, who had betrayed their lack of *Landespatriotismus* through their flight across the Rhine, many Rhinelanders responded in a vein similar to the inhabitants of the Channel Islands one-and-a-half-centuries later, when confronted with a similar challenge: with a great deal of bitterness and resentment to those preaching to them from a position of safety. In October 1794, officials in the occupied Electorate of Trier, responding to earlier threats against collaboration issued by the exiled government from across the Rhine, gave vent to their frustration: the officials claimed they were motivated only by love for their sovereign and their 'Fatherland' (*Vaterland*), that the Elector, or rather, his evil advisers, were placing them in the impossible position of having to expose themselves to either retribution from the French or the government-in-exile, that this was unjust, and that if they resigned from their public responsibilities, other less scrupulous elements would take over. The officials concluded their statement with the bitter, if disingenuous, observation that the warning against collaboration must have been drafted without the Elector's knowledge, as its outrageous contents questioned the loyalty of officials working under French occupation. The warning and threats, they continued, had arrived as a bolt from the blue. Whilst they were being showered by French bombs and howitzer shells, they had at least expected sympathy and moral support from those sheltering behind fortifications on the opposite bank of the Rhine![24] Similar resentment existed in the other French-occupied territories. Johann Adolf Kopstadt of Cleves, writing during the Restoration, noted how the inhabitants of his city had been abandoned by members of the Prussian élite on the eve of the French occupation. These acted purely out of their own interest, and not of that of the city.[25] Such behaviour by the old-régime rulers only reinforced the view that they were essentially absentee landlords whose own interests were not synonymous with those of the Rhenish cities and the Rhenish *Länder*. Hence they did not possess the moral authority to call for resistance. Rather, the interests of the *Länder* and cities – true patriotism – demanded some form of engagement with the French occupation, if only to prevent worse.

Of course, there were many other motives for collaboration other than either the extremes of ideological commitment to the French Revolution or, alternatively, a patriotic desire to act in the best interests of the community. Some of these motives were revealed in an investigation into collaboration conducted by the government of the Electorate of Mainz following the temporary expulsion of the French from Mainz in early 1793.[26] The survey revealed that for many, 'collaboration' stemmed from pragmatic, not ideological, considerations. Fear and peer pressure were crucial in governing behaviour, especially amongst groups particularly vulnerable to pressure from the occupying forces: those in public employ, dependants on public relief, and unpopular minority groups traditionally dependent upon the authorities for protection, like the Jews. Yet others were less motivated by pressures than by the commercial opportunities that were presented by occupation: tavern owners, who displayed revolutionary symbols in order to attract lucrative custom from French soldiers, for example. As in other examples that could be drawn from other lands and eras, collaboration (and indeed its opposite, resistance), could be motivated by a plethora of considerations.

The revolutionary decade gave way to the Napoleonic period in November 1799, when General Bonaparte launched the Brumairian coup that terminated the Directory and instituted the Consulate. The new French régime faced massive challenges in the occupied German territories when it came to power, but it is fair to say that it mastered most of them relatively quickly.[27] These challenges included the need to support a large occupation army at the expense of an exhausted region, which meant a continuation of the crushing burden on the native population. This, combined with a lack of legitimacy enjoyed by French rule, undermined administration in the territories. Both problems – the legitimacy deficit and deployment of an occupation army – were solved at a stroke by Napoleon's victory in the War of the Second Coalition. This removed the need to station a vast army in the Rhineland to counter the Habsburgs, and instead allowed for the redeployment of forces for the ongoing struggle against the British. Victory also resulted in the Treaty of Lunéville (9 February 1801). This was of significance for the occupation, in that it legalized French rule in the Rhineland.[28] This was of no mean importance in a region whose political culture and traditions of conflict resolution had become increasingly legalistic in the eighteenth century. Indeed, respect for imperial law had been a key ingredient of the *Reichspatriotismus* that remained strong in the Rhineland to the bitter end. Lunéville, at a stroke, neutralized this strong alternative focus of loyalty.

Victory alone, however, was insufficient to consolidate direct French rule over the new German departments. Lunéville might have removed the competing focus of allegiance represented by the Empire. That represented by the other power with universalistic pretensions, the Roman Catholic Church, remained. However, this too was largely resolved by the Concordat, concluded between Napoleon and Pius VII, and published on 18 April 1802. Certainly, problems remained on the religious front: the dissolution of most Rhenish monasteries that was rubber-stamped by the Concordat produced a large number of embittered and impoverished ex-regular clergy who formed a constituency opposed to French rule. On the plus side, the secularization of monastic and other church lands, and their auctioning off to wealthy Rhinelanders, produced another constituency with a vested interest in the preservation of at least this aspect of French rule.[29]

Napoleon overcame other challenges in solidifying French rule. One was the attitude of Frenchmen themselves. The approximately 150 000 French troops stationed in the Rhineland at any one time in the 1790s had not treated its inhabitants as anything other than a conquered people. This had not initially been so, but attitudes had hardened over the winter of 1792–93 when it became clear that they would not, as expected, be welcomed as liberators. All armies suffer from a degree of indiscipline, but this appears to have been especially the case with the revolutionary army of the 1790s.[30] At least under the Terror, soldiers had to an extent been kept in check by the fearsome People's

Representatives-on-Mission. Following Thermidor, however, no effective civilian check existed on the field armies in the occupied territories. This changed under the Consulate.

This statement might appear to go against accepted wisdom that Napoleonic France was highly militarized. In many respects, and compared to modern western democracies, it no doubt was. However, it is possible to interpret things slightly differently. Take, for example, the elegant uniforms and flamboyant ceremonial that were the hallmarks of the Napoleonic prefectoral administration, introduced in 1800. Prefects, subprefects, even humble mayors, not to mention their adjuncts and municipal police officers, as well as tax officials, and even, eventually, the presidents of consultative assemblies and electoral colleges, were prescribed their own unique uniform. Different colours marked out different branches of the administration, with the more braid indicating higher rank. At one level, this might be dismissed as the kind of show often associated with upstart régimes lacking historical legitimacy. It might also be interpreted as the introduction of military values into civilian administration. Or, and this interpretation seems to fit the evidence available from the Rhineland, it could be seen as one way of restoring the prestige of civilian officials in the eyes of the population. For, as some senior senators and councillors of state noted on their fact finding tours to the new Rhenish departments, the majority of inhabitants judged the position of an individual in the hierarchy according to his appearance. They would not respect a shabbily dressed mayor or subprefect, especially when forced aside by the passing carriage of an army officer in resplendent uniform. Local notables, Napoleon recognized, would not collaborate by assuming official responsibilities until their status was visibly raised. Official etiquette might be thought of as a subordinate issue, but judging from the volume of paperwork devoted to it, it was seen as essential. The representational role of the chief civilian administrators in the departments, the prefects, and the struggle some of them waged to put the military in its place, should not be overlooked when assessing civil/military relations in Napoleonic France. It is a lesson that other occupying powers attempting to restore the primacy of civilian rule would be well advised to study.[31]

The establishment of peace with the other powers, the legitimization of French rule in international law, the Concordat, the sale of secularized properties, the assertion of the primacy of civilian administration, the restoration of the prestige of public posts including those likely to be occupied by natives, not to mention the restoration of law and order by the newly introduced gendarmerie: all this encouraged Rhinelanders to make their peace with the new régime. Many went further, and sub-sequently accepted official positions within the new hierarchy by the end of the Consulate. By the time of the establishment of the Empire in 1804, Napoleon had succeeded in making French rule acceptable, if not popular, for the overwhelming majority of Rhinelanders.

There was another, more profound reason, for the successful consoli-dation of Napoleonic rule on the Rhine. Napoleon once sneered at the Habsburgs for having out-of-date ideas; but, as Blanning observes, at least they had some.[32] Arguably, the very ideological flexibility – or, more unkindly put, lack of principle – inherent in Bonapartism was a key to its success (at least in the short-to-medium term). A hallmark of French government in the 1790s had been its tendency to divide individuals into either allies, defined narrowly as those who subscribed to the political agenda of whatever régime happened to be in power, or enemies, composed of everybody else. The politics of the short-lived 'sister republic' of Mainz – the first modern republic on German soil – is illustrative of how this kind of governing principle operated when exported to the occupied territories. Its inhabitants were presented with two registers, one of which they were compelled to sign: a red one, denoting support for the freedom promised by the French, and a black one, decorated with chains and denoting the slavery of the Old Regime. Proposals for moderate reform, drafted by representatives of the guilds, were dismissed as counter-revolutionary; indeed, their author – an individual who would later serve as mayor of Mainz under Napoleon – was expelled from the city for his efforts.[33]

Bonapartism, in contrast, was not about confronting people with stark ideological choices. Nor was it about deliberately provocative symbols that simply provided people with opportunities to register their opposition to the régime. The flavour of the new régime became apparent soon after Brumaire, when the government ordered that only those public festivals on which popular opinion was 'unanimous' would henceforth be celebrated. Liberty trees were quietly removed from those towns and villages where they had caused most offence.[34] Experience in Corsica, Italy and Egypt had taught Napoleon that the world was not composed solely of people occupying extreme opposite poles marked 'collaborator' or 'resister', but that the majority preferred to position themselves in the spectrum in between; and, within the system he constructed, all but the most extreme and dangerous opponents could find their place. Aristocrats who had fled in the 1790s were allowed to return, so long as they adopted French citizenship. Even if they hated the new régime, and refused all dealings with it, they were left in peace to sulk in self-imposed internal exile. At the other end of the spectrum, enthusiastic supporters were encouraged to compete for Napoleon's favour by serving the Empire in a military or civilian capacity. Their reward might include membership of the *Légion d'Honneur*, elevation into the imperial nobility, a bursary for a son to enter a *lycée*, or nomination to the Senate.

Collaboration does not imply necessarily a relationship between equals. It does, however, imply that the potential collaborator possesses something the occupier wants. Usually, if not always, the existence of collaborators allows for cheaper government than can be supplied if the entire administrative structure and personnel need to be shipped in from outside. There can never have been a power in history so secure in its omnipotence that it has not attempted to enlist the services of collaborators. As John Breuilly has observed on the subject, even the Nazis sought out collaborators to help run the death camps.[35] At another level, the British, in the nineteenth century, became experts in running the largest empire in history on the cheap by going through local élites.[36]

Obviously, Rhinelanders were in a stronger bargaining position than concentration camp inmates, but how indispensable were they, and what was Napoleon willing to pay for their services? On what did the price depend? It depended in large measure on the nature of the élites that he confronted. The Rhineland, though a region of limited size, had previously contained a large number of polities, each with its own élite. These differed in nature, so that in microcosm the region represents in certain respects the kind of diversity that one might expect to encounter in a much larger area – even an entire continent. Research on élites under Napoleonic rule suggests that from the occupiers' perspective, there needs to be just the right level of social cohesion amongst the élites of an occupied area for the administration to operate most effectively. Too little social cohesion – social disintegration, as for example, Napoleon encountered in Spain – is disastrous. In such areas the occupier might identify and even win over the élite. The trouble is, the élite is not attached to anything, and is thus useless. Rather than provide support, it itself needs military protection.[37] In extreme cases, the entire élite might be destroyed, or emigrate en masse. This almost appears to have happened in Cleves, at the northern end of the Rhineland, a former Hohenzollern possession, and the one area where the local élite did form an attachment to a dynastic state – in this case, Prussia – that superseded attachment to the *Land*. A more dramatic example of the élite simply emigrating confronted Napoleon when he occupied Moscow in 1812.

At the other extreme is a case of complete social cohesion amongst the élite. Such was the case in the former imperial city of Cologne. It possessed an élite that had successfully integrated new elements over previous decades, that had no rivals, and that was internally cohesive thanks to marriage ties and a basic union of interests.[38] In such a situation, the élite was in a strong position, as the French were presented with no alternatives other than bringing in their own men from outside, and that was always expensive. A more dramatic example of such social cohesion might be found in the Tyrol.[39] From the French point of view the best environment was like that found in Aachen, another imperial city but one that had not been especially successful in incorporating new elements – notably, Protestant businessmen – into its élite in the eighteenth century.[40] Here, the French could outflank the existing political élite by promoting new elements into positions of authority who then owed their status entirely to the French – a variation of divide and rule.

Napoleon recognized the importance of propaganda in encouraging collaboration. Jean Tulard possibly goes too far in writing that the French cultural imperialism, as represented by the eighteenth-century Enlightenment, paved the way for the military imperialism of Napoleon; the present consensus denies the exclusively French nature of the Enlightenment, but instead emphasizes the unique characteristics of the Enlightenment – or better still, 'enlightenments' – in Europe's diverse nations and regions.[41] That accepted, one can nonetheless adopt Jacque Ellul's formulation that the loose set of ideas commonly associated with the Enlightenment that circulated in much of educated Europe in the decades before Napoleon represented a form of indirect or sociological propaganda: 'the penetration of an ideology by means of its sociological context', something that informed not simply opinion, but lifestyle.[42] This 'sociological' propaganda was subsequently built upon by direct Napoleonic propaganda, which sought to portray France as the sole repository of enlightened progress, and the enemies of France as backward or anarchic. Hence, the French authorities in the Rhineland went out of their way to associate themselves with agricultural improvement societies, statistical surveys, infrastructure projects, the restoration of ancient monuments such as the famous Porta Nigra in Trier or the cathedral in Aachen, and so on.[43] Certainly, some of these policies served directly to strengthen France, especially those related to attempts to achieve autarchy as a means of destroying the British. However, there was more to it than that. Rhinelanders 'collaborating' with the French authorities by, for example, providing some of the raw

data that went into the compilation of the great departmental topo-
graphical descriptions prepared under the Consulate, could congratulate
themselves not so much for collaborating with a foreign occupier, but
rather for contributing to the progress of humanity as a whole. Napoleonic
patronage of Freemasonry can also be seen in this context. Lodges were
founded in most major Rhenish cities during the course of the eighteenth
century, but some at least had suffered harassment by the Old-Regime
authorities, especially in the security crackdown ordered following the
outbreak of the French Revolution. Lodges were refounded following
the French occupation, and integrated into the Napoleonic Masonic
structure after Brumaire. Rhenish freemasons could view themselves as
favoured children of the Emperor, with whom they were collaborating
in encouraging enlightened progress.[44]

It was easy enough for the élite to collaborate with the French in an
area of mutual benefit, such as economic improvement, or small-pox
vaccination. What about where interests diverged? This was the case in
areas such as taxation, which had been lower under the Old Regime, military conscription, which had not existed before the French period, and
over the tariff barrier the French extended to the Rhine in 1798, which
disrupted traditional trade flows. Rhenish resistance to the tariff barrier
in the form of smuggling and customs fraud reached epic proportions,
as has been demonstrated in particular by Roger Dufraisse, and
implicated a whole cross section of society, from wealthy merchants and
bankers to humble porters and boaters, and from tavern owners to public officials.[45] Should we categorize this as resistance to French rule?
Napoleon certainly viewed it as a crime against the state: not only did
customs fraud deny the treasury substantial revenue, but the smuggling
of illegal wares threatened to undermine the strategy for defeating
Britain. Hence, its categorization as one of those crimes to be dealt with
by special non-jury courts, crimes that included forgery, attacks against
purchasers of *biens nationaux*, and armed insurgency. Beyond that,
smuggling, as one official wrote, was not simply a crime in itself, but
a phenomenon that was so widespread and involved such a large
proportion of the population that it undermined all forms of authority.[46]
But can we see it as a form of resistance against the French?

We return to the definition of resistance provided by Peter Davies:
'... an act of resistance was, basically, anything that, in the mind of
the person or group executing the act, *felt* like an act of resistance'.
Certainly, smuggling felt like resisting the law: it was something that
had to be conducted illicitly, under cover of darkness, not out in the
open. But did it feel like resisting the French? Admittedly, the vast

majority of the customs men – the despised *douaniers* – were native Frenchmen; the special customs courts eventually established by Napoleon also contained a preponderance of native Frenchmen, unlike the ordinary courts which counted larger numbers of Rhinelanders.[47] So, on the face of it, smuggling was something that appears to have pitted Rhinelanders against Frenchmen. However, sources then remind us that smuggling involved not only Rhinelanders, but also native Frenchmen, including even high officials and military officers. Indeed, even the commander of the Gendarmerie in the Rhenish departments, Georgeon, was implicated, whilst on another occasion a French military officer involved ordered his men to fire at *douaniers* who were interfering in an operation.[48] Ironically, smuggling was something that Frenchmen and Germans could collaborate in. In that sense, perversely, it might have assisted in the long-term aim of integrating the new departments into France. The most that can be conceded is that smuggling represented 'functional resistance': it was not motivated primarily by the desire to undermine French rule, but by profit.

The same conclusion can be reached with respect to opposition to military conscription, which manifested itself as draft evasion and desertion. Fortunately, we have quite good statistics on the incidence of both draft evasion and desertion within the entire French Empire, broken down by year and department.[49] These statistics, provided by the general direction for conscription, allow us to build up a map illustrating where resistance to the draft was most serious. The Rhenish departments, though newly annexed and though they had never experienced conscription before, appear amongst the most reliable departments from the government's point of view. After a slow start, they quickly provided an above average quota of troops in relation to their population.[50] It is estimated that in all, 80 000 Rhinelanders served in Napoleon's armies at one time or another, representing about 30 per cent of the age groups concerned. Draft dodging was slightly above the national average, but desertion below. The one really worrying statistic, from the government's perspective, was the tiny proportion of draft dodgers actually arrested, at least in the years covered by the statistics, which end in 1810: the average in the Rhenish departments was 6–8 per cent and 11–20 per cent for the Empire as a whole; and, as Alan Forrest correctly notes, draft dodging was less about individual choice and more about social cohesion: for it to succeed, it required community support.[51] The statistics suggest this was provided in the Rhineland.

Reference to 'collaboration' and 'resistance' suggests a relationship between two parties: the people, however defined, and some form of authority, be it a government or occupying military power. It is recognized that the people are not homogeneous, but composed of numerous individuals and communities, and that these are positioned at various points on the spectrum between the extremes of collaboration and resistance. Nor, however, should we assume that governments or states are homogeneous. What do we mean when referring to the 'French', or 'Napoleonic state', or 'government'? After all, there were within the Napoleonic administration several, competing bureaucratic hierarchies: the customs administration, subordinate to the finance ministry in Paris; the regular administrative chain, running from mayors and adjuncts at the bottom, via the subprefects and prefects to the interior minister at the top; there was another parallel hierarchy running up to the police minister, and something analogous subordinate to the justice ministry. In many respects, the Catholic Church, with its 'mayors in black' (parish priests) and 'prefects in purple' (bishops) represented just one more Napoleonic hierarchy, subordinate to the Ministry of Cults. Collectively, these administrations represented the French state, but not individually.[52]

How do we rate Rhenish opposition to one or two of these administrations (the customs administration and indirect tax collection agencies were, predictably, the least popular) coupled with support for another (and here the judiciary should be highlighted)? Does such a combination add up to resistance, or collaboration?

This was essentially the point that one eminent Rhinelander, Georg Friedrich Rebmann, made when accused after 1814 by German nationalists of collaborating with the French. Rebmann had served as a senior judge under Napoleon. Following Napoleon's defeat, he was employed by the newly installed Bavarian authorities as a writer and journalist to counter the Prussian-backed nationalist press that attacked not only French rule in the Rhineland, but also those German states such as Bavaria that had allied themselves with Napoleon within the framework of the Confederation of the Rhine. In a balanced way, Rebmann listed the pros and cons of French rule. The former included the abolition of the vestiges of feudalism, the removal of fiscal privileges, state encouragement of agriculture, and the civil and commercial codes. More generally, Rebmann argued that Napoleonic rule had been essential to the southern and western part of Germany, as it had allowed this area to modernize its antiquated structures. This was in contrast to Prussia, he admitted, where Napoleonic domination had resulted only in oppression and exploitation. Amongst the disadvantages of Napoleonic rule in the Rhineland listed by Rebmann were the increasingly authoritarian tendencies of the régime, as manifested in the penal code and the special non-jury courts.[53]

Rebmann's background as an eminent judge gave his comments on Napoleonic legal institutions great weight. Of all the institutions bequeathed by Napoleon to the Rhineland, none, arguably, was more important than the law codes and the hierarchy of courts that enforced them. Defence of this legacy was something that Rhenish liberals united around throughout the first half of the nineteenth century, leading a socially broad-based coalition against attempts by the Prussian successor régime to replace it with its more antiquated alternative. In this, they proved successful: the French codes remained the basis of law in the Rhineland until replaced by a new all-German code at the beginning of the twentieth century.[54]

Rhinelanders' support for the Napoleonic code opened them up to accusations by later German nationalist historians like Treitschke of somehow being Francophile, and disloyal to the German nation.[55] The positive reception given to the codes does seem convincing evidence of Rhenish acceptance of French rule: surely it justifies locating the region securely within the inner empire.[56] Yet, there is an alterative explanation. Firstly, we need to consider what Rhinelanders liked about the Napoleonic legal system. This is not so difficult, thanks to a thorough investigation conducted by the Prussian authorities after 1815. The investigative commission solicited the opinion not only of Rhenish jurists, but of people more widely. This revealed that the French system was popular not so much because of the contents of the civil code or penal code, but rather because of the procedures of the French courts: the oral, public proceedings in front of juries, the principle of equality before the law, and the independence of the judiciary from political interference. Of course, what the Prussians were investigating was only part of the legal system established by Napoleon; they were not investigating the various special tribunals that he had established to try those crimes that were of peculiar interest to the state, and where juries might acquit. Crimes such as forgery of official documents, fraud in the conscription process, and smuggling, for example. These courts, which operated without juries and generally included military officers amongst those sitting in judgement, collapsed immediately upon the French army's evacuation of the Rhineland in 1814. They had never been popular. Thanks to Napoleon's defeat, the region had been fortuitously shorn of those elements of Napoleonic governance – not just the special courts, but also the customs men and special police commissioners, to name some – that had caused most public disquiet. What remained intact was only a part of the Napoleonic edifice, but it was the most benign part that quite naturally attracted popular support.[57]

Of course Prussophile German nationalists like Joseph Görres, or Ernst Moritz Arndt, or indeed, the Freiherr vom Stein, tended to overlook such subtle distinctions in their hatred of the French, and condemned anything emanating from Napoleonic despotism. In their eagerness to de-Napoleonize, as Rebmann put it – '*Entnapoleonisierung*' – they threatened to throw out the baby with the bathwater. Those, like Rebmann and many other Rhinelanders who supported aspects of the Napoleonic inheritance faced condemnation as Francophile traitors. This label, to an extent, stuck, being repeated by representatives of the Borussian school like Treitschke, writing in the hyperpatriotic (and anti-French) atmosphere that prevailed in the final decades of the nineteenth century, and by a later generation of historian, in the years after the First World War. In conclusion, Rhinelanders can neither be classified as collaborators nor resisters. Instead, they treated Napoleonic rule as an *à la carte* menu: they picked and chose, selecting those Napoleonic institutions and innovations that they liked best, and opposing the others. In so doing, they were motivated by hard-nosed self interest, not broader ideological considerations.

Notes

1. S. Gilliatt, *An Exploration of the Dynamics of Collaboration and Non-Resistance* (Lewiston, NY, 2000), p. 131.
2. P. Davies, *France and the Second World War. Occupation, Collaboration and Resistance* (London, 2001), p. 49.
3. For example, L. Taylor, *Between Resistance and Collaboration. Popular Protest in Northern France, 1940–45* (Basingstoke, 2000), *passim*.
4. Though it should be noted, at this point, that a strand of the current German historiography of the Holy Roman Empire now views that entity less as an incoherent, loose collection of essentially sovereign territories and more as a 'state' in its own right – indeed, a precursor of the German nation state. See especially G. Schmidt, 'Das frühneuzeitliche Reich – komplementäres Staat oder föderative Nation', *Historische Zeitschrift*, CCLXXIII, no. 2 (October, 2001), pp. 371–99; and H. Schilling, 'Reichsstaat und frühneuzeitliche Nation der Deutschen oder teilmodernisiertes Reichssystem: Überlegungen zu Charakter und Aktualität des Alten Reiches', *Historische Zeitschrift*, CCLXXII, no. 2 (April, 2001), pp. 377–95.
5. For a brief survey of the territorial order in the pre-revolutionary Rhineland, see M. Rowe, *From Reich to State: the Rhineland in the Revolutionary Age, 1780–1830* (Cambridge, 2003), pp. 14–15.
6. This would become dramatically apparent when the French revolutionaries attempted to impose their new republican calendar and festivals on the region in the late 1790s. For more on this, cf. M. Rowe, 'Forging "New-Frenchmen": state propaganda in the Rhineland, 1794–1814', in B. Taithe and T. Thornton (eds), *Propaganda* (Stroud, 1999), pp. 115–30.

7. The current historiography of the Holy Roman Empire (referred to in note 4) marks the culmination of a longer process of rehabilitation that began at least as early as the 1960s. For a review of the early revisionism, cf. G. Strauss, 'The Holy Roman Empire revisited', *Central European History*, XI, no. 4 (December, 1978), pp. 290–301.

8. For the military potential of the *Reich*, see P. Wilson, *German Armies: War and German Politics, 1648–1806* (London, 1998).

9. Plenty of examples of the civic pride (and indeed arrogance) of Cologne's burghers are provided by J. Hashagen, *Das Rheinland und die französische Herrschaft: Beiträge zur Charakteristik ihres Gegensatzes* (Bonn, 1908), pp. 9–24, 29–45, 47–50, 72.

10. For a relatively accessible indication of the kind of role imperial institutions played in the preservation of urban privilege, see C. Friedrichs, 'Urban conflicts and the imperial constitution in seventeenth-century Germany', *Journal of Modern History*, LVIII (1986), supplement, pp. 98–123. For much more detailed examinations of the imperial courts, see B. Diestelkamp, *Rechtsfälle aus dem alten Reich: denkwürdige Prozesse vor dem Reichskammergericht* (Munich, 1995), and also H. Gross, *Empire and Sovereignty: a History of the Public Law Literature in the Holy Roman Empire, 1599–1804* (Chicago, 1975).

11. T. Nipperdey, *Germany from Napoleon to Bismarck 1800–1866* (Dublin, 1996), pp. 272–3. The German national anthem of Hoffmann von Fallersleben was also a product of this crisis.

12. U. Möllney, *Norddeutsche Presse um 1800. Zeitschriften und Zeitungen in Flensburg, Braunschweig, Hannover und Schaumburg-Lippe im Zeitalter der Französischen Revolution* (Bielefeld, 1996). For a classic analysis of the rise of the public sphere, see J. Habermas, *Strukturwandel der Öffentlichkeit* (6th edn, Neuwied, 1986). See also the works of H. Bödeker, and in particular, H. Bödeker, 'Prozesse und Strukturen politischer Bewußtseinsbildung der deutschen Aufklärung', in H. Bödeker and U. Hermann (eds), *Aufklärung als Politisierung – Politisierung als Aufklärung* (Hamburg, 1987), pp. 10–31.

13. Frederick's victory over the French at Rossbach in 1757 appears to have had an especially big impact throughout Germany. Cf. D. Showalter, *The Wars of Frederick the Great* (London and New York, 1996), p. 191.

14. Two recent contributions include, W. Hardtwig, 'Vom Elitebewußtseins zur Massenbewegung. Frühformen des Nationalismus in Deutschland 1500–1800', in W. Hardtwig (ed.), *Nationalismus und Bürgerkultur in Deutschland 1500–1914. Ausgewählte Aufsätze* (Göttingen, 1994), pp. 34–54; Winfried Schulze, '*Sua cuique nationi discrimina*: nationales Denken und nationale Vorurteile in der Frühen Neuzeit', in S. Krim and W. Zirbs (eds), *Die Deutschen und die Andern: Patriotismus, Nationalgefühl und Nationalismus in der deutschen Geschichte* (Munich, 1997), pp. 32–66.

15. M. Schnettger, '*Impero romano – Impero germanico*: Italienische Perspektiven auf das Reich in der Frühen Neuzeit', in M. Schnettger (ed.), *Imperium Romanum – Irregulare Corpus – Teutscher Reichs-Staat: das Alte Reich im Verständnis der Zeitgenossen und der Historiographie* (Mainz, 2002), pp. 53–75.

16. Readers of English are well-served when it comes to the Rhineland in the 1790s, with T.C.W. Blanning, *The French Revolution in Germany: Occupation and Resistance in the Rhineland, 1792–1802* (Oxford, 1983).

17. The Rhenish press's initial response to news of the Bastille's fall is well documented in J. Hansen (ed.), *Quellen zur Geschichte des Rheinlandes im Zeitalter der Französischen Revolution, 1780–1801* (Bonn, 1931–8), I, pp. 380–5.
18. Blanning, *French Revolution in Germany*, p. 84.
19. Hansen, *Quellen*, II, pp. 668–9, 728–32, 848–50.
20. Electoral order no. 2398, 14 July 1794, in J. Scotti, *Sammlung der Gesetze und Verordnungen, welche in den ehemaligen Herzogthümern Jülich, Cleve, und Berg, und in dem vormaligen Grossherzogthum Berg über Gegenstände der Landeshoheit, Verfassung, Verwaltung und Rechtspflege ergangen sind. Vom Jahr 1475 bis zu der am 15. April eingetretenen Königlich Preußischen Landesregierung* (Düsseldorf, 1821), II, p. 742.
21. Hansen, *Quellen*, II, pp. 618–21.
22. Hauptstaatsarchiv Düsseldorf (hereafter HStAD), Oberpräsidium Köln, 1534.
23. Gilliatt, *Dynamics of Collaboration*, pp. 11, 14.
24. Hansen, *Quellen*, III, pp. 280–2.
25. J.A. Kopstadt, *Über Kleve: in Briefen an einen Freund aus den Jahren 1811 und 1814* (Frankfurt am Main, 1822), pp. viii–x.
26. This investigation is brought to light by K. Wegert's fascinating study, *German Radicals Confront the Common People: Revolutionary Politics and Popular Politics 1789–1849* (Mainz, 1992), pp. 26–37, upon which the remainder of this paragraph is based.
27. The author is mindful of the danger of believing everything spouted by Napoleonic sources on the preceding Directory, a régime the new rulers of France had a vested interest in denigrating. That said, with respect to the occupied territories, and especially the Rhineland, the Consulate represented a definite improvement over what had preceded. For a positive assessment of the Directory's achievements in France proper, see M. Lyons, *France under the Directory* (Cambridge, 1975); and, more recently, M. Crook, *Napoleon Comes to Power: Democracy and Dictatorship in Revolutionary France, 1795–1804* (Cardiff, 1998).
28. Previous treaties referring to the Rhineland, such as Basel (1795) and Campo Formio (1797), were concluded by the French Republic and individual German princes with an interest in the region. Lunéville, however, bound the Holy Roman Empire, the body with ultimate sovereignty in the Rhineland. Hence the agreement's importance.
29. There has been a considerable amount of research into the secularization process in the Rhineland. Especially important, in terms of the sheer amount of scholarship it is built upon, is W. Schieder (ed.), *Säkularisation und Mediatisierung in den vier rheinischen Departements 1803–1813: Edition des Datenmaterials der zur veräussernden Nationalgüter* (Boppard am Rhein, 1991).
30. For the endemic indiscipline in the French army in the Rhineland in the 1790s, see Blanning, *French Revolution in Germany*, pp. 15–16, 93–8, 123.
31. Rowe, *Reich to State*, pp. 92–3.
32. T.C.W. Blanning, *Joseph II* (London, 1994), p. 203.
33. Much has been published on the Republic of Mainz. One of the best books remains F. Dumont, *Die Mainzer Republik von 1792/93: Studien zur Revolutionierung in Rheinhessen und der Pfalz* (Alzey, 1982).
34. For the relative success of Napoleonic propaganda in the Rhineland, see Rowe, 'Forging "New-Frenchmen". For Napoleonic propaganda more

generally, consult R. Holtman, *Napoleonic Propaganda* (Baton Rouge, Louisiana, 1950).

35. J. Breuilly, 'Napoleonic Germany and State-formation', in M. Rowe (ed.), *Collaboration and Resistance in Napoleonic Europe: State-Formation in an Age of Upheaval, c.1800–1815* (Basingstoke, 2003), p. 125.
36. S. Potter, 'British Overseas Expansion', in S. Ellis (ed.), *Empires and States in European Perspective* (Pisa, 2002), pp. 125–6.
37. In Spain, as Esdaile demonstrates, the degree of social disintegration also impeded organized resistance to the French. Cf. C. Esdaile, 'War and Politics in Spain, 1808–1814', *The Historical Journal*, XXXI (1988).
38. W. Herborn, 'Der Graduierte Ratsherr. Zur Enticklung einer neuen Elite im Kölner Rat der frühen Neuzeit', in H. Schilling and H. Diederiks (eds), *Bürgerliche Eliten in den Niederlanden und in Nordwestdeutschland: Studien zur Sozialgeschichte des europäischen Bürgertums im Mittelalter und in der Neuzeit* (Cologne, 1985), pp. 337–74.
39. Though even here there were underlying rural-urban tensions. Cf. F.G. Eyck, *Loyal Rebels: Andreas Hofer and the Tyrolean Uprising of 1809* (Lanham, New York, 1986), pp. 1–17, 27–35, 37–41, 68–9, 109, 158–9.
40. M. Sobania, 'Das Aachener Bürgertum am Vorabend der Industrialisierung', in L. Gall (ed.), *Vom alten zum neuen Bürgertum. Die mitteleuropäische Stadt im Umbruch 1780–1820* (Munich, 1991), pp. 218–22.
41. Cf. especially R. Porter and M. Teich (eds), *The Enlightenment in National Context* (Cambridge, 1981).
42. J. Ellul, *Propaganda: the Formation of Men's Attitudes* (New York, 1968), pp. 15, 30, 62–70.
43. The French did the same in the northern, Hanseatic departments, annexed in 1810. Cf. A. Joulia, 'Der Departementalverein Ober-Ems (1812): ein Erbe der Aufklärung oder ein Produkt des napoleonischen Dirigismus?', *Osnabrücker Mitteilungen*, LXXVIII (1971), pp. 151–9.
44. For more on this, cf. Rowe, *Reich to State*, pp. 139–42. Also, W. Dotzauer, *Freimaurergesellschaften am Rhein: Aufgeklärte Sozietäten auf dem linken Rheinufer vom Ausgang des Ancien Régime bis zum Ende der napoleonischen Herrschaft* (Wiesbaden, 1977). For the same theme, but with reference to one of the German satellite states, cf. H. Gürtler, *Deutsche Freimaurer im Dienste napoleonischer Politik: die Freimaurer im Königreich Westfalen 1807–1813* (Struckum, 1988).
45. R. Dufraisse, 'La contrebande dans les départements réunis de la rive gauche du Rhin à lé poque napoléonienne', *Francia*, I (1973), pp. 508–36.
46. *Ibid.*, pp. 513, 529–32.
47. For the national balance within the Napoleonic judiciary, cf. S. Graumann, *Französische Verwaltung am Niederrhein. Das Roërdepartement 1798–1814* (Essen, 1990), pp. 182–8, 192–3.
48. Dufraisse, 'Contrebande', pp. 519–25; J. Bourdon, 'La Contrebande à la frontière de l'Est en 1811, 1812, 1813', *Annales de l'Est*, 5th series, II, no. 4 (December, 1951), pp. 273–305.
49. G. Vallée, *Le Compte Général de la conscription de A.A. Hargenvilliers* (Paris, 1937).
50. For a more in-depth account of Napoleonic conscription in the Rhineland, and the opposition it provoked, cf. Rowe, *From Reich to State*, pp. 158–92.

51. A. Forrest, *Conscripts and Deserters: the Army and French Society during the Revolution and Empire* (Oxford, 1989), pp. 135–6.
52. F. Ponteil, *Napoléon Ier et l'Organisation Autoritaire de la France* (Paris, 1956), *passim*.
53. The above paragraph on Rebmann is based on K. Faber, *Die Rheinlande zwischen Restauration und Revolution: Probleme der Rheinischen Geschichte von 1814 bis 1848 im Spiegel der zeitgenössischen Publizistik* (Wiesbaden, 1966), pp. 46–55. For more on Bavaria's propaganda drive, designed to counter accusations in the Prussian-backed nationalist press that it and the other southern states had betrayed Germany through their allegiance to Napoleon, cf. W. Piereth, *Bayerns Pressepolitik und die Neuordnung Deutschlands nach den Befreiungskriegen* (Munich, 1999).
54. M. Rowe, 'The Napoleonic legacy in the Rhineland and the politics of reform in Restoration Prussia', in D. Laven and L. Riall (eds), *Napoleon's Legacy: Problems of Government in Restoration Europe* (Oxford, 2000), pp. 129–50.
55. H. von Treitschke, *History of Germany in the Nineteenth Century* (London, 1915), pp. 31–2, 59, 73, 107, 138, 146, 149, 200–3, 219.
56. For the concept of an inner and outer Napoleonic empire, cf. M. Broers, *Europe under Napoleon 1799–1815* (London, 1996).
57. For much more detail on all this, cf. part III of Rowe, *From Reich to State*, pp. 213–81.

5
Popular Resistance in Catalonia: *Somatens* and *Miquelets*, 1808–14

Antonio Moliner Prada

A strongly independent-minded region with long traditions of political, judicial and cultural autonomy, Catalonia entered the nineteenth century with a proud record of self-defence that was above all founded on the idea of the 'people-in-arms'. Thus, at the heart of Catalan military organization lay two forces which were in essence composed of armed civilians. Of these the first were the *miquelets* – volunteers contracted in time of war for a certain period of time for permanent service on a province-wide basis who drew their name from the followers of the sixteenth-century Catalan solider of fortune, Miquel de Prats. As for the second, it consisted of the *somatens* – men raised by ballot as a homeguard for service in their own localities alone who were expected always to be on the *qui vive* against danger (hence the name, *somatén* being a contraction of *som atent* – literally, 'be alert'). The heart and soul of the war effort in the Catalan revolt of the 1640s and the later struggle against Phillip V, these forces had for obvious reasons disappeared for most of the eighteenth century. However, the special circumstances thrown up by the Revolutionary and Napoleonic Wars led to their revival. In the so-called *guerra gran* – the war against the Convention of 1793–95 – for example, the *somatén* reappeared, but we are here concerned only with the *guerra del francés* of 1808–14. In this struggle – the Catalan experience of the Peninsular War – the wheel turned full circle. The professional army having largely disintegrated in the wake of Duhesme's occupation of Barcelona, the Supreme Junta of Catalonia, which was constituted at Lérida on 18 June 1808, promoted both the formation of *tercios de miquelets* and a general *somatén*, whilst similar moves had already been witnessed on the part of the local *juntas de corregiment*. Thereafter, meanwhile, both forces were tolerated and made use of by the military, whilst their actions often overlapped with those of the guerrilla bands that also appeared in Catalonia.[1]

At the beginning of the war against France the use of irregular forces was particularly prominent, this being so much the case that one of the chief contemporary chroniclers of the struggle, the regular army officer, Francisco Javier Cabanes, described the period from May to September 1808 as the '*somatén* era'.[2] Nor is this surprising: most of the garrison of Catalonia had fallen into the hands of the French when the latter had occupied Barcelona, whilst it was some time before reinforcements reached the principality from the Balearic Islands, the latter being the principality's nearest source of fresh troops. With few other means of protection, in fact, the insurgent authorities had no option but to turn to Catalonia's own military traditions. The first Catalan *somatén* – in this context the word means irregular band – was therefore formed in early June 1808. Citizens of Igualada, Manresa and other neighbouring towns raised such a force in the Bruc mountains with the aim of halting General Schwartz's march on Zaragoza. The skirmish, which took place on June 6, had the desired effect and succeeded in putting the imperial troops to flight. Made famous by the incident of the so-called 'drummer of Bruc', this was an important psychological victory – it was, indeed, the first defeat that Napoleon's army suffered in Spain – and was to become a symbol repeatedly exploited by the civil and military author-ities in their anti-French propaganda campaign. And, of course, it was a stimulus to further efforts of this type: following the Bruc battle, other villages that had previously not raised *somatens*, like Vilanova i la Geltrú, quickly did so.[3]

Very soon, then, *somatens* were in action in many parts of Catalonia. On 10 June the *somatens* of Vilafanca del Penedès, La Segarra and Urgell, attacked the French division commanded by Chabrán at Vendrell, who in reprisal looted and set fire to the whole town. On 14 June another French attempt to force the pass of El Bruc was repulsed with many cas-ualties. On 17 June the *somatens* again confronted the French at Mon-gat, in which action a woman named Susana Claretona, who was the wife of a *somatén* sub lieutenant, D. Francesc Felonch, so distinguished herself that she was named co-commandant, along with her husband, of the band to which she belonged, and later helped prevent the French from taking Capellades. On 4 July forces under the command of Franc-esc Deu de Llisá and Josep Colomer y Riu attacked the French at Con-gost. But perhaps the *somatens'* greatest glory was that which they attained in the successful defence of Gerona against repeated French assaults in the period from June to August 1808: with the city originally garrisoned only by a single understrength infantry battalion and a few artillerymen, it would undoubtedly have fallen to the French had not the local inhabitants stood to arms and manned the walls alongside the regulars.[4] Meanwhile, several thousand *miquelets* and *somatens* took part in the final relief of the city on 16 August 1808, the defence of the city also being notable for the involvement of a number of women, including Teresa Balaguer and Isabel Pi from Bagur, Esperansa Llorens from Cadaqués and Maria Plajas from Calonge.[5]

It was not long, meanwhile, before the *somatens* were joined by fresh forces. Notwithstanding successes of the sort as that obtained at Bruc, it was clear that an irregular militia that took to arms only when its own homes and families were in danger and at best served only for a few days, was hardly sufficient as a means of defence against the forces of Napoleon. Though some measure of relief was obtained by stipulating that men called up for the *somatén* should serve for a certain period of time and by forming the various local bands into larger units called *divisiones*, what was needed was clearly a permanent force that would be capable of carrying out special actions and of serving anywhere it was needed. No sooner had it assembled at Lérida, indeed, than the provincial junta that had been formed in the wake of the uprising decreed the formation of an army of 40 000 men. Needless to say, this was envisaged in terms not of regular troops but of *miquelets*, of which there were to be 40 *tercios* or regiments. Each one of these units was to be based on a particular town or district, whilst the men were all to be volunteers who were expected to serve for the duration of the war. The third article of the orders established that, once each town had met the numbers assigned to it – Lérida was supposed to raise 1000 men; Cervera, 500; Tarragona, 1500; Tortosa, 1200; Manresa, 500; Vic 400; Vilafranca, 150 and Igualada, 110 – the other men recruited should form a reserve and 'serve as *somatens* whenever need be, to which end companies and tercios shall be formed, and drill in the use of arms'. As this suggests, the *somatén* was not forgotten, but there is nonetheless a distinct hint that what was envisaged was the militarization of at least some of the bands of militiamen springing up around the region, the decree that established the *miquelets* referring to them as an army of *somatens* and giving commissions in their ranks to a number of men who had acted as commandants in the latter force (examples here include a notary from Lérida named Joan Baget; a canon from Manresa named Montanya; and a lawyer from Igualada named Riera).[6] Yet, in general, the principle that the defence of Catalonia should rest in the hands of its own citizens was not forgotten, as witness, for example, the fact that the leadership cadres of both the *somatens* and the *miquelets* continued to draw on men who could either have found no place in the old regular army, or had simply chosen other careers for themselves. There were, true, a number of retired and supernumerary officers such as Francisco Miláns del Bosch and Joan Claròs. But commanding some *somatens* were clergymen like Francisco Campos, who reputedly carried out a number of exemplary actions in the region of the Empordà, and Francesc Rovira, who later went on to establish hiimself as one of Catalonia's first guerrillas. And also prominent were the clothier, Josep Mansó, the merchant, Antoni Franch, and the proprietor, Esteban Pascual y Casas, all of whom were wealthy notables with a considerable stake in society.[7]

Yet were the *miquelets*, in particular, really a people's militia? It was true that there were certain differences from the old army. Setting aside the fact that the men were all volunteers, all officers up to the rank of captain were appointed by the local juntas (in theory more senior positions were in the gift of the Captain General, but here, too, one suspects that the civil authorities held the whip hand). Yet the men were paid wages, and, however simply, uniformed (regulations promulgated in August 1808 speak of grey jackets with red facings and round hats bearing the national cockade; to distinguish the regiments one from another, meanwhile, the soldiers' collars bore the initial of the towns from which they were raised). As for the officers, they were paid generous salaries – captains received 20 *reales* a day, lieutenants 16 and sub lieutenants 12 – whilst they were given the same rights and prerogatives as the regular army, and thereby admitted at least to the military estate, if not the army itself.[8] In the end, then, it is hard to see how the *miquelets* amounted to anything other than regular troops even if the regimental standards that they carried continued to mark them out as regular troops who were specifically Catalan and had forms and origins that were distinct from the rest of the Spanish infantry.

The formation of the new force was not without its difficulties. Tortosa had provided 1200 men by early October 1808 and Vic another 800, but there were complaints that towns further from the French zone of control were not acting with the same speed.[9] At the same time the response was certainly patchy: some areas, such as Manresa, Seu d'Urgell and Puigcerdà produced rather more men than those required by the draft, while others fell short, like Mataró, La Marina, the Vall d'Aràn and Camprodón. Acccording to Oman, indeed, at the beginning of August only 6000 men had been raised for service with the *miquelets*, whilst there were difficulties in arming and officering even such men as had come forward.[10] Of the 40 000 men called up in the month of June, no more than 23 000 were actually assembled. But there is no doubt that many *tercios de miqueletes* were soon ready to take the field. Thus, Esdaile indicates the creation of a total of 27 *tercios* in 1808: two in Tarragona, four in Lérida, three in Gerona, one in Manresa, two in Cervera, one in Tortosa, two in Vic, one in Mataró, one in Seu d'Urgell, one in Berga, two in Talarn, one in Cerdanya, two in the Vall d'Arán, one in Barcelona, one in the Ampordà, one in Igualada, one in Figueres and one in Granollers (in the case of the Barcelona and Figueres *tercios*, one assumes that what is meant is that the troops came from the towns, rather than actually being raised in them).[11]

If the brunt of the June fighting had fallen upon the *somatens*, from July onwards their endeavours were increasingly shared by the *miquelets*. Knowledge of the terrain, particularly in the hills, enabled the two forces to cause the Napoleonic army heavy losses. With the aid of the local population, the patriots carried out a defensive war of attrition, accepting no real battle unless they had clear numerical superiority. The rest of 1808, then, was characterized by a long list of raids and skirmishes. For obvious reasons, it is impossible to detail all these actions here, but, in brief, whilst large forces of irregulars including the 'divisions' of *somatens* commanded by Arzú and Baget and the *tercios de miquelets* of Berga, Manresa and Igualada, blockaded Barcelona, whither Duhesme had retired with the bulk of his forces following his failure to capture Gerona, others closed in on the isolated garrison of Figueras and even raided the French frontier.[12] Amongst the most active leaders at this time was Milans del Bosch who in September 1808 alone is reported to have attacked the invaders at Moncada, Badalona and San Feliu de Guixols.[13]

As the summer of 1808 wore on, however, so the war in Catalonia began to change. In August substantial forces of regular troops began to arrive at Tarragona from the Balearic Islands, and by October the Spaniards had put together a substantial army. Known as the 'Army of the Right', this was commanded by Juan Miguel de Vives. For many of the *miqueletes*, in particular, their experience of the war now began to change. Thus, now some 20 000 strong, many of their units were integrated into the ranks of Vives' troops, of which the Vanguard Division contained the first and second *tercios* of Gerona, the first *tercio* of Tarragona, and the *tercios* of Igualada Cervera and Figueres, and the Fourth Division the first *tercio* of Lérida and the *tercios* of Vic, Manresa and Vallés.[14] Meanwhile, with the French shut up in Barcelona and Gerona, there was now much less need for the *somatens* and, to the fury of some of the *juntas de corregimiento*, many were either sent home or drafted into the *miquelets*. But the move towards more formal methods of waging war was only temporary. Having first captured the petty fortress of Roses, on 9 December a large French force under Marshal St Cyr drove away the irregulars blockading Figueras and then headed for Barcelona, and for the next few days assorted groups of *miquelets* and *somatens* harassed the march of the French columns or sought to hold strategic positions blocking the route to the *ciudad condal*. Despite their courage, however – at one point St Cyr himself was almost captured whilst personally trying to find a vital goat track – the French were not to be checked. Thanks in large part to Vives' incompetence, indeed, a detachment of the Army of the Right was beaten at Cardedeu on 16 December, and Barcelona relieved the next day. Nor was this all: on 21 December St Cyr sallied out of Barcelona and routed the Spanish troops still lining the banks of the River Llobregat immediately to the south and west of Barcelona.[15]

Known as the battle of Molins de Rei, this last battle was almost fatal to the Army of the Right. 'Having been responsible', we are told, 'for a thousand excesses in the towns they passed through, [the soldiers] reached Tarragona naked, disordered, starving and possessed by an inexplicable terror and panic'.[16] According to Oman, meanwhile, the *miquelets* 'mostly dispersed to their homes'.[17] Yet by the same token Molins de Rei also gave a new fillip to 'people's war'. Desperate to win time to reorganize his battered forces, the new Spanish commander in Catalonia, General Teodoro Reding, sought to revive the *somatens* as the best means of continuously harassing the enemy. With large swathes of the province now under enemy control, calling them up was by no means as easy as before but a call went out for men who had been serving in *somatens* that had been dispersed or disbanded to come forward to fight the French once more and this produced a small irregular force – in effect a guerrilla band – that was given to a regular brigadier named Iranzo. Under the direction of another general named Martí, meanwhile, a plan was drawn up to reorganize the *miquelets* on a much less costly basis and to turn the *somatens* into a reserve. Disrupted though these efforts were on 25 February 1809 by a fresh defeat at Valls, which saw the death of Reding, they continued unabated for most of the year that followed. The system of conscription already used for the *somatens*, it was agreed, should be extended to the *miquelets*, and both bodies were subjected to a common inspector general in the person of Joan Clarós. The *somatens* were divided into four divisions: the Ampurdán division, which was to operate from the frontier to the Ter; the Montseny, to cover the area between the Ter and the Tordera; the Vallès, from the Tordera to the Besós, and the Llobregat, to operate from the capital as far as the Penedès (the renowned irregular commander, Rovira, was given the first division, and the other three were placed under the command of the governors of Vic, Mataró and Vilafranca, respectively). And on a local level juntas such as that of Vilafranca del Penedès tried to make service in their *somatens* more attractive by giving them the aspect more of a regular civic guard than a band of irregulars.[18]

Thanks to these efforts, the *somatens*, in particular, continued to play a part in the war. Led by a priest named Mas and one Otzet, peasants from Sallent, Moià and other villages carried out significant defensive actions, while Collbató and Capellades witnessed effective cooperation from bands led by Baltasar de Eixalà and Josep Matheu.[19] Outstanding in the Priorat region, meanwhile, was the *somatén* of Porrera. Led by Josep Pellicer i Fort, this participated in the campaign of Valls and later captured much food and ammunition from a French convoy that it attacked in late 1809 as well as preventing an enemy column from occupying Falset.[20] In March and April 1809 the *somatens* of the Vallès Oriental made life uncomfortable for the enemy troops that had occupied Terrassa and Sabadell. Indeed, the action of the *somatén* of the latter city, commanded by Turull de Sentmenat, forced the French to withdraw, but they returned on Easter Wednesday, with more men and took full revenge: 'Thieving, pillaging, the most horrific violence to women young and married filled Sabadell with wailing and consternation on a day as saintly as any celebrated by the Church.'[21] In the villages of the Baix Camp, Alt Camp and Conca de Barberà (Albiol, Vimbodi, Coll de Alforja and Prades) regions of Tarragona, Jaume Palliser and Marià Palies led 300 men of the *somatens* in a series of strikes in March 1809 which forced the imperial troops to fall back on Montblanc.[22] And, finally, whilst the walls of the city were manned, among other units, by *tercios* of *miquelets* drawn from Gerona, Vic, Cervera and the Vall de Talarn, the third siege of Gerona (June–December 1809) saw large forces of *somatens* being employed in the various attempts that were made to raise the siege and get convoys of food through to the defenders.[23]

According to some observers, meanwhile, all this encouraged a certain bravado. Let us take, for example, a letter cited by the chief contemporary chronicler of events in Barcelona as having been written by a *somatén* commander named Fernando Chaparro. Thus, Chaparro was particularly impressed by the attitude adopted by the irregulars *vis-à-vis* the once-feared enemy cavalry:

Every day the somatens provide fresh proof of their dash, and surely glory is deserved by these men whose occupation two months ago was the innocent tasks of farming, but who now know other tools than the mattock and the plough...and have humiliated the Saint-Cyrs, the Chabrans, the Lechis and other swarms of their generals? They now laugh at them wearing their cuirasses, which inspire about as much fear in them as the Easter processions, and pay them no attention other than to argue about who should have first dibs on them when it comes to taking them home to their villages. All the more is this the case since they have learned from experience that a musketball pierces the cuirass from more than 100 paces, killing the cuirassier and coming out of his arse. The somatens know full well that, once the cuirassiers have been knocked from their horses, they are little different from turtles, and are reduced to laughter by the clumsiness of men dressed up...in such junk.[24]

For a French view of all this, meanwhile, we might turn to a Frenchman named Maffre-Baugé who refers in his memoirs to the trap the Catalan *somatens* prepared for him when, towards the end of 1809, a detachment of his troops was heading towards the monastery at Montserrat: 'The Catalans rushed us in a mob, whilst from the top of the rocks they opened a harassing fire that caused us much loss...without us being able to hit back with any success.'[25]

Unlike the *miquelets*, which, as we shall see, were soon to disappear altogether, the *somatens* continued to operate for most of the war. Following the capture of the fortress of San Fernando de Figueres by Rovira in April 1811, for example, a general *somatén* was ordered of some 6400 men, with the target quotas being distributed as follows: Tarragona, 1000; Montblanc, 400; Cervera, 1500; Lérida, 500; Manresa, 1500; Vilafranca, 1500. And when Tarragona was besieged two months later, the Junta attempted to call up another 12 500 men.[26] At this time, indeed, the *somatén* again experienced a revival of interest in its fortunes. With large parts of the regular forces all set on departing for Valencia in the wake of the loss of the city that had been Catalonia's temporary capital since 1808, Jacinto Buniva de Morera, a sub lieutenant in the Baza Infantry Regiment, proposed a general *somatén* – in effect, a national guard – coupled with the deployment of the available manpower into four divisions that would take it in turns to be ready to combat the enemy at a moment's notice.[27] As for the *somatens'* main successes in the latter part of the war, the most important was Rovira's capture of the great citadel of San Fernando de Figueres. Thus, at the head of 2000 irregulars, on the night of 9 April 1811 Rovira got into the fortress with the help of three young Catalans who had secured employment in its magazines. Having knocked out the Neapolitan troops defending the gate and detained the sleeping governor, the Spaniards found that they had taken 850 prisoners, provisions for 2000 men for four months, 16 000 muskets, immense supplies of clothing and shoes, and 400 000 francs. Following a four and a half month siege, in August the French took the fortress back but not before they had lost 4000 men to dysentery and malaria.[28]

Thus far, we have been talking about popular resistance in terms of Catalonia's traditional system of militias. In the Spain of 1808–14 there had emerged an entirely separate phenomenon in the form of the independent guerrilla band. With more and more of the principality under enemy occupation – Gerona fell at the end of 1809, Lérida in the spring of 1810 and Tarragona in the summer of 1811 – it was but logical that Catalonia should also have been affected by this development. As elsewhere, then, we see attempts to form *cruzadas* – literally 'crusades', though a better term would be 'bands of crusaders' – composed of members of the clergy. In June 1809, for example, we find a canon of the collegiate church at Pons named Joan Pau Constans submitting a proposal for such a force to the Junta Central.[29] These schemes rarely came to fruition, however: although his plan had the support of both the then Captain General of Catalonia, General Joaquín Blake and the Junta Central, Constans was unable to overcome the numerous obstacles he came up against in both the Junta of Catalonia and ecclesiastical circles, whilst the *cruzada* proposed by another priest named Joan Ferrer, who was chaplain of the Escuelas Pías School at Moià, met with a similar lack of success.[30] In so far as can be ascertained, then, most of the guerrilla bands that were formed in Catalonia were wholly secular, though their leaders did sometimes come from the clergy, two examples that we might cite here being Josep Bertran, the parish priest of Llorà, and Canon Francesc Rovira, who in 1811 had managed to gather together a band of stragglers and deserters from Manresa, Solsona, Cardona and Sant Llorens de Morunys at the head of which *tercio de expatriados*, as he called them, he was able to attain the rank of brigadier.[31] If Rovira's status as a priest was quite rare, this was less so with respect to the fact that he had been fighting the French since 1808. Thus, most of the Catalan guerrilla commanders were men who had earlier led troops belonging to either the juntas or the regular army and attained a considerable amount of promotion. As an example, we might cite the retired army officer, Joan Clarós, whose activities quickly gained him great notoriety (in September 1810, for example, he joined with Rovira in a raid on the Cerdagne, which caused the French authorities much alarm not just on account of the 30 000 francs that were extracted in ransoms for the various hostages taken by the Catalans, but also with respect to the cooperation which they were afforded by many of the local inhabitants).[32]

Unlike many other such forces, we happen to know a considerable amount about Clarós's *partida*. On 3 August 1811 his 'division', as it was known, comprised a total of 279 men, of whom 203 were soldiers from the First Regiment of Cervera, 38 stragglers from a variety of different corps, and 40 peasants who had rallied to his standard. The captains were José Cuadros and P. Barrios, who had both been appointed by Clarós; the lieutenants José Moya (an officer of the Granada Regiment, who had been captured by the French and later escaped), Ignacio Surés (an officer of the Soria Regiment, who was, again, a fugitive from French imprisonment), Francesc Franch (a straggler from the Catalan Legions, who had joined Clarós), and Ramón Marcos (an officer of the Third Regiment of Cervera, who was another escaped prisoner); and the sub lieutenants, Juan Vert (an officer of the light company of the First Regiment of Gerona), Juan Requena, Agustín Saberres and Mariano Borrás (all of whom were stragglers from the Volunteers of Tarragona), Miguel Viñes (a straggler from the Almogávares battalion), José Baleta (a deserter from the Savoya Regiment) and Miguel Darder (a deserter from the Iberia Regiment).[33]

Whether this somewhat patchwork appearance was typical of the guerrillas, we do not know. But we have already seen that Rovira's band was largely recruited from men who had fled the French zone of occupation, whilst this is something that also appears to have been the case with the *partida* called the company of *almogovares* – a term used in the early-modern period to decribe Spanish light horse – formed in Olot in January 1810 under the command of Narcís Gay, the 378 men whom Gay had gathered together by 31 May of the same year for the most part coming from the Empordà (i.e. the district around Figueres).[34]

Thus far, then, thus good. Popular resistance in Catalonia was found in many forms both old and and new, whilst it also appears to have been constant. In this respect, the praise that even the most jaundiced British historians have lavished on the Catalans appears to have been well merited. Let us take, for example, the extremely anti-Spanish William Napier. Thus: 'Their patriotism was purer and their efforts more sustained: the *somatens* were brave and active in battle, the population of the towns firm and the juntas apparently disinterested.'[35] Similar views were, meanwhile, entertained by many Spanish historians, as well as by the contemporary chronicler, Father Raimundo Ferrer.[36] And at the time of the war itself, it was very clearly the 'official' line. As the Junta of Catalonia's gazette put it, for example:

> There is no difference between men in Catalonia, all are soldiers, in the fields, on the roads, in places, in the cities occupied by the enemy, wherever the Catalans show profound hatred for the French, an inextinguishable zeal for the Fatherland, a loyalty beyond question . . . Supplies, munitions, the French convoys fall to the valiant patriots that cover every inch of ground, and in the towns and villages where they have superiority in weapons, it is the houses and walls that are captive, not the hearts, which constantly exalt their loyalty in the most energetic, most heroic demonstrations.[37]

But there is also another side to the story. From source after source come details that challenge or undermine the traditional version of events, whilst the Catalan archives are full of evidence that suggests a very different *guerra del francés*, and it is this to which we must now turn our attention.

Let us begin with the *somatén*. In this respect it is a little disturbing to find that the famous defence of El Bruc was the work not just of heroic armed civilians, but also of large numbers of deserters from the garrison of Barcelona, including a detachment of the Swiss Wimpffen regiment commanded by Lieutenant Francisco Krutter preparing an ambush for the French. Dressed though these men may have been in Catalan *barretina* caps, if it is true, as at least one source claims, that the number involved came to around 500, then a very different view must be entertained of the defence of the pass.[38] Reinforcing such doubts is the fact that service in the *somatén* does not appear to have been that popular. Thus villages along the French frontier or close to areas of French occupation were concerned at the idea of sending off their menfolk and thereby depriving themslves of their only means of defence.[39] From all parts of Catalonia came significant number of petitions from private citizens requesting that their sons be declared exempt from service.[40] And later on, as at Vacarises, draft evasion was a problem with many men choosing to run away to join guerrilla bands such, in this instance, as that commanded by José Boadas.[41] Finally, the local authorities themselves might make difficulties, as occurred at Vizcondado de Bas and Sant Joan de Les Fonts where the justices protested at complete strangers demanding costly contributions and the raising of *somatens* 'on they knew not what authority'.[42] Nor was the situation with the *miquelets* any better. Not only did recruitment fall well short of the mark set by the Junta of Catalonia, but there were complaints of even such men as had enlisted destroying their weapons so that they would not have to go to war.[43]

It was not just a question of obtaining recruits, however. Thus, no sooner had many men enlisted or been called up, than they were looking for opportunities to escape, this being a problem that afflicted the *somatens* and *miquelets* alike. As the landowner Antoni Bellsolell recalls in his memoirs, for men with a little money one way out was to buy their freedom, and this happened with some frequency.[44] But for many of the poorer combatants, there was no hope of availing themselves of this privilege with the result that they turned to desertion. A problem throughout Spain – taking the country as a whole it may have affected 20 per cent of the army's manpower at one time or other – in Catalonia it was even more prominent. The papers of the Junta of Barcelona (a somewhat fugitive body that led a chequered existence not in the *ciudad condal* but in various towns in the hinterland) contain details of a number of cases that occurred in 1810. Amongst the citizens of Barcelona who had fled were Miquel Ferreras, who was thirty-three and a barber; Joan Llubregat, who was nineteen and another barber; Benet Miravet, who was seventeen and a painter; Isidre Valba, who was twenty-two and a shoemaker; and Josep Sola, who was thirty-six. For a closer look at such a man, meanwhile, we might take the case of Miquel Estop, who was a soldier of the First Catalan Legion, nineteen years old, the son of Antoni and Serafina, five foot one in height, and possessed of dark brown hair, brown eyes, a broad nose, dark skin and a scar. Estop having deserted on 2 May 1810, the Junta's military commission was ordered to arrest him: 'It is urgent that with due zeal you endeavour to collect the said individual by whatever means you deem prudent, and if that is not possible you should imprison the father, mother, brother, uncle or closest relative until he is produced and report that you have thus done so'.[45] How the commission was to accomplish this feat in the midst of a city filled with French troops was not made apparent, but that is by-the-by. What matters is simply the fact that flight was an ever present reality. As Rovira informed the Junta of Manresa in January 1810, for example, the desertion going on around him was so 'continued and scandalous' that 'in a short time I am likely to be left with no men but myself'.[46] Still worse, meanwhile, the population were all too happy to connive at this activity, the situation not being helped in this respect by the fact that many magistrates not only failed to uphold the law but even went so far as to shelter both their own sons and those of their wealthier neighbours.[47]

As time went on, so a refuge other than home and hearth offered itself to would-be deserters. Thus, in November 1811, the arrest was ordered of Jaume Borrull, a citizen of Sant Climent, for having recruited men in a number of villages in order to form a guerrilla group, on the promise of exemption from the draft.[48] In this instance, the dodge was foiled, but the fact is that joining one of the many extra-official *partidas* that began to spring up was a wonderful way out of trouble for many soldiers, especially as these bands were generally in reality nothing more than *companías de brivalla* – literally 'rabble companies' – living by theft and highway robbery whose ransacking of village after village kept the entire population in a state of alarm. There were frequent tussles between the different bands and on occasions they even joined the French, whilst the local authorities were often forced to beg the Junta of Catalonia to help them keep them in order.[49] For a good example of such a force one might cite the gang raised by a wealthy farmer named Pere Rovira y Galcerán, which was in theory raised to assist in the blockade of Barcelona in the autumn of 1808, but in practice devoted itself to smuggling goods into the city and running a variety of protection rackets.[50] In theory, authorized bands – those, for example of Gay and Rovira – were not supposed to allow deserters to enlist with them, but in practice it was not easy to distinguish between men who had run away from their units (*desertores*) and men who had returned to their homes or been scattered across the countryside after some defeat (*dispersos*). Nor did it help, meanwhile, that men who were willing to rejoin the army were often offered better pay than those who had stuck it out through thick and thin, and that food was often far more plentiful in irregular units such as that of Gay than it was in the rest of the army.[51] Indeed, it was in part for this very reason that, despite his protests, Gay's command was disbanded in August 1811.[52]

Assuming the status of a guerrilla was a useful tactic and there is plenty of evidence from other parts of Spain to suggest that many outlaws and deserters made use of it at one time or another. But, of course, the phenomenon of banditry was anything but new. And in Catalonia, in particular, gangs known as *parrots* or *brivalles* had a long tradition in the region going back to the seventeenth century. In short, banditry already had a solid base in 1808, and was in consequence a natural response to the misery suffered by the lower classes in these years of war. Not surprisingly, meanwhile, the number of such malefactors grew throughout the *guerra del francés*. As for the war, many of the gangs made no pretence of having any interest in the struggle. Thus, in July 1811 we find Lieutenant Pedro Antonio Alvanés reporting that a detachment of troops that he was with had just been attacked at Arbolí, in the Baix Camp by a group of deserters who had their stronghold in caves at L'Alforja. Formed up in two groups, they had swept down on the soldiers, seized sixteen mules loaded with flour that had just been taken from the French, and mercilessly killed the commander of the detachment as he lay wounded on the ground. As for Alvanés, he managed to save himself by hiding in the house of the village priest. Determined to find him, the bandits had then turned all the houses upside down. Frustrated in this object, they had then destroyed all the weapons they could find (so as, one presumes, to frustrate the possibility of pursuit), and finally left to the accompaniment of claims to the effect that they had a monopoly on violence in the area. To quote the leader of the ruffians, 'Any deserter or armed villager we find that does not join us will be shot.'[53]

Something of the extent of the problem faced by Catalonia is conveyed by the report of an officer of the Cazadores de Cataluña battalion named Manuel Errando who was sent out with a small detachment comprising a sergeant, a corporal and eight men to hunt down deserters and thieves in central Catalonia in the early summer of 1812:

> In the present month of April we arrested fully armed the thief, Juan Quincles, alias Man, on the road that goes from Vic to Manresa, and a fortnight later we took his two companions, Manuel and Francisco Serrat...In the Sierra de Collespina five deserters who we took to Vique. Near Vidrá in a house called El Barretó we caught three deserters who we also took to Vic. Between La Fontella and Vilada and the parish of Malañeu we took three more, one of whom was wounded in the thigh whilst trying to escape...This month we have arrested as a thief and deserter, Antonio Sala y Golobandas, alias Solé, who is an inhabitant of Prats de Llusanés. In Llusá we took Juan Basa, alias Animota, the reason being, once again, that he was a deserter and thief. And in Berga we happened to chance on Josef Montorno, alias Tatxa, an inhabitant of Prats de Llusanés.[54]

The activities of Manuel Errando's column were very effective and gave the bandits no respite. Thus, in June he also managed to arrest a well-known thief and deserter named Casadesús at Marlés, four deserters at Igualada, and five more deserters at Vic, as well as killing two or three members of a band of 12 thieves and smugglers that was operating from

Viladecaballs.[55] Yet to the end of the war Catalonia remained overrun with *brivalles*, whilst this allowed the French to maintain that the *somatens* and guerrillas were all bandits *ipso facto*. On 16 June 1810, for example, four young men, accused of numerous acts of violent robbery on the highroads, were sentenced to death in Barcelona by a French military commission, their names being Geroni Albás, aged thirty-three, who was a gunsmith and resident of Olot; Jaume Fargas, twenty-four, a shoemaker, also from Olot; Rafael Fluxeny, twenty, a butcher from Molins de Rei; and Pau Smith – curiously – who originally hailed from Alsace, and was currently an agricultural labourer in Mongat.[56] What 'violent robbery on the highroads' actually meant in this instance is unclear, but for the French there was no doubt: a brigand was a brigand, and the only good brigand a dead one. Whether a brigand was also a freedom fighter is another matter: at first sight one is tempted simply to say 'no', but consideration of the contemporary Balkan example of the *hajduks* – the insurgent bands that long harassed the Turks in their European dominions and headed the Serbian revolt of 1804 – suggests a more cautious answer. Thus, by their very banditry, men such as Albás and his companions dislocated society and thereby discredited French rule, and in this respect it is interesting to find the French commissioner of police in Gerona complaining that the deserters who infested the countryside were bringing commerce to a complete standstill.[57]

But this is beside the point. The bandits took to the hills not to fight the French but because they were starving, and because violence was an easy option in the context of the *guerra del francés*. Meanwhile, to return to our discussion of the Catalan forces, a further fact that strikes the historian very forcibly is that there was little or no difference between the behaviour of the *somatens, miquelets* and guerrillas when they were in their ranks and that which they displayed when they were out of the control of the authorities. Of this the evidence is legion. The abbot of the monastery of Sant Pere de Camprodón, for example, was insulted and mistreated by a band of *miquelets*.[58] The citizens of Vic were regularly subjected to extortion by *miquelets* passing through the town.[59] The tradesmen of Gerona were, in the words of General Nogués, all too frequently robbed and abused 'by our troops, our *miquelets* and their supporters'.[60] The inhabitants of La Bisbal experienced frequent cases of theft, disorder and crime of all forms at the hands of soldiers denied what they demanded.[61] The Vallès region was devastated by bands of soldiers roaming its territory.[62] And in 1810 Narcís Gay, the man behind the Cuerpo de Almogávares, reported: 'The Figueres and Expatriado *tercios* are scattered about the hills, along with some draftees and deserters that have escaped various Army corps; most of these people are pillaging the countryside and murdering travellers. In order to halt as far as is possible so many excesses, I have seen the Rev. Rector of Llorá and we have agreed to pursue...these people who are so pernicious for society'.[63]

If it is impossible to argue that the Catalan forces were models of discipline, it is also difficult to show that they were of very much value in military terms. In places such as the pass of El Bruc where the French could not deploy their cavalry the *somatens* were able to gain the occasional success, whilst they were also able to put up a good show behind the walls of such towns as Gerona and Roses. As sentinels and pickets, too, they were fine, but every time they had to confront the French in open battle they were swept away with heavy losses: thus, the action at Mongat in which Susana Claretona supposedly so distinguished herself was actually a run-away French victory in which the *somatens* fled after a few shots. Nor were the *miquelets* much better. In one skirmish at Sant Jeroni de Murtra in October 1808, for example, we are told that 'the *miquelets* and their officers, far from withdrawing in good order...ran and scattered to the hills in shameful flight'.[64] Nor is any of this surprising. As the contemporary military analyst, Francisco Javier Cabanes, explained in his *Historia de las operaciones del ejército de Cataluña*, while masses of militia might have been valuable in the War of Succession 100 years before, they could not adjust to the more sophisticated tactics of the Napoleonic era, and were in consequence utterly insufficient to Catalonia's needs.[65] For such troops, guerrilla warfare was more of an option, but even here there are questions that have to be answered, the image presented by contemporary documentary evidence being very critical of the guerrilla bands, for example, on account of their instability, fragility, high cost and limited effectiveness.[66]

Faced by this situation the military authorities were in no doubt: Catalan traditions and Catalan sensibilities alike would have to give way to the demands of the war effort. Until the end of 1809 the heroic defence of Gerona shielded the military and political authorities from the full realities of the situation, but the loss of that city brought a new realism, and all the more so as Catalonia possessed a new Captain General in the person of the energetic and ambitious Enrique O'Donnell. For this officer, the way forward was quite clear. As he wrote to the provincial junta soon after taking over the army with respect to a particularly blatant case of mass desertion amongst the Castellterçol *somatén*, 'This scandalous desertion on the part of the *somatens* clearly indicates that they cannot be counted on for the defence of the principality, and that it is necessary to adopt other measures with which to increase the strength of the army.'[67] Meanwhile, much the same reaction was elicited by that news that over 4000 of the 5500 men then commanded by Rovira had absconded: 'God willing, the disenchantment of those who have to rely on these undisciplined people will stimulate Your Excellency to adopt swift measures in order to fill this army's ranks and thus free this great country from the ruin that threatens it. The love I profess for the Principality and the love I profess for my homeland make me desirous of seeing the organization of real military forces, for these are the only means of making war.'[68] In rapid succession, there followed a number of measures, including, not least, the imposition of the hated system of conscription known as the *quinta*, and the dissolution of the *miquelets*, the few men who remained in their ranks being absorbed into a new set of regiments called Catalan Legions in line with proposals that had been submitted to the Junta in June 1809 by, amongst others, Milans del Bosch. Minor concessions were made to Catalan sentiment – service in the new units was to be for two years only whilst the rank and file were to enjoy thirty days' leave a year – but the principality's earlier particularism was much circumscribed whilst by the end of the war even the Catalan Legions had vanished in favour of ordinary units of the regular army even if they were allowed to go on bearing names that were clearly Catalan in their affiliations.[69] On taking over the Captain Generalcy of Catalonia after the fall of Tarragona in June 1811, the arrogant and thrusting Luis Lacy would have gone still further, and he in fact issued orders that would have forcibly incorporated all men serving in irregular forces of one kind or another into the regular army, but such was the desertion that resulted that he was forced to retract the order, or at least to restrict it solely to deserters.[70] As for those soldiers who continued to abscond, Lacy dealt with the phenomenon in predictable fashion, circulating very strict orders that deprived deserters of all their rights and threatened the application of the strictest penalties.[71]

As can be imagined, the Junta of Catalonia did not go along with this programme of militarization with any enthusiasm. Yet much of what O'Donnell and Lacy were trying to do was not repugnant to it. Thus, with respect to the problem of public order, as early as 11 July 1808 the Junta of Catalonia agreed to the creation in the principal town of each local Junta of a picket of 15 mounted soldiers led by an officer and a sergeant, whose task it would be 'to prevent disorder of any kind, and to capture and take as prisoners...disturbers of the public peace, thieves, spies and any other wrongdoers'.[72] Slightly later, meanwhile, it also agreed to proposals for the formation of an urban guard.[73] Nor, meanwhile, did the Junta have any issue with the need to round up deserters: in July 1811, for example, it agreed to the request of the parish priest of La Palma, Adrià Ochando Ros, that he be allowed to form a force of 1000 men from peasants, draft dodgers, prisoners who had escaped from the French and deserters native to his locality (interestingly, however, Ochando was not allowed, as he wished, to set himself up on the banks of the Ebro, but was instead directed to take such men as he got together to join Clarós).[74] Content with the fact that it had been permitted to keep the *somatén*, the Junta therefore agreed to promulgate new regulations that sought not just to govern its operations but also to put an end to the problems of earlier years. Indeed, the new orders were very precise: 'The somatens will be warned to keep strict discipline as any excesses will be punished.' The villages would keep them supplied, and the magistrates ensure proportional shares in this respect. The objective would be to harass the enemy by all means possible, 'especially in the mountains, with parties going into place in their rear to intercept convoys'. As for organization, 'The *somatén* will be organised in companies of 100 men, who will choose their own commanders in the persons of a captain and a lieutenant and the corresponding sergeants.' Making up the *somatén* were to be all men aged eighteen to fifty that could bear arms, with the only exceptions being magistrates and those priests who did not wish to do so. And finally, the *somatens* were to be ready for action at the first sound of the bugle.[75] Nor was this the only measure that was introduced to curb the indiscipline of the *somatén*. On 29 August 1811, the Junta of Catalonia's *comisión de armamento* – literally, 'armament commission' but the title is probably better rendered as 'mobilization commission' – came up with a further list of rules and regulations. Particularly significant is the decision to apply the code of military justice and the army's other *ordenanzas* to the *somatens*, whilst the latter were reminded that 'subordination is the basis of all military instruction'. Also worth noting is the treatment afforded to dubious behaviour of various sorts:

> Disorder on the march, arson, forgery, violence to women, heinous crimes, false witness, rebellion, hiding or otherwise assisting deserters, cowardice, and theft will all be punished according to the sentences of army orders, it being understood that, although sacking and pillaging are allowable [in certain circumstances], they are never permitted ... except by order of the general. Whilst pillaging may be sometimes be necessary for reasons of state, it is necessary for it to be contained within certain limits so as to ensure that the laws of

humanity are not lost sight of, nor still the respect due to all that profess the Holy, Roman, Catholic religion of the Apostles.[76]

What this rather confusing passage seems to add up to is, on the one hand, recognition that the *somatens* might on occasion have to live at free quarters – in other words to be fed and housed by the local populace – and could also expect from time to time to be let off the leash in respect of the enemy and his collaborators, and, on the other, an insistence that these pleasures could not be expected as of right. Whether this was sufficient to reassure public opinion in respect of the *somatens'* behaviour is a moot point, but there is at least some suggestion that the traditional militia system continued to receive much support. Thus, in January 1810 we find one Antonio Borrás blaming most of the problem on the *somatens'* officers, whom he regarded as corrupt and immoral; suggesting that such problems as were to be found amongst the men could be dealt with by revivalist missions and better religious instruction; and arguing that the *somatén* should actually be increased in numbers and equipped with cannon on the grounds that 'a nation armed en masse is invincible' and the *guerra del francés* a conflict that had begun 'not with the military but with the peasants'.[77] And as late as 1811 a letter to the Junta signed by someone styling himself 'The Patriot of the mountains' attributed all Catalonia's ills to the inefficiency of the regular army which he attributed to the fact that its officers had adopted French forms of dress, turned their backs on religion, surrounded themselves by concubines, been grossly self indulgent, mistreated the populace and devoted all their time to playing games of chance.[78]

It was all very well to have faith in the heroism of the Catalan people and the efficacy of its traditional forms of military organization, however. What observers such as Borrás completely failed to tackle was the the failure of the inhabitants to live up to their expectations. Thus, like it or not, volunteers were few in number, conscription deeply unpopular and desertion general. But if this situation cannot be denied, can it be explained? In answer to this question, one needs to look at the experiences of Catalonia's citizen soldiers and the circumstances in which the struggle was waged, the first point to note here being that the combatants were hardly well treated by the authorities. One of the claims made by 'The Patriot of the Mountains' quoted above, for example, is that the soldiers' pay was frequently in arrears.[79] And the commanders Clarós and Mansó both protested bitterly about their men having to go half-naked for want of uniforms for months on end.[80] On top of all this there is also the issue of the amount of faith that could be placed in the military command. In the light of the evidence that we have from the rest of Spain, for instance, there seems little reason to doubt that many of the men who officered the Catalan forces did indeed cut a very poor figure, and certainly not one that was inclined to persuade militiamen, volunteers and conscripts to fight to the death. And, as disaster was heaped on disaster, so it became clear that the generals and other commanders were not much better, in which respect we can do no better than to quote some of the popular sayings of the day. Thus, 'The Baron of Eroles is a game of bowls...Gay never gets there...Milans fails to advance...Mansó plays the goose.'[81]

Whether this is enough of an explanation is a moot point. But, whatever the reason may have been, the facts are clear enough. Thus, the revival of Catalonia's traditional military institutions occasioned by the outbreak of the *guerra del francés* in 1808 proved short lived. On the one hand, the Junta of Catalonia's hopes for the creation of an army of volunteer *miquelets* were only fulfilled in part, whilst on the other militia embodied by the *somatens* proved of only limited use in the struggle, the result being that the principle behind both forces had in the end to be abandoned: by the end of the war Catalonia's manpower was subjected to the same system of conscription as that of the rest of Spain and forced to serve in units that were indistinguishable from those seen in the rest of the country (as we have seen, in 1811 the last remnants of the *miquelet* system were swept away in favour of ordinary units of infantry and cavalry, whilst in 1814 the *somatén* was absorbed into the national guard). It could be argued here that the Catalan military system never had a fair chance thanks to the lack of money and weapons that dogged the Junta of Catalonia (which was itself superceded in 1812 by the new arrangements initiated by the *cortes* of Cádiz) right from the start. But on this the last word must probably go to Francisco Javier Cabanes, who, as we have seen, pointed out that in the Napoleonic era – and, by extension, the modern era in general – mere 'crowd armies' were of no avail. Perpetuated in the form guerrilla bands, the principles underlying the *somatens* and the *miquelets* may therefore at best be said to have kept the Patriot cause alive in Catalonia, but even here the waters are muddied by the links with banditry which can again be seen in other parts of Spain. Setting aside the issue of whether the population was possessed of sufficient in the way of national consciousness to be much interested in a war against Napoleon in 1808, the issue that dogged the Junta of Catalonia and its subordinate *juntas de corregiment* was therefore how to balance the demands of war with those of Catalan tradition. In this they failed – but then so did their successors of 1936.

Notes

1. Please note that in this chapter, Catalan forms are used throughout (hence *somatens* and *miquelets* instead of *somatenes* and *migueletes*). With respect to place names, however, whilst minor places – e.g. Molins de Rei – have been treated in this fashion, places likely to be famliar to English readers have been allowed to retain their Castillian names (hence 'Gerona' rather than 'Girona').
2. F.X. Cabanes, *Historia de las Operaciones del Ejército de Cataluña en la Guerra de la Usurpación: Campaña Primera* (Barcelona, 1815), pp. 13–42.
3. Conde de Toreno, *Historia del levantamiento, guerra y revolución de España* (B.A.E. edn; Madrid, 1953), p. 92.
4. For the fighting of June–July 1808, cf. J. Priego López, Guerra de la Independencia, 1808–1814 (Madrid, 1972–2003), II, pp. 98–115, 303–27. The story of Susana Claretona may be found in A. Delvillar, *El somatén: su origen, su historia, su organización, su espíritu* (Barcelona, n.d.), p. 34.
5. Delvillar, *El somatén*, p. 36.
6. Decree of Junta of Catalonia, 19 June 1808, Archivo de la Corona de Aragón (hereafter ACA), 74; for further details, cf. R. Ferrer, *Barcelona cautiva, osea diario exacto de lo ocurrido en la misma ciudad mientras la oprimieron los franceses, esto es, desde el 13 de enero de 1808 hasta el 28 de mayo de 1814* (Barcelona, 1815), II, Appendix 2, p. CLVI.
7. The details respecting Francisco Campos come from the *memorial* which he submitted to the Junta of Catalonia on 24 August 1808, which may be found in Archivo de la Corona de Aragón, Sección de la Junta Suprema de Catalalunya, (hereafter ACA. JSC.) 69. Otherwise I owe this information to the generosity of my esteemed colleagues, Charles Esdaile and Leonor Hernández Enviz, who have extracted it from the data base discussed elsewhere in this work.
8. Various, ACA. JSC. 68.
9. Various, ACA. JSC. 3, 68.
10. C. Oman, *A History of the Peninsular War* (Oxford, 1902–30), I, p. 322.
11. C. Esdaile, *The Spanish Army in the Peninsular War* (Manchester, 1988), p. 205.
12. The blockade of Barcelona is covered in J. Gómez de Arteche, *Guerra de la Independencia: Historia Militar de España de 1808 a 1814* (Madrid, 1868–1903), III, pp. 181–214. For some details of the situation in the frontier districts, cf. J. Sarramon, *Napoléon et les Pyrénées: les Chasseurs des Montagnes et la Couverture de la Frontière, 1808–1814* (Selgues, 1992), pp. 36–44.
13. J. Mñ oz Maldonado, *Historia Política y Militar de la Guerra de la Independencia contra Napoleón Bonaparte desde 1808 a 1814* (Madrid, 1833), I, pp. 281–4; *ibid.*, II, pp. 68–70; E. Rodríguez Solis, *Guerrilleros de 1808: Historia Popular de la Guerra de la Independencia* (Madrid, 1887), I, iii, pp. 43–4.
14. Oman, *Peninsular War*, I, pp. 635–6.
15. For all this, cf. *ibid.*, II, pp. 36–72; J. Priego López, *Guerra de la Independencia* (Madrid, 1972–2002), III, pp. 335–64.
16. ACA. JSC. 76.
17. Oman, *Peninsular War*, II, p. 72.
18. ACA. 76, various; Delvillar, *El somatén*, p. 49.
19. Delvillar, *El somatén*, p. 41.
20. E. Fernández i Pellicer, *Un guerriller liberal al Priorat* (Barcelona, 1972), pp.16–20.
21. Ferrer, *Barcelona cautiva*, III, p. 223.

22. *Ibid.*, p. 207.
23. For the third siege of Gerona, cf. Oman, *Peninsular War*, III, pp. 19–66.
24. Ferrer, *Barcelona cautiva*, III, p. 207.
25. M. Molières, *Guerra a cuchillo: la Guérilla pendant la Guerre d'Indépendance Espagnole, 1808–1813* (Paris, 2002), p. 140.
26. J. Perez Unzueta, *El sometent a través de la història* (Barcelona, 1924), pp. 368–370.
27. 'Plan o arreglo para el mejor regimen y salvación de la provincia de Cataluña, sacado nuevamente a luz pra. la instrucción y guía de los que desean su defensa, y presentado á la Superior Junta de Gobierno de dicha provincia por Don Jacinto Buniva de Morera, subteniente del Regimienitode Infantería de Baza, en el mes de Julio de 1811', ACA. JSC. 89.
28. Oman, *Peninsular War*, IV, pp. 490–6, 536–8. According to some sources the number of prisoners taken in the fortress amounted to 2000 men, of whom half died of starvation and mistreatment during the siege, but this seems a wild exaggeration given that the garrison was no more than a single battalion.
29. Cf. 'Vindicta y reglamento del cuerpo religioso y militar de la Cruzada de Cataluña, formado por orden de su Majestad, por Don Juan Pablo Constans, sacerdote canónigo de la Iglesia de Pons, obispado de Urgell', ACA. JSC. 89.
30. P. Pascual, *Curas y frailes guerrilleros en la Guerra de la Independencia: las partidas de cruzada reglamentadas por el carmelita zaragozano, P. Manuel Traggia* (Zaragoza, 2000), pp. 31–35.
31. Various, ACA. JSC. 87.
32. For Clarós' raid on the Cerdagne, cf. Sarramon, *Napoléon et les Pyrénées*, pp. 108–17.
33. Various, ACA. JSC. 87.
34. Various, ACA. JSC. 76.
35. W. Napier, *History of the War in the Peninsula and the South of France from the Year 1807 to the Year 1814* (London, 1828–1840), I, p. 57.
36. E.g. M.A. Príncipe, *Guerra de la Independencia: narración histórica de los acontecimientos de aquella Epoca* (Madrid, 1842–7) II, p. 285. For Ferrer's views, cf. Ferrer, *Barcelona cautiva*, III, pp. 93, 350.
37. *Gazeta Militar y Política del Principado de Cataluña*, 17 August 1809, Ferrer, *Barcelona cautiva*, II, pp. 68–69.
38. A. Carner i Borràs, *Les tropes suïsses a Catalunya durant la guerra 'de la independència'* (Barcelona, 1976), pp. 24–31; J.M. Torras i Ribe, *Sometents, exércit i poble a les batalles del Bruc: apunts sobre l'organització de la resistència contra els francesos l'any 1808* (Bruc, 1982), p. 7.
39. Various, ACA. JSC. 68.
40. Various, ACA. JSC. 69.
41. Peres Unzueta, *El sometent*, p. 285.
42. Justices of Vizcondado de Bas and Sant Joan de les Fonts to Junta of Catalonia, 24 August 1810, ACA. JSC. 76.
43. Junta of Mataró to Junta of Catalonia, ACA. JSC. 4.
44. A. Simon Tarres (ed.), 'La Guerra del Francès segons les memòries d'un hisendat del Corregiment de Girona (Memòries d'Antoni Bellsolell)', in *L'Avenç*, no. 113 (1988), pp. 42–7.
45. Various, Institut Municipal d'Història de Barcelona, Secció de Consellers, C-XVI-316.

46. F. Rovira to Junta of Catalonia, 18 January 1810, ACA. JSC. 76.
47. E.g. J. Manso to Junta of Catalonia, 2 June 1812, ACA. JSC. 86.
48. Various, ACA. JSC. 87.
49. E.g. E. Beulas and A. Dresa, *La Guerra del Francès a Mataró, 1808–1814* (Barcelona, 1989), pp. 115–16. The most well-known example of an irregular who went over to the French is constituted by the notorious Josep Pujol i Barraca. Generally known as 'Boquica', he had originally been a smuggler and had in 1808 taken part in the fringes of the *guerra del francés*, before leading his men over to the enemy, and becoming the head of an irregular force known as the Cazadores Distinguidos de Cataluña. For another example, cf. J. Bertran to Junta of Catalonia, 16 July 1810, ACA. JSC. 76.
50. Junta of Mataró to Junta of Catalonia, 29 March 1810, ACA. JSC. 76.
51. E.g. Barón de Eroles to Junta of Catalonia, 4 August 1811, ACA. JSC. 87.
52. Cf. N. Gay to Junta of Catalonia, 20 August 1811, *ibid.*
53. P.A. Albanés to Junta of Catalonia, 11 July 1811, ACA. JSC. 87.
54. M. Errando to Junta of Catalonia, 19 May 1812, ACA. JSC. 86.
55. M. Errando to Junta of Catalonia, 12 June 1812, *ibid.*
56. Ferrer, *Barcelona cautiva*, V, Appendix no 45, pp. CLXXXIV–CLXXXVI.
57. H. de Beaumont Brivazac, *Rapports addressés à S.E. le Général en Chef, Comte Decaen, Gouverneur-Général de la Catalogne, et à Monsieur le Général de Division, Comte Maurice Mathieu, Commandant Supérieur, par H. de Beaumont Brivasac* (Barcelona, 1813), I, p. 19.
58. Various, ACA. JSC. 3.
59. Junta of Vic to Junta of Catalonia, 27 October 1808, ACA.JSC. 68.
60. S. Woolf, *La Europa Napoleónica* (Barcelona, 1992), pp. 309–310.
61. Various, ACA. JSC. 87.
62. Various, ACA. JSC. 71.
63. N. Gay to Junta of Catalonia, 22 May 1810, ACA. JSC. 76.
64. Junta of Granollers to Junta of Catalonia, 13 October 1808, ACA. JSC. 68. For a French view of this action, cf. *Diario de Barcelona*, 12 October 1808, pp. 1231–2.
65. Cabanes, *Ejército de Cataluña*, pp. 41–2. Also worth consulting here is E. Canales, 'Militares y civiles en la conducción de la guerra de la Independencia: la visión de Francisco Javier Cabanes', in J.A. Armillas (ed.), *La Guerra de la Independencia: Estudios* (Zaragoza, 2001), II, pp. 985–987.
66. Cf. M. Ramisa, *La Guerra del Francès al corregiment de Vic* (Vic, 1993), pp. 112–13; M. Ramisa, *Els catalans i el domini napoleònic* (Montserrat, 1995), pp. 433–40.
67. E.g. O'Donnell to Junta of Catalonia, n.d., ACA. JSC. 7.
68. O'Donnell to Junta of Catalonia, 20 January 1810, *ibid.*
69. Oman, *Peninsular War*, III, pp. 313–14; *ibid.*, IV, p. 540.
70. Cf. Pérez Unzueta, *El somatent*, pp. 290–1.
71. *Ibid.*, p. 286.
72. Ferrer, *Barcelona cautiva*, I, Appendix no. 12, p. CLXXVIII.
73. .Cf. *memorial* of T. Artiés, 31 July 1808, ACA. JSC. 68.
74. Cf. *memorial* of A. Ochando Ros, 10 July 1811, ACA. JSC. 87; Pérez Unzueta, *El somatent*, pp. 288–9.
75. Decree of Junta of Catalonia, 11 July 1811, ACA. JSC. 89.
76. 'Leyes penales para los Cuerpos de Reserva o cuando esten de servicio militar', ACA. JSC. 88.

77. Antonio Borrás, 'Memoria sobre somatens de la Provincia de Cataluña', 29 January 1810, ACA. JSC. 76.
78. Anon. to Junta of Catalonia, n.d., ACA. JSC. 89.
79. *Ibid.*
80. J. Clarós to Junta of Catalonia, 31 May 1812, ACA. JSC. 86; J. Mansó to Junta of Catalonia, 12 July 1811, ACA. JSC. 87.
81. A. Blanch, *Historia de la Guerra de la Independencia en el Antiguo Principado* (Barcelona, 1968), p. 475. The Catalan runs as follows: 'Lo baró d'Eroles, es un joch de boles . . . En Gay, no hi arriba may . . . En Milans, ja no ataca com abans . . . En Manso, ja fa el ganso.'

6

The Anatomy of a Research Project: The Sociology of the Guerrilla War in Spain, 1808–14

Charles J. Esdaile and *Leonor Hernández Enviz*

The identity of the Spanish guerrillas of 1808–14 is not a subject that has ever gripped the attention of the historical community. Whilst there has been general agreement that popular resistance played a considerable role in Spain's struggle against Napoleon, the men and women who actually took up arms against the invaders have remained cloaked in anonimity. Proud of the heritage of their *patrias chicas*, a number of local historians have sought to uncover the identities of the leaders of the guerrilla bands that operated in their own provinces, whilst the eagerness of the nineteenth-century Republican, Rodríguez Solis, to emphasise the heroism of the Spanish people encouraged him to embark on an extensive catalogue of the *partidas* and their exploits that to this day remains an important introduction to the subject.[1] Other writers, meanwhile, have concentrated on painting a picture of individual *cabecillas* and in the process have afforded us a series of more or less useful introductions to the *guerrilla* in one part of Spain or another. However, this work is but a beginning. Whilst it has given us a picture of the main leaders, and here and there even provided us with the names of a few of their followers, it made no almost attempt to analyse such questions as age, occupation, social class or geographical origin (in fairness to Rodríguez Solis, he does provide some statistical detail on both the provinces that the men he uncovered operated in and the period in which they were active, but his data is so random, unreliable and unscientific that his figures are of little use). For a long time, meanwhile, there was little interest in taking matters further, whilst such historians who did feel the need to say something on the subject were reduced to making vague generalizations. Let us take, for example, the words of Gabriel Lovett:

Who were the guerrillas and their leaders? A cross section of the whole Spanish nation, they included men from all walks of life. They were peasants, shepherds, students, smugglers, dispersed soldiers, or simply deserters who preferred to fight in groups untrammelled by military regulations and discipline to serving in the ranks of the remaining regular army units. There was an occasional nobleman and there were quite a few clergymen, but on the whole the bulk of these groups was made up of the sons of the humblest classes, especially peasants.[2]

In a general sense these remarks are probably sensible enough, but they are clearly based on nothing better than 'guesstimation'. Nor, of course, do they offer us anything in the way of figures. Only very recently, indeed, has greater exploration of the immense wealth afforded by Spain's national, provincial and municipal archives, together with the spread of information technology, prompted an interest in taking matters further, in which respect mention must be made of two names in particular. In Andalucía the present author's esteemed friend and colleague Francisco Luis Díaz Torrejón has spent the past few years combing the municipal archives of such towns as Osuna for evidence of irregular resistance in the provinces of Cádiz, Málaga and Seville, and great things are to be expected from his research, the result of which is due to be published in the not too distant future. And from his base in Valencia the distinguished British historian of the Spanish Civil War, Ronald Fraser, has for the past ten years been engaged in the elaboration of a social history of the Spanish War of Independence, which has incorporated a certain amount of work on the guerrillas. The results of this work having just been published in the Spanish journal, *Historia Social*, it seems appropriate to give them here for the purposes of comparison. Thus, Fraser cites a total of 1091 individuals, including 748 men whom he lists simply as guerrillas and another 343 whom he lists as men condemned to death as guerrillas or bandits by the special law courts set up by the *josefino* régime to try crimes relating to highway robbery and irregular resistance. As might be expected, these individuals are then characterized according to various headings, the first of these being the type of *partida* to which they belonged, in which respect we learn that 49 per cent belonged to groups which sprang up without any official organization, and the remainder – separate figures are not given – to bands set up with the sanction of the Patriot authorities, some of which were secular (*corsarios*) and others religious (*cruzadas*). We then move on to questions of occupation and social class. For reasons which are unclear, but which are probably related to the fact that the papers of the *juntas criminals extraordinarias* – the *josefino* tribunals examined by Fraser – contain almost no details of the background of the prisoners who came before them, these are calculated solely in terms of the 748 'guerrillas', or rather the 209 members of this group of whose occupation and place in society the author claims to have some knowledge (interestingly, the sources of the names concerned, nor, still less, the definition according to which they were compiled, are never specified, whilst we are also never provided with a clear numerical breakdown of the figures). However, from this we learn that 20.9 per cent of the individuals on the list were members of the privileged classes whilst another 25.6 per cent came from the populace. Groups involved in the former category include clergy (8.3 per cent), military (5.5 per cent), civil authorities (2.4 per cent), professionals (2.3 per cent), students (1.3 per cent) and *rentistas* (1.1 per cent), and those involved in the latter peasants (12 per cent), day labourers (0.5 per cent), shepherds (3.4 per cent), muleteers and carters (1 per cent) artisans (4.3 per cent), bandits and smugglers (2.4 per cent), and others (2 per cent). If analysis is confined to *partidas* that ostensibly emerged without any official authorization, the percentage representing the privileged classes drops to 18.8 per cent, whilst that representing the masses rises to 29.8 per cent (this begs an important question, however: we need to know far more about Fraser's classification of the *partidas* he has looked at as many so-called *partidas* – good examples are those of Villacampa and Julián Sánchez – were actually units of the regular armed forces, and in consequence in no need of any such authorization). These figures are then contrasted with the contents of the only document in the twenty or so *legajos* in the Archivo General de Simancas pertaining to the *juntas criminales extraordinarias* that contains detailed information on the identities, place of residence and occupational backgrounds of a substantial group of guerrillas. Composed of 19 men – ten of them deserters from the regular army – from the bands of Juan Mendieta (El Capuchino) and Isidro Astorga captured in a raid near Valladolid in January 1810, we hear that of them one was a friar, six were peasants (*labradores*), three shepherds, one a market gardener, two barbers, one a butcher and one a shoemaker (the occupations of the last four are not recorded). To these we may add the occupations of the two leaders, neither of whom were captured. Thus, Mendieta, as his nickname suggests, was a friar and Astorga a butcher. Though Fraser does not point this out specifically, an obvious difference is apparent. Thus, the 19 men captured from the French in very large part come from beyond the ranks of the élites, whereas, of the two *cabecillas* concerned, this is the case of only one of them. Nor is this surprising in view of the analysis which Fraser provides us of the 118 commanders (out of 333) whose occupation he has been able to establish. Indeed, the figures given above for the 748 guerrillas as a whole are found to be reversed, 28.2 per cent of the *cabecillas* coming from the privileged classes and 20.3 per cent coming from the masses, whilst Fraser further notes that the 'men of quality' whom he has been able to find fighting in the rank and file of the guerrilla movement was, by contrast, a much lower percentage of the figure than the 20.9 per cent which they constituted of the list as a whole. In brief, then, what we get is a movement whose rank and file was drawn largely from the rural lower classes (in many instances after they had fought for a while in the regular army: deserters, indeed, are said to have represented between one third and one half the total number) but whose leadership came from the élite, which is a picture not dissimilar from the one sketched out for us by Lovett.[3]

To quote an English proverb, 'Great minds think alike.' At the very same time that Fraser was producing the figures that we have just looked at, the current author was by coincidence engaged on a very similar project. In the course of many years research in Spain, he had come across a range of primary documents that suggested that it might be possible to construct a sociological study of the guerrilla movement. Having been awarded a two-year research fellowship by the Leverhulme Trust in May 2000, he was able to put this to good use and elaborate a database that by September 2002 contained the details of no fewer than 1166 individuals. In amassing this figure, however, much stricter parameters were imposed than those that seem to have been made use of by Fraser. For example, whilst the same volumes of documents relating to the *juntas criminals extraordinarias* were consulted, a very careful selection was made of their contents, and the men tried by the French were only added to the data base if there was strong evidence to suggest that they had been members of a *partida* (by which was meant a military force that, even if it was eventually militarized and subsumed into the ranks of the regular army, was in its origins independent of the regular structures of the state). At the same time, meanwhile, great care was taken to exclude forces which were made up of local militias and home guards, such as the Catalan *somatén*, or units of the regular armed forces, including the many new volunteer and conscript units raised in 1808, the result of this having been the omission of a great many familiar names. To take just one example, no mention will be found of the famous Leonese leader, Julián Sánchez García, on the grounds that he obtained a commission in 1808, albeit in a new regiment, and for the whole of

1809 operated as part of the regular Spanish forces based on the western frontiers of the province of Salamanca, only becoming a 'guerrilla' when the area was occupied by the French in 1810 (and, by the same token, reverting to fighting as part of the local field army when it was liberated two years later). In so far as can be ascertained, meanwhile, the range of sources was much wider: amongst the papers made use of, for example, was the copious personal archive of General Francisco Copons y Navía; held in the Real Academía de Historia in Madrid, it being ascertained that no one had accessed these papers since the current author had made use of them as a young doctoral student in the summer of 1982.

What we have, then, is a study that is both very different and entirely independent from that of Fraser. Yet, broadly speaking, its conclusions were very similar. Thus, after extensive cross-checking, it was found that there were 322 men whose occupation in 1808 was known with a reasonable degree of certainty. Of these, no fewer than 204 (63.35 per cent) may be said in one sense or other to have been the representatives of property, power and social success as students, professionals, landowners or wealthy tenant farmers, serving or retired army officers, or members of the clergy (the remaining 118 include such groups as taverners, butchers, stall holders, municipal employees, muleteers, peasants, day labourers, artisans, common soldiers, smugglers, bandits and escaped prisoners). Too much emphasis should not be placed on such figures, for members of the Church, the army or the propertied classes were far more likely to leave a trace in archive or written record than members of the *populacho*. However, even if every single one of the remaining 844 names whose occupation remains a mystery were to turn out to have come from the populace, we would still have a situation in which groups representing fewer than 10 per cent of the population provided 17 per cent of the guerrilla movement. Also significant, meanwhile, is the identity of men who at one time or another commanded a *partida*, for, out of the 371 such leaders identified in the study, 103 came from middling or upper echelons of society, and only 37 from the *populacho*, the backgrounds of the remainder being unknown.[4]

Amassing these figures was, of course, an interesting exercise, whilst it is gratifying to learn that they have been in some measure confirmed by the independent work of Mr Fraser. Yet their generation also gave rise to considerable frustration. In the first place, and most obviously, there was the question of all the missing information. Who were, for example, the 829 men of whom we had little more than a name? When, too, had many of the men who were listed as *militares* enlisted in the armed forces? In the second place, meanwhile, there was a need to come up with more names: it is impossible to establish exactly how many guerrillas took the field against French, but estimates for the total number in action have ranged up to 50 000, whilst a list of 22 *partidas* that was published in various Spanish newspapers in 1812 claimed that in October 1811 these alone amounted to 38 520 combatants.[5] In the third place, it could not but be felt that the selection of the material was random in the extreme: garnered in the pursuit of an entirely different project, it was determined not by considerations that were germane to itself, but by the dictates of what was required for the elaboration of *Guerrillas, Bandits and Adventurers* (for this reason it would be absurd to attempt to draw conclusions from it with regard to, say, the geographical origins of the guerrillas). In the fourth place, there were many sources which had of necessity been left untapped, a good example here being Spain's many municipal archives. And, last but not least, studying the guerrillas suggested that there were many questions that might be illuminated by a more extensive database: one possibility, for example, would be to cross reference known guerrillas with the names of those executed for banditry after 1815, whilst a second might be to compare the social base of the guerrillas with that of the regular army.

To pursue these goals, however, would clearly be quite impossible without the aid of dedicated research assistance, and to this end from the autumn of 2000 onwards, application was made to a variety of funding bodies in the hope of obtaining the necessary support. In May 2002 these efforts paid off, the Arts and Humanities Research Board awarding the current author a grant of £51 000, of which the chief purpose was the employment of a Spanish research assistant. Initially, funding was sufficient only for one year, but a further grant of approximately £19 000 has since been obtained from the British Academy. Work therefore continued until the summer of 2004, and the findings of the project are shortly to be made available to the academic community by means of the internet, all that remains to be said at this point in proceedings being to thank both the Arts and Humanities Research Board and the British Academy for their generosity, not to mention the many scholars in both Britain and Spain who have given 'Guerrillas and Bandits' their advice and support.

Let us now turn to the question of 'nuts and bolts'. The starting point for any database is that it should be accessible and easy to manipulate, in which respect matters are greatly facilitated by the widespread availability of Access and Windows. Such is the dominance of these products that there was no need to consider any other system, and the bulk of the designers' attention has therefore been directed more towards achieving the greatest possible degree of coherence in the construction of the database, in which respect particular attention was paid to, first, considering the sort of information that might be gathered on the subject of the Spanish guerrillas, and, second, rationalizing the headings under which it would be entered. With this in mind, especial heed was also taken of the likely purposes for which the database might be used by future research projects. In the short term, meanwhile, it was agreed that the basic questions which the database should address were essentially two-fold. First of all, there was the issue of 'quantity'. How many *partidas* existed? How many men fought in them? How frequently were they to be encountered? In what areas did they operate? Secondly, there was that of 'content'. Who joined the guerrillas? How old were they? What were they? Were did they stand with regard to issues of politics? And, finally, there was that of 'activity'. For how long was each *partida* active? In what actions did they fight the French? How many men could they muster at various moments of their existence? In addressing these questions, however, it was obvious that many difficulties would have to be faced. The documentation, for example, is extremely fragmentary, whilst much of the information that is required is not usually recorded: indeed, we generally only have full details only of a small number of very prominent figures. Given these problems, it might have been thought that one solution would have been to reduce the number of questions to be asked in respect of each individual to a bare minimum, but this temptation was resisted: as research continues, there is always the hope that the gaps might gradually be filled as fresh information becomes available or fresh archives are tapped, and it was therefore be judged to be much better at least to create the option of adding such material rather than to preclude all chance of doing so right at the beginning of the project. It will further be noted, meanwhile, that the scope of the database is much wider than that of the primitive 'pilot' model developed in the period 2000–02, the new model being designed so that it can accommodate not just armed civilians, but also the militias, home guards and regular troops who took part in *la guerrilla* alongside them, the object here being first to spread the net as wide as possible in terms of information gathering and second to enable scholars to draw sociological comparisons between different aspects of resistance to the French. However, that said, it will further be noted that great care has been taken to keep the 'true' guerrillas separate from other combatants in the struggle.

Before moving on to a discussion of material that has been entered into the database, it is worth highlighting two other issues that have caused the designers much debate. The first is the obvious one of language. As it cannot be expected that all those who consult the database will have access to Spanish, it was decided that it would have to be prepared in duplicate, and, further, that in the English version all accents and other language marks should be suppressed. The second is a somewhat less obvious question of geography in that there have been repeated changes in Spain's territorial organization since the Napoleonic era, and in this respect it was eventually agreed that towns, villages and such should be listed under their current affiliations.

In so far as the organization of the material is concerned, it is arranged so that it may be consulted under a number of headings. A full list of these, together with the possible answers that may be returned in response to each query, is appended as an appendix to this paper. Needless to say, the number of permutations that enquiries may take is virtually infinite. It is, for example, possible to ask the database to give details of the number of ecclesiastics in the full list, the number of ecclesiastics who commanded *partidas*, the number of ecclesiastics who held subaltern rank, the number of ecclesiastics who fought as members of the rank and file and the number of ecclesiastics who were killed in action or executed by the invaders, and all this in connection with the whole war or some period thereof, and the whole of Spain or some part thereof. And, should it be wanted to go still further, the ecclesiastics could be broken down into their different categories – seminarians, deacons, priests, friars, archdeacons and so forth.

The sources used for this study have included both primary sources and the published works of other historians. With regard to the former, considerations of time have forced the designers to concentrate on archival centres which contain large concentrations of material such as the Archivo Histórico Nacional, the Archivo General Militar, the Archivo General de Simancas, the Archivo de la Corona de Aragón, the Real Academia de Historia and the Archivo Municipal de Zaragoza. Collections consulted, meanwhile, include the 1007 volumes of pamphlets and other printed material known as the Colección Documental del Fraile, the papers of the Junta Central, the Junta Superior de Cataluña and the Juntas Criminales Extraordinarias, and the papers of Generals Blake, Castaños, Palafox and Copons y Navía. Where possible, material has also been incorporated into the database from English-language sources, the Wellington Papers and the extensive memoir material associated with the Peninsular army both containing many references to *la guerrilla*. With regard to secondary sources, meanwhile, the work of a wide range of authors has been carefully 'trawled' to provide as much information as posible, and the results checked against the original documents (a process which has proved to be immensely time consuming: many works on *la guerrilla* are, at best, intensely hagiographic).

What, though, of the question of results? Given the huge obstacles posed by the nature of the material, progress in amassing the data has been much slower than the designers would have wished. At the time of writing, the number of guerrillas entered in the database stands at 3024, of which 656 were commandants, 39 seconds-in-command, 2135 'subalterns' (by which is meant all officers other than commandants and their seconds, all non-commmissioned officers and all members of the rank and file), 167 unknown and 27 civilian collaborators (Figure 7.1). Limited though these figures are, however, they have yet produced a number of interesting points. Of these, the first is clearly the fact that activity was not constant across the full length of the war. On the contrary, from 1809 onwards there was was a steady fall in the number of individuals active in any given year. Thus, in 1809, 628 of the combatants on the list were active, whereas in 1811 the number was 557 and in 1813 only 136 (Figure 7.2). Meanwhile, the guerrilla bands seem to have become fewer in number: in 1809 commandants constituted 42.4 per cent of the number of combatants, whereas by 1813 this figure had fallen to 19.1 per cent (Figure 7.3). This itself is very interesting, confirming as it does the very considerable anecdotal evidence that suggests that there was a steady decline in the popularity of the war, and, by extension, the apathy of the civilian population. This is, perhaps, most graphically expressed by Figure 7.4, which shows the percentage of the survey known to have been in arms at any given time.

Given that it may be interrogated with regard to both the number of *partidas* and the number of combatants operating in any given province, interesting details may also be obtained from the database with regard to the response of different regions of Spain to French occupation. In brief, in certain areas the response appears to have been much more enthusiastic than in others. Navarre, for example, accounts for 215 of the 3024 combatants (7.1 per cent), whereas in 1808, at 221 728, its population numbered only 2.1 per cent of that of Spain as a whole. Yet Andalucía had 1 909 422 inhabitants (18.1 per cent) and could only produce 290 combatants (9.6 per cent), whilst Galicia did still worse with 1 142 630 inhabitants (10.8 per cent) and 66 fighters (2.2 per cent). When it comes to the number of bands that have been traced, however, these figures are more or less reversed in that, at 129 (19.7 per cent) and 38 (5.8 per cent) Andalucía and Galicia have a much larger share than the number of men that they turned out would seem to warrant, and

Navarre, by contrast, a much smaller one, the figure here being a mere 24 (3.7 per cent).[6] In short, the less popular enthusiasm there was for the struggle, the smaller and more numerous were the guerrilla bands. Also evident, meanwhile, is the close connection that exists between this point and the extent to which militarization took hold amongst the guerrillas, almost all the bands that were eventually transformed into units of the regular army – examples include those of Espoz y Mina, Longa and Juan Martín Díez – coming from areas where support for the struggle appears to have been above the average. For all this, readers are referred to Figures 7.5 and 7.6.

In so far as such questions as occupation and social class are concerned, as Figures 7.7 and 7.8 show, the database records the details of some 534 individuals (as opposed to the 315 considered at an earlier date by the present author or the 209 analysed by Fraser). Unfortunately, differences in the manner in which the data has been compiled and analysed make the elaboration of direct comparisons a slightly problematic task, but what stands out is the very high percentage of the men concerned who in some way were associated with either the Church, the Bourbon state or the social élite. Thus, 178 (33.3 per cent) come from the ranks of the Church, 122 (22.8 per cent) from those of the armed forces, 43 (8.2 per cent) from those of the administration and the judiciary and 28 (5.5 per cent) from commerce and the free professions. Given that 18 (3.4 per cent) are described as rentiers and 11 (2.2 per cent) as students, some 400 (75.4 per cent) may be said to have come from the establishment or the upper echelons of society, whilst this figure may almost certainly be increased still further by the addition of at least some of the 59 individuals who were involved in agriculture, the ranks of the latter undoubtedly including a number of prosperous tenant farmers or even landowners (for comparison, the corresponding figures in Fraser and Esdaile *primítivo* were 20.9 per cent and 63.35 per cent). What all this suggests, of course, is that participation in *la guerrilla* of those with some stake in society – something to lose, indeed – was far higher than that of those on its margins, this figure being strengthened still further by consideration of the fact that only 10.2 per cent of the individuals whose estate is known were definitely *pecheros* (Figure 7.9).

There is, meanwhile, a further way of dissecting *la guerrilla*, and that it is to to look at the way in which it was composed in military terms. If the database is consulted with regard to the number of *partidas* that it lists, it will be discovered that there is mention of some 656. Not all of these units are bands of irregulars of the sort envisaged in the traditional historiography, however. On the contrary, the term is used rather to mean simply an independent force of armed men. On occasion, this might be a band of armed civilians who had come together to fight the French, but, then again, it might not. Thus, it will be found that combatants are listed under many other headings, including the volunteer and conscript units that were raised to supplement the regular army and the various local militias that were organized to help fight the French in Catalonia, Galicia and other areas. All this is reflected in Figure 7.10, which shows the members of four different categories of *partida* over the course of the period 1808–12, and, more particularly, how generally only a minority of combatants were members of the group that has been defined as 'unmilitarized *partidas*' – in other words bands of armed civilians – at any given time (the one exception, by a short head, appears to be 1810). Especially noteworthy, too, is the collapse in support for the Catalan *somatén*, this being a force that has been much vaunted in traditional accounts of the war. This, however, is by-the-by, what matters at this point being rather the way in which a large part of *la guerrilla* can be seen to have depended on and been controlled by the Patriot authorities, rather than having been the spontaneous work of the armed *pueblo*. Moreover, many of the bands that did spring up from the ranks of the civilian population were themselves headed by members of the élite, rather than the commonalty, the fact being that figures such as the peasants Juan Martín Díez and Francisco Espoz y Mina were far less common than the legend suggests.

It cannot be stressed strongly enough that great care must be taken with these figures, which are beyond doubt seriously distorted by the stronger footprint that property, education and social status will always leave in the archives. To believe, indeed, that the populace was absent from *la guerrilla* would be patently ridiculous. In Navarre archival evidence suggests that one third of the male population eventually took part in the struggle, whilst, even if this province is completely atypical – Navarre was one of the few areas in the country where many of the inhabitants of the countryside were reasonably prosperous – it is quite clear that the bulk of the rank and file were of humble stock (particularly noteworthy are the frequent references to the presence of large numbers of deserters from the regular army).[7] Absence of evidence, then, is not the same as evidence of absence. But what is clear is that to paint a picture of the Spanish people rushing into the hills to take up arms in defence of *díos, rey y patria* is distinctly unwise, and all the more so given the great weight of evidence that exists in the archives to suggest that large numbers of recruits joined the *partidas* because they were starving, because they wished to clothe a life of crime with a veneer of respectability or because taking the chance of service in their ranks was preferable to being marched off to France as a prisoner of war, because they wished to avoid service in the regular army or simply because they were conscripted. Still more can this be seen to be the case, meanwhile, if one takes into account the fact that the database shows that comparatively few participants in *la guerrilla* fought in the bands of armed civilians of legend.

To conclude, then, what do we see? First of all, it is clear that, despite the old saw that the Spanish guerrillas, as a popular phenomenon, left no trace in the archives, a considerable amount of archival information is available on their identity and background. Not only is it available, moreover, but it may be woven together to provide a surprisingly clear picture of popular resistance to the French. In so far as can be ascertained, meanwhile, that picture is inclined to confirm both the rather vague generalizations that have hitherto been all that the historian has had to go on so far as the social composition of the guerrillas is concerned, and the increasingly iconoclastic line that the present author has taken over the years with regard to the participation of armed civilians in the struggle against Napoleon – a line, moreover, that is pressed home still further in his monograph, *Fighting Napoleon: Guerrillas, Bandits and Adventurers in Spain, 1808–14.* That said, however, to pretend that the results of the research project currently under review have been entirely satisfactory would be dishonest. Setting aside the fact that a much wider selection of data would be welcome, one is in the end constrained to recognize that many problems are suggested even by such material as has been generated. Setting aside the issue of whether or not the data that has been collected can in any sense be relied upon, the fact remains that the privileged classes were always certain to be over represented in the findings of any exercise such as the one currently under discussion. This, of course, may be corrected easily enough in our interpretation of the figures, but, if the figures are to be corrected, how far, in the end, have we advanced from the 'guesstimation' with which this chapter commenced? But this, perhaps, is something that is rather to be welcomed, suggesting, as it does, that 'number crunching' has its limitations, and that there can in the end be no substitute for painting visions of the past.

Notes

1. E. Rodríguez Solís, *Los Guerrilleros de 1808: Historia Popular de la Guerra de la Independencia* (Madrid, 1887). For an example of such a regional study, cf. R. Guirao and L. Sorando, *El Alto Aragón en la Guerra de la Independencia* (Zaragoza, 1995).
2. G. Lovett, *Napoleon and the Birth of Modern Spain* (New York, 1965), p. 672.

3. For all this, cf. R. Fraser, 'Identidades sociales desconocidas: las Guerrillas Españolas en la Guerra de la Independencia', *Historia Social*, no. 46 (2003), pp. 3–23.
4. For full details, cf. C. Esdaile, *Fighting Napoleon: Guerrillas, Bandits and Adventurers in Spain, 1808–14* (Yale University Press, 2004), pp. 92–3.
5. *El Redactor General*, 3 November 1812, Hemeróteca Municipal de Madrid 6/3.
6. Please note that all population figures are taken from the 1797 census. This is notoriously unreliable, the total of 10 541 221 that it gives being at least a million short of the reality, which has been calculated at 11 595 343, but it seems more logical to rely on this rather than on the earlier census of 1786–87.
7. For detailed discussion of the exceptional case presented by Navarre, cf. J. Tone, *The Guerrilla War in Navarre and the Defeat of Napoleon in Spain* (Chapel Hill, North Carolina, 1994), pp. 9–41 *passim*, and F. Miranda, *La Guerra de la Independencia en Navarra: la Acción del Estado* (Pamplona, 1977), pp. 119–35.

Appendix: fields contained in the database

1   Identity: name, surname and nickname.
2   Age in 1808.
3   Marital status: single, married, married with children, widowed, widowed with children, ecclesiastic, unknown.
4   Origin: place of birth/residence.
5   Professional particulars: active, retired, unknown.
6   Occupation: lawyer; postal official; fiscal official; mason; mayor; archdeacon; muleteer; barber; chemist; canon; chaplain; butcher; carpenter; clergyman; merchant; coachman; smuggler; *corregidor*; leather worker; priest; priest with benefice; priest without benefice; deacon; ecclesiastic; tobacconist; student; baize manufacturer; corn factor; tailor's assistant; public prosecutor; friar; Agustinian friar; Benedictine friar; Bernardine friar; Capuchin friar; Carmelite friar; Carthusian friar; Franciscan friar; Mercenary friar; Trinitarian friar; customs guard (tobacco administration); day labourer; peasant; doctor; messenger; innkeeper; soldier; soldier (corporal); soldier (*Guardia de Corps*); naval officer (first lieutenant); soldier (retired); soldier (captain); soldier (colonel); soldier (private); naval officer (second lieutenant); notary; customs official; *gensdarme*; municipal official; shepherd; teacher; rentier; gravedigger; bartender; weaver; military accountant; clerk in minor orders; leather worker; shoemaker.
7   Professional group: agriculture; government; clergy; regular clergy; secular clergy; commerce; construction; smuggler; army; education; functionary; artisanate; navy; other occupations; free professions; *rentier*; transport.
8   Rating: apprentice; craftsman; master.
9   Social class: commoner; ecclesiastic; noble; soldier.
10 Economic class: tenant; large-property owner; medium-property owner; small-property owner.
11 Cultural characteristics: illiterate; literate; university graduate.
12 Military particulars in 1808: serving soldier; retired soldier; civilian; ecclesiastic; unknown.
13 Rank in 1808.
14 Unit in 1808.
15 Combat experience prior to 1808: War of the Oranges (1801); Revolutionary War (1792–95); War against Britain (1796–1808); colonial campaigns (America), etc.
16 Month and year of first appearance in the 'little war'.
17 Reason for enlistment: commissioned by the civilian or military authorities; dispersed; deserted; failure of the national army; revenge; unknown; granted permission to form a band; granted permission to form a *cruzada*; home defence; escaped French imprisonment; escaped from justice; *juramentado* taken prisoner by the guerrillas; carried off by force; transferred to land service for want of naval resources and/or objectives; requested permission to form a band; ordered by the Patriot authorities to join the guerrillas; freed from prison to fight the French; personal violence.
18 Initial status: commandant; second commandant; subaltern; unknown; civilian collaborator.

19 Province and region in which activities began.
20 Family members serving with the guerrillas.
21 Military service, 1808–14 (by month).
22 Status, 1808–14: commandant; second commandant; subaltern; unknown; civilian collaborator.
23 Category of combatant in 1808: bandit; gendarmerie (*resguardo*); insurgent; local militia (*alarma*); local militia (*cruzada*); local militia (*milicia honrada*); local militia (rising); local militia (*somatén*); regular army (*migueletes*); militar-ized guerrilla band; unmilitarized guerrilla band; regular army (new regiment); regular army (pre–1808); Royal Navy (Spanish); unknown.
24 Region/s of operation (by year).
25 Band/unit (by year).
26 Changes in status (by year).
27 Combats (by month).
28 Province or provinces of operation by month.
29 Strength of band/unit.
30 Political preferences: absolutist; liberal.
31 Career after 1814, date and place of death.
32 Fate (1808–14): garrotted by *junta criminal*; hung by French army; amnestied; died in combat; died of wounds; went over to enemy; imprisoned by Patriot authorities; captured by the French army; sent to France as prisoner of war; retired to civil life; executed by other guerrillas; executed by the French army; executed by the Patriot authorities; exiled to Portugal; exiled to France; exiled to Britain; wounded in battle; band dissolved by the Patriot authorities for misconduct; band dispersed by the French; captured by other guerrillas; sentenced to death by *junta criminal*; sentenced to death by hanging by *junta criminal*; imprisoned by *junta criminal*; surrendered to the French; returned to the ranks of the regular army.
33 Fate (post–1814): stayed on in the army; fought against the absolutism of Fernando VII; took part in the Carlist War; returned to civil life; emigrated to Britain; fought against the liberals; participated in the Navarrese uprising of 1814.
34 Sources: primary; secondary.

Rank	No.	%
Commandant	656	21.7
Second commandant	39	1.3
Subaltern	2135	70.6
Collaborator	27	0.9
Unknown	167	5.5
Total	3024	100.0

Figure 7.1 Combatants in *la guerrilla* analyzed by status

Rank	1808		1809		1810		1811		1812		1813		1814	
	No.	%	No.	%	No.	%	No.	%	No.	%	No.	%	No.	%
Commandant	85	8.0	266	42.4	238	35.1	195	35.0	91	20.4	26	19.1	4	14.8
Second commandant	1	0.1	17	2.7	18	2.7	14	2.5	8	1.8	1	0.7	0	0.0
Subaltern	981	91.9	283	45.1	379	55.9	308	55.3	334	75.1	107	78.7	22	81.5
Collaborator	1	0.1	5	0.8	13	1.9	12	2.2	9	2.0	2	1.5	1	3.7
Unknown	0	0.0	57	9.1	30	4.4	28	5.0	3	0.7	0	0.0	0	0.0
Total	1068	100.0	628	100.0	678	100.0	557	100.0	445	100.0	136	100.0	27	100.0

Figure 7.2 Combatants in *la guerrilla* analyzed by year and status, 1808–14

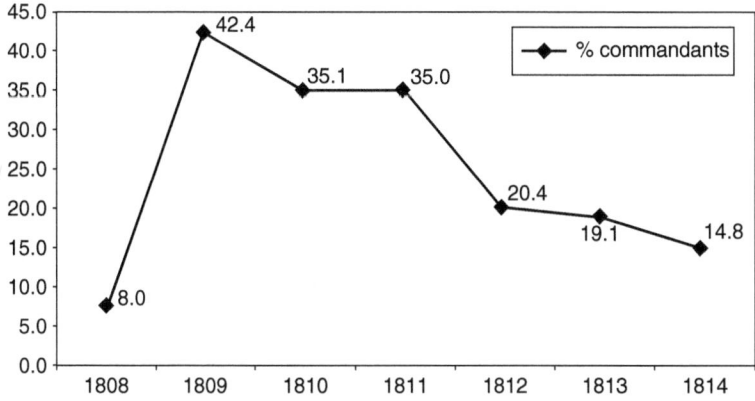

Figure 7.3 Commandants as a percentage of combatants in *la guerrilla*, 1808–14

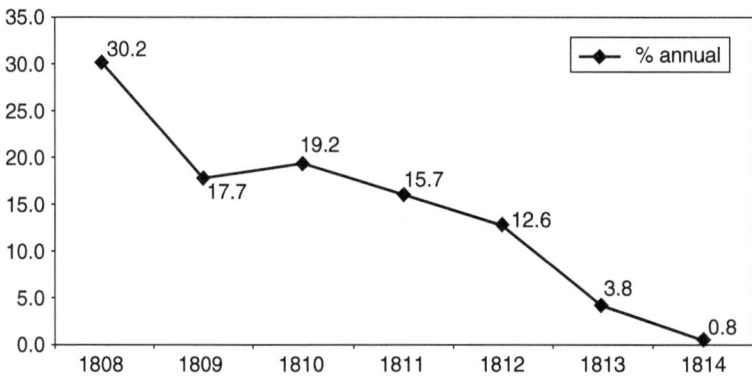

Figure 7.4 Combatants in *la guerrilla* analyzed by year, 1808–14

Regions	No.	%
Andalucía	290	9.6
Aragón	1089	36.0
Asturias	59	2.0
Cantabria	48	1.6
Castilla La Mancha	208	6.9
Castilla León	367	12.1
Cataluña	238	7.9
Extremadura	50	1.7
Galicia	66	2.2
La Rioja	104	3.4
Madrid	32	1.1
Murcia	0	0.0
Navarra	215	7.1
País Vasco	74	2.4
Valencia	150	5.0
Unknown	34	1.1
Total	3024	100.0

Figure 7.5   Combatants in *la guerrilla* analyzed by region, 1808–14

Regions	No.	%
Andalucía	129	19.7
Aragón	88	13.4
Asturias	20	3.0
Cantabria	7	1.1
Castilla La Mancha	67	10.2
Castilla León	67	10.2
Cataluña	78	11.9
Extremadura	19	2.9
Galicia	38	5.8
La Rioja	40	6.1
Madrid	10	1.5
Murcia	0	0.0
Navarra	24	3.7
País Vasco	27	4.1
Valencia	36	5.5
Unknown	6	0.9
Total	656	100.0

Figure 7.6   Commandants in *la guerrilla* analyzed by region, 1808–14

Occupation	No.	%
Actor	1	0.2
Alderman	2	0.4
Archdeacon	1	0.2
Bandit	3	0.6
Barber	2	0.4
Blacksmith	4	0.7
Botanist	1	0.2
Butcher	1	0.2
Canon	4	0.7
Carpenter	2	0.4
Chaplain	3	0.6
Chemist	2	0.4
Clergyman	5	0.9
Clerk in minor orders	1	0.2
Coachman	1	0.2
Corn factor	1	0.2
Corregidor	2	0.4
Custom Guard	1	0.2
Customs official	1	0.2
Day labourer	11	2.1
Deacon	1	0.2
Doctor	5	0.9
Ecclesiastic	6	1.1
Fiel de fechos	1	0.2
Fiscal official	3	0.6
Foreman	1	0.2
Friar	101	18.9
Gensdarme	3	0.6
Goverment official	2	0.4
Gravedigger	1	0.2
Gunsmith	1	0.2
Income administator	3	0.6
Innkeeper	1	0.2
Judge	5	0.9
Lawyer	9	1.7

Occupation	No.	%
Leather worker	1	0.2
Manufacturer	3	0.6
Market gardener	1	0.2
Mason	2	0.4
Mayor	13	2.4
Merchant	3	0.6
Messenger	1	0.2
Military chaplain	1	0.2
Military accountant	1	0.2
Muleteer	1	0.2
Municipal official	1	0.2
Notary	10	1.9
Peasant	58	10.9
Postal official	1	0.2
Priest	53	9.9
Procurador sindico	1	0.2
Public prosecutor	1	0.2
Rentier	18	3.4
Seaman	1	0.2
Seminarian	1	0.2
Servant	5	0.9
Shepherd	10	1.9
Shoemaker	3	0.6
Skinner	1	0.2
Smuggler	5	0.9
Soldier	122	22.8
Spinner	1	0.2
Student	11	2.1
Surgeon	2	0.4
Tailor's assistant	1	0.2
Tailor's cutter	2	0.4
Taverner	1	0.2
Teacher	2	0.4
Tobacconist	1	0.2
Weaver	3	0.6
Total	534	100.0

Figure 7.7 Combatants in *la guerrilla* analyzed by occupation, 1808–14

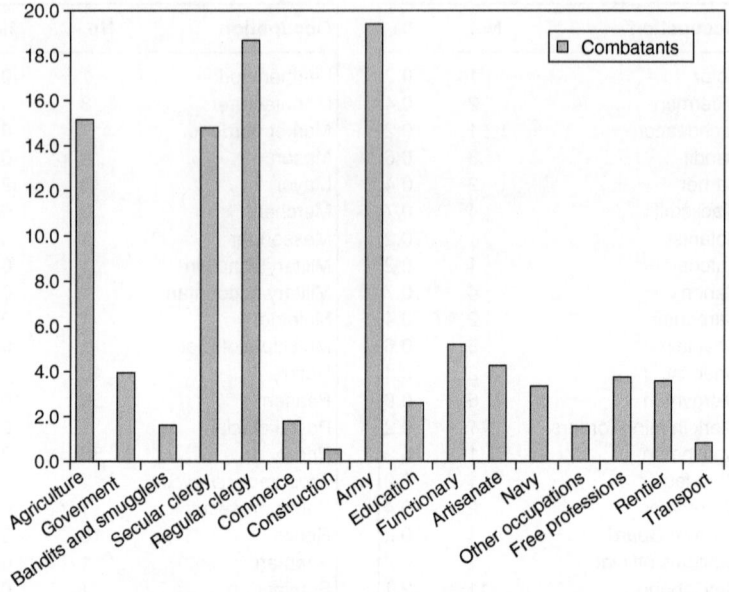

Figure 7.8 Combatants in *la guerrilla* analyzed by professional group, 1808–14

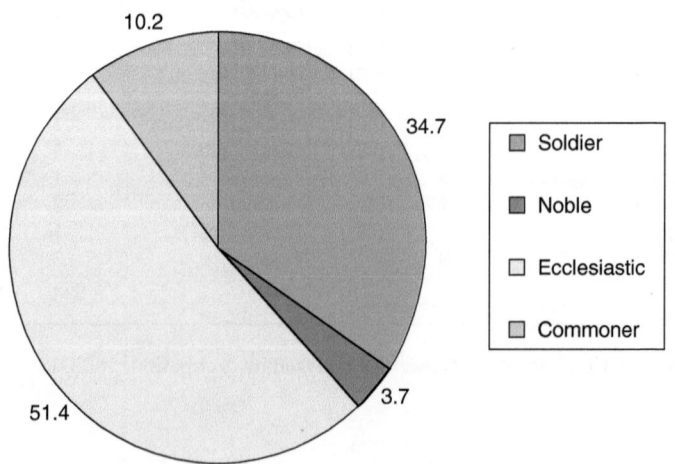

Figure 7.9 Combatants in *la guerrilla* analyzed by estate, 1808–14

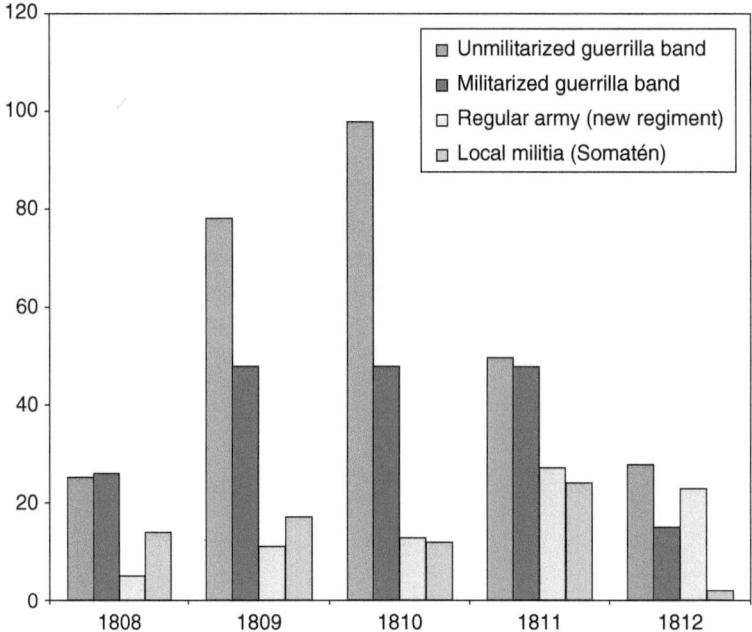

Figure 7.10 Members of four different categories of armed force in *la guerrilla*, 1808–14

Notes

Changes in the rank, status and affiliation of many individual combatants over the period 1808–14 makes the elaboration of overall figures of this sort very difficult. To make it possible at all, it has been necessary to establish certain 'census points'. Taking Figure 7.1 as an example, we therefore find that it has been computed on the basis of the first appearance of each individual in the tables: in consequence, the figure for commandants does not include men such as the famous Espoz y Mina who originally enlisted in a *partida* in a subordinate capacity, but then established bands of their own. This principle of 'first appearance' has also been followed with regard to Figures 7.5 and 7.6, but in other cases, including, most notably, Figure 7.2, the base has rather been the number of combatants registered year by year. And in still other cases (Figures 7.7, 7.8 and 7.9), it has been possible simply to take the global totals without reference to any further analysis. Finally, attention must also be paid to issues of distortion. In Figure 7.5, for example, it will be noted that Aragón accounts for a very large number of the combatants. This is by no means surprising: Aragón was under continuous French occupation longer than almost any province other than Navarre and the Basque provinces. But it also has to be recognized that Aragón is an area whose *guerrilla* is better known than almost any other, and the authors would here wish to pay particular tribute to the work of the Spanish historian, Ramón Guirao, whose monograph *Guerrilleros y Patriotas en el Alto Aragón* (Huesca, 2000) contains the names of literally hundreds of men who enlisted to fight the French in the Huesca area.

7
Regulating the Irregulars: Spanish Legislation on *la guerrilla* during the Peninsular War

Vittorio Scotti-Douglas *

Whether irregular warfare holds – together with prostitution – the dubious merit of being the most ancient form of human activity is something that can never be known for certain. However, all that need concern us here is that it is a very old and well-established way of fighting, usually employed against overwhelming odds. Tracing its long history is not the purpose of this chapter, and all the more so as the current author has written on this subject elsewhere.[1] But talking about the concept of *guerrilla* does require at least a short philological introduction that will give us some insight into the origin and the meaning of this word.

As is well known, *guerrilla* is a word that comes to us from Castillian. In this language, it is very old, whilst it is obviously derived as a diminutive from *guerra* ('war'). We encounter it recorded for the first time in the famous *Tesoro de la Lengua Castellana, o Española* by Sebastián de Covarrubias Orozco, published in Madrid in 1611. Found under the heading for *guerra*, it is defined as 'a quarrel between private citizens that . . . causes them to split into rival bands and in consequence to incur severe punishment at the hands of the ruler of the state'.[2] Note, then, that *guerrilla* is at this stage is a private conflict, and, being a breach of the peace, something that worries rulers, who thus punish it. Slightly more than a century later, in the first edition of the Real Academia's dictionary, we find some change, albeit a minor one: 'Small armed conflict, or difference in opinions of little importance.'[3] There is also another definition of *guerrilla* relating to a carefully described game of cards, but this has no military connection other than the fact that,

---

* I would like to thank my good friend, Dr Charles Esdaile, for his splendid work in editing this chapter; he has respected my thoughts absolutely whilst giving the chapter an accessible English form.

judging from similar games played in other countries, it was probably
first played by soldiers.[4]

We can read the same things in the editions of the dictionary published
in 1780, 1783 and 1791. But in the meantime, in 1780 there appeared
the first Spanish translation of a treatise on the art of war that was, in
its time, a real European 'bestseller'. Entitled *La Petite Guerre, ou Traité
du Service des Troupes Légères en Campagne*, this had been written by
a Frenchman, Augustin Thomas de Grandmaison, and originally
published in 1756. In this work one could find explained the origins,
development theory and practice of a particular way of waging war
that, as the title suggests, the author defined as *petite guerre* – in other
words 'small', 'petty' or 'little' war. As is well known *petite guerre* was the
answer adopted by military theorists – and most especially French
theorists[5] – to the problems caused for regular armies by the irregular
forces met in a variety of campaigns from the Thirty Years War
onwards. In so far as France was concerned, particularly important here
was the War of the Austrian Succession of 1741–48, in which French
troops suffered heavy losses at the hands of Maria Theresa's Croat
irregulars, but it should be noted that most armies faced such problems
whilst they were not confined to Europe, as witness the problems faced
by the British in North America in the Seven Years' War (1756–63) and
the American War of Independence (1775–83). Grandmaison's treatise
was neither the best, nor, still less, the only one on the subject, but it
nevertheless proved an incredible success.[6] As noted above, the first
Spanish translation was published in 1780, whilst its title was *La Guerrilla,
ó Tratado del Servicio de las Tropas Ligeras en Campaña*.[7] The logical
consequence of this was to establish an equivalence between *guerrilla*
and *petite guerre*, whilst the expression *partidas de guerrilla* was used to
designate the small detachments and cavalry employed in surprise
attacks, intelligence gathering or advanced reconnaissance. In addition,
meanwhile, the term might be applied to troops deployed in skirmish
order on the battlefield, such men being described as being deployed
en guerrilla.[8]

Coming back to our own period, we find that the terms *guerrilla* and
partida were employed throughout the Peninsular War. We find them,
for instance, in General Castaños' bulletin after the battle of Bailén,[9] in
a biography of the Empecinado published in 1814,[10] and in memoirs
written at the time but not published till long afterwards.[11] In the course
of the struggle, however, their meaning changed. At the beginning of
hostilities, the word *guerrilla* referred specifically to regular soldiers,
and this meaning continued in use for some time. But at the same time

it began to be used in connection with another meaning, this being that of the armed struggle of civilians, organized in irregular bands, against an invading enemy and/or against a government that was unjust or, as in Spain, illegitimate.[12] This is, of course, the modern understanding of the term 'guerrilla warfare' and it is in this sense that it has entered languages other than Castillian.

How, though is all this relevant to the current chapter? In brief, the link is found in this very change of meaning. Thus, nearly always spontaneously born and headed by local leaders, throughout the Peninsular War the new form of *partida* was frequently in conflict with the authorities, both civilian and military. First of all we have to consider what happened when insurrection first broke out against the French in May 1808. How did the authorities react to this development? The general attitude was to try and soothe the people by recommending calm, peace, prudence and obedient submission. Let us here cite, for instance, General Don Gregorio García de la Cuesta, Capitán General de Castilla la Vieja y León, who on 29 May 1808 wrote to the Leonese authorities, explaining that, as both Carlos IV and Fernando VII had renounced the crown, Spaniards had been freed from any fidelity to them, and that obedience was now due to the provisional government – the Junta de Gobierno – that for the time being ruled Spain in Napoleon's name, whilst at the same time stressing the need for calm and the uselessness of resistance.[13] We may discuss the reasons and even understand the grounds on which such decisions were taken, but there is no doubt that such blindness broke the bonds of trust that must necessarily unite rulers and ruled. And, needless to say, the expectation of passivity on which it was based was swept aside by the success of the uprising. Thus, on 6 June 1808 we find the Junta of Seville publishing a document entitled *Prevenciones*, in which it was suggested that general actions should be avoided in favour of a strategy in which the enemy would be attacked by small bands that would never let them rest, but always hang on their flanks and rear, wearing them out, intercepting their convoys, destroying their stores, and cutting their communications.[14]

Although it also contains passages which seem to suggest that much reliance should also be placed on organized home guards that could leap to the defence of bridge, city wall or mountain pass at the first sign of the French, this document can be seen as an unequivocal invitation to engage in irregular warfare. To put it another way, the Junta was specifically encouraging the perpetuation of the popular fury that had in many places administered rough justice – sometimes in a barbarous way – to all those held responsible, whether justly or not, for the country's supposed betrayal to the French.[15] Contained within it, meanwhile, is an assumption on the part of the Junta, a revolutionary reincarnation of an ancient and traditional institution, of the army's near uselessness, a popular uprising being held to be the only way – albeit a desperate one – of countering the troops of the great emperor. However, after the unexpected victory at Bailén on 19 July 1808, the supreme Spanish authorities somewhat changed their minds, as is shown by the exaggeratedly optimistic tone of the *Manifiesto a la Nación Española*. A proclamation designed to legitimize the rule of the new Spanish government – the Junta Suprema Central de Gobierno del Reino – this is one of the most celebrated works of the writer, Manuel Quintana, and may almost be regarded as the Spanish equivalent of the United States' declaration of independence.[16] Setting aside its political aspect – it was couched in terms that were strongly liberal – the *Manifiesto* spoke not just of 'fighting the enemy with success', but of driving the French beyond the Pyrenees, and compelling them to free the king and the royal family, and acknowledge Spain's freedom and independence.[17] And as for how all this was to be done, the proclamation only spoke of armies and regular troops, and specifically states that it is only from them that the people has to expect its safety. Not a word was devoted to the first exploits of the *guerrilleros*, although stories were circulating that in some cases – most notably, El Empecinado – they had begun to attack the French even before the uprising of the Dos de Mayo. And all the more is this strange given that other episodes had already shown the importance of popular participation in the struggle: led by such figures as El Empecinado, the first guerrilla bands had emerged in the summer of 1808, whilst one should also remember the success of the Catalan *somatenes* at El Bruch, and the heroic defence of towns and cities such as Valdepeñas, Zaragoza, Gerona and Tarragona, not to mention the events of the Dos de Mayo in Madrid.

The irrelevance of Quintana's approach was revealed very quickly. Thus, the general situation had started to deteriorate even before the proclamation had become widely available, whilst it continued to worsen very quickly in November and December. The list of battles against the French is a sequel of defeats – Zornoza (31 October), Gamonal (10 November), Espinosa de los Monteros (10–11 November), Tudela (23 November), Somosierra (30 November) – and all this culminated in Madrid's capitulation to Napoleon on 4 December. Nor was this an end to the story: within a month of the fall of Madrid, the British were forced to re-embark at La Coruña; the Spaniards led by General Vives compelled to raise the blockade of Barcelona; and the French allowed once again to besiege Zaragoza. But whilst the nobility, bureaucracy and a portion of the intelligentsia did choose the French side, for different and sometimes honourable reasons, there were increasing number of guerrillas attacking the French, at first with daggers, knives and a few ancient blunderbusses and fowling pieces, and then with muskets and bayonets taken from the enemy, whose dead were also stripped of their uniforms and shoes. These men were generally grouped together in bands known as *partidas*. A totally irregular formation, a *partida* normally owed its origin to the decision to fight the French of one man who, for a variety of reasons – personal prestige, acknowledged courage, previous military service honourably discharged, or more simply because of what today we label as charisma – was able to gather together a band of individuals who were ready to follow him. Of course, some bands were unsuccessful and soon fell apart or were overcome, but where success was achieved it was a different story. Thus, victory increased the enthusiasm of the first members of the band, brought in new recruits, and increased the fame of the *partida*, and very soon the leader would become known not by his own name, but by a nickname, if he did not have already one.

As the bands proliferated, however, the Junta Central began to hear complaints and protests about their independence. These were the work of a variety of provincial juntas and regional military commanders. What does the Junta do in the face of this growing clamour? Despite the fact that it was in a desperate military situation, it promulgates a *reglamento* or ordinance. Issued in Seville on 28 December 1808, this text is of the utmost importance from the historical, political, military and juridical point of view.[18] It has a short but important foreword, 34 articles or rules and a final declaration. Let us begin with the foreword, especially as this merits quotation in full:

> Spain abounds with subjects endowed with extraordinary bravery, who, exploiting the great advantages provided by their knowledge of the country, and the implacable hatred of all the nation against the tyrant who wants to subdue it by the most iniquitous means, are able to spread terror and consternation within his armies. To make it easier for them to attain so noble an aim, supply them with the means of honourably enriching themselves with the enemy's booty, and allow them to immortalize their names with heroic deeds deserving an undying fame, His Royal Majesty [i.e. the Junta Central] has deigned to create a new kind of armed force, which is to go under the name of *partidas* or *cuadrillas*.[19]

The statute's articles dictate (or rather, as we shall see, try to dictate) the rules organizing the band, its ranks, discipline, pay, in a word the bureaucratic structure of the *partidas*, leaving only two articles, Articles 22 and 23 for detailing the military aspect that is the paramount aim of its birth. Some attention is also merited by Article 29, which runs as follows:

> Many subjects of distinguished bravery and undauntedness having, for want of a means of making use of their military talents in a worthy manner . . . devoted themselves to smuggling, they shall be pardoned and will be employed in another kind of *partida* called a *cuadrilla* . . . in order to make them useful to the state and give them the glorious career offered them by the circumstances of the day.[20]

And Articles 30 and 31 give in detail the rewards for smugglers who, volunteering to serve in a *cuadrilla*, arrive armed and with a horse, whilst laying down that, if they still had smuggled goods, these should be bought 'at a price granting them [the smugglers] a moderate profit'.[21] Also interesting, and for that reason worth quoting in full, is the final statement, which openly reveals the desire to connect the *partidas* with the regular military apparatus of the state that we shall go on to see. Thus:

> Everybody wishing to enlist . . . under the above rules, must present himself immediately to his local provincial junta . . . or Captain General, and then proceed to the commander of whichever field army happens to be stationed in the area in order to be sworn in, assigned to a unit and given his marching orders. The existence of each *partida* and *cuadrilla* having been checked out, the Intendent shall then issue an order for them to be granted the relevant pay in accordance with a monthly review instituted by the Commissary, or failing him, the local magistrate.[22]

The historical importance of this document is quite clear. The first text that attempts to legitimate a combat form totally irregular by its own nature, waged by civilians armed with every kind and description of arms, including agricultural implements, which, after being used to kill passing Frenchmen, are returned to their peaceful fields, is also the confession of a government that cannot trust its army, and tries to use laudatory words to win the support of 'subjects of distinguished bravery and undauntedness' and even smugglers, whose crimes are explained away by the fiction that they are men of natural military talent who could not find an outlet for their skills under the *antiguo régimen*. Just as obvious, meanwhile, is its political, military and juridical importance, the point being that the independence of the guerrilla movement was being vitiated at the very moment that it was ostensibly legitimized as a phenomenon. Yet from the practical point of view, it was a dead letter from the start, the majority of historians agreeing that compliance with the *reglamento* was almost nonexistent. It is not clear if it was this failure that pushed the Junta into accepting a project, concocted by Vicente Alcalá Galiano, that took the form of another set of regulations, but at all events on 17 April 1809 there duly appeared the *Instrucción para el Corso Terrestre contra los Ejércitos Franceses*.[23]

Here again a simple reading of the text offers us some very interesting points for our consideration. First of all, however, a short explanation is needed for the name given to the guerrillas in this document. This is very well clarified in the letter that was written to Martín de Garay, who was the Secretary of the Junta Central, by the author of the proposal. The brother of a naval officer who was killed fighting fighting heroically in the battle of Trafalgar, he seems to have been thinking primarily in terms of psychological warfare and even bluff. Thus:

> Unless I am very much mistaken, this plan ought to give even the emperor pause, whilst at the same time spreading fear and terror among his soldiers … Always inclined to set much store by the new, the French nation can be relied on not to look calmly at the situation, and the troops will immediately imagine the countryside to be full of corsairs ready to rob and murder them the moment they relax their guard.[24]

As for the term itself, it stands, of course, for 'land piracy', the model on which it was based being that of naval privateering. For a definition, let us turn to the *Shorter Oxford English Dictionary*. In this we read that a privateer is 'an armed vessel owned and officered by private persons, and holding a commission from the government, called 'letters of marque', authorizing the owners to use it against a hostile nation, and especially in the capture of merchant shipping'.[25] Whilst still to all intents and purposes a pirate, the holder of the 'letters of marque' therefore became a kind of authorized and legal combatant.

Now, then, we have a completely different situation. The call to arms was still universal, but the individual guerrilla was no longer an agent of the state. On the contrary, he was now an entrepreneur who might benefit the state by his actions but was really acting on his own account. And, as the combatants were now specifically intended to spread terror amongst the enemy, it followed that there should be no restriction on their actions: no reference, in short, could be made to either the laws of war or the principles of common humanity. Much of this is clear from Article 1 of the new decree. Thus:

> Every inhabitant of the provinces occupied by the French troops who can arm himself, is authorized to do so ... in order to attack and to plunder the French soldiers, when in favourable conditions, whether they are found alone or in groups, seizing the victuals and supplies meant for their maintenance, and, in short, inflicting all the evil and damage possible on them, with the understanding that this service will be considered as rendered to the Nation, and rewarded in proportion to its extent and results.[26]

It is easy to see, from the very beginning, that a very different spirit informs all the text, from the long introduction – an impassionate and stirring patriotic appeal, full of hatred against the French – to the 18 short articles, with few bureaucratic rules and many promises for the fighting patriots. As for the author, in contrast to his predecessor, he comes over not as an official worried by red tape and the question of law and order, but as a Spaniard whose central interest is that of inflicting on the enemy 'all the evil and damage possible'. This is further emphasized by the clarity of the general instructions contained in the introduction: the struggle will be longer and more costly if the Patriots do not succeed in making it difficult 'for the French troops to acquire victuals and the other means necessary for surviving in the Country'; all communications must be cut or destroyed; a close eye must be kept on the enemy's movements, aims and combinations; and the latter's troops must be kept in a state of 'continuous stress and alarm'. As for the Spaniards, meanwhile, they should at all times demonstrate 'firmness and stead-fastness', but who is the appeal directed to? In brief, the people, in which respect one statement is especially interesting:

> As Napoleon has succeeded with the basest and vilest arts in destroying and disorganizing Spain's military force, in seizing her major fort-resses and taking prisoner her king, is it not very clear that it is now necessary for the civilian population to band together to fight her enemies?[27]

One of the most important and noteworthy results of the *Instrucción* was the birth of the 'Corso Terrestre de Navarra', led by Martín Javier Mina y Larrea, better known by his nicknames of 'El Mozo' or 'El Estudiante'. In this respect the document may be said to have had fundamental results – the resistance movement which Mina founded eventually became the most impressive in the whole of Spain – and it may well be for this development that the new measure will be chiefly remembered.[28]

Whilst still on the subject of the Junta Central, a few words should perhaps be devoted to a third set of rules that it issued with respect to the guerrillas. We come here to the question of the *cruzadas*, or 'crusades'. In principle, these consisted of guerrilla bands made up entirely of priests, monks and friars, and the idea of such forces, which surfaced repeatedly in the course of 1809, may be regarded as an attempt at one and the same time to inject fresh energy into the guerrilla movement and to control its excesses.[29] Whatever the exact thinking behind the idea may have been, the Junta Central evidently felt it to be worth pursuing for on 30 December 1809 it issued a set of rules 'for the creation of the *cruzadas*'.[30] In theory, these bands should have been formed only of ecclesiastics, regular or secular, to the number of 50 to every *partida*. Yet there is no proof whatsoever of even one of these bands ever having been created. We know that many clerics – both regular and secular – did participate individually in the guerrilla bands, and that some of them succeeded in becoming famous leaders, the best known of whom is probably Jerónimo Mérino.[31] But as an attempt to influence the development and behaviour of the guerrillas, the scheme got nowhere and may therefore be discounted.

A close analysis of the *Instrucción*, especially if done in combination with the *Reglamento*, would offer us many interesting insights with respect to various other important points concerning the state of the Patriot Spain, good examples of such subjects being what they have to say with regard to desertion, the ever increasing problem of how the guerrillas should be supplied, and the situation of the rural and urban population, but these are not questions pertaining to the subject of the current paper. Returning to this latter issue – the attempts that were made to regulate the guerrilla bands – the two *reglamentos* of 1808–9 were followed by a number of local decrees and codes of conduct. Of these, however, only a brief mention of just one example need suffice. For this purpose we shall look at a set of rules published by the then Captain General of Catalonia, General Luis Lacy on 9 September 1811. Entitled *Reglamento para las Partidas Patrióticas*, this consists of 15 articles, and is very similar to the 1808 *Reglamento*.[32] Thus, its contents are nearly all military and without anything of particular relevance, bar a hint about cooperation between the *partidas* and the *somatenes* – the Catalan home guard[33] – at Article 15, and the significant contents of Article 14, which states that one of the main objects of the *partidas* should be 'the pursuit and capture of deserters, robbers and wrongdoers, who must be brought to the nearest division's commander'.[34]

If we accept that the *Reglamento para los Cuerpos Francos o Partidas de Guerrilla* of 28 July 1814 was clearly concerned solely with the demobilization of the guerrillas, the last important legislative provision concerning the guerrillas is the *Reglamento para las Partidas de Guerrilla* of 11 July 1812.[35] By the time that the former document was issued, the situation in Spain had changed enormously. Although 1812 was in all of Spain the 'year of hunger', from the military point of view there were increasing hopes of victory, thanks on the one hand to the news of Wellington's successes, and on the other to the withdrawal of 30 000 French troops to fight in Russia. What we have in July 1812 is therefore not a desperate cry for popular involvement in the war effort, though it is notable that the text stresses the importance of propaganda and, especially, the task of keeping the populace informed with regard to the latest provisions of the authorities and the latest war news.[36] Rather what we see is a well-considered piece of legislation that sought to repeat and improve upon the 1808 norms, and in particular to emphasize and develop their military aspects. Whilst there are no tactical or strategic innovations – the need to gather information, cut the enemy's communications and engage in other such tasks is simply restated – there are new and more fastidious prescriptions on how to deal with the problem of booty when it concerns goods pertaining to Spaniards. 'Good Spaniards', of course, were not to be molested at all, whilst they were guaranteed the return of any goods taken from them. 'Bad Spaniards' were a different matter, but even they now got a better deal. Thus: 'When they capture bad Spaniards...all the money, jewels, clothing and goods found on them shall be totally theirs, but they must be able to present detailed proof of their guilt.'[37] But who should decide as to which Spaniards were 'good' and which Spaniards were 'bad'? It is very clear from the text that the final decision lay with the leaders of the bands, and, that, proof or no proof, they had therefore acquired enormous liberties. More positively, however, much effort was devoted to regularizing the relationship between *partida* and *pueblo*, and, in particular to avoiding exactions and other kinds of abuses. Thus, a complicated system was established whereby guerrilla bands could be issued with certificates of good conduct 'that will serve as recommendation for the commanders, always provided that the justices of the same *pueblos* have not at a different time made separate complaints against them'.[38]

This was, therefore, the corpus of legislation that, at least theoretically, ruled the guerrillas and governed their legal status (there are four other provisions that in some way or other deal with the issue, of which three were issued in 1809 by the Junta Central and the fourth in 1811 by the Regencia, but they do not change the sense of this chapter[39]). But what, in fact, actually happened? What were the relationships between the *partidas* and the civilian and military authorities? It is this scarcely charted and difficult territory that we must now explore. The task, however, is not an easy one, not the least of the problems being that the civilian authorities were all too often divided amongst themselves, and, even more so, at odds with their military counterparts. Before going any further, indeed, we must look at these problems. Let us begin with the civil power. The disappearance of a strong central authority in the first days of the insurrection led, as is well known, to the creation of local governments which under the name of 'juntas' took over the civilian power in their respective regions. This produced a reaction, and when the Junta Central was formed in September 1808, it was seen in some quarters as a solution to the atomization of political power. However, the reality was very different, as the Junta Central generally lacked any effective means of enforcing its authority, even in those areas that were not occupied by the French. Even if the theory was that all the district and provincial Juntas should submit to the new central government, this therefore in the end depended on the local authorities' good will. But it was not just the central power that was weak. Thus, the disintegration of authority had snowballed to such an extent that the provincial Juntas found it difficult to control their provinces and the district juntas difficult to control their districts. Especially in the case of communities rich in historical privileges or traditions of self-government, what mattered was therefore the *pueblo*, and it was often only at this level that questions of defence were considered.[40] Moving on now to the issue of civil–military relations, we find that these were even more troubled. In this respect the fierce quarrel between the Marquess of La Romana and the Junta of Asturias is especially well known. However, it is not the only instance, and in this respect it is worth pointing out that the guerrillas were in fact one of the chief bones of contention when it came to clashes between army officers and the juntas. Thus, particularly if they had helped arm and recruit them, many juntas were inclined to regard guerrilla bands operating in the vicinity as *de facto* private armies, and were therefore extremely unwilling to see them receive orders from the general in command of the district or even act on their own initiative. Meanwhile, such interference carried on even when *partidas* had been militarized (i.e. organised into regular units and granted the status of troops of the line). On top of this there was the issue of the formation of new *partidas*. By 1810 many army officers were deeply suspicious of the value of the 'classic' guerrilla band and were actively opposing the formation of fresh *partidas*. Yet for the civilian authorities the issue was seen quite differently. On the one hand there was less awareness of the military problems thrown up by the irregulars, whilst on the other the creation of fresh *partidas* strengthened the hands of local and provincial juntas with regard to patronage and at the same time reinforced their power and influence. And here, of course, lay the basis for a very deep split with army officers accusing the juntas of selfishness and egotism, and juntas accusing army officers of lack of faith and vision.[41]

Yet, whilst they might look with favour on the guerrillas, this did not mean that the civil authorities were blind to the problems which they threw up. On the contrary, there was also a more or less clear fear that the *partidas* could become nests of bandits and robbers, and, in a word, a menace to the civilian authorities, the maintenance of peace and the social order. Such fear is absolutely obvious in the parliamentary debate held on the subject in the *cortes* on 9–10 of August 1811, even if the discussion concluded with the unanimous rejection of the new set of rules for guerrillas proposed by the Minister of War. One sees here the ambivalence that characterized the view of the guerrillas entertained by the leaders of civilian society in Patriot Spain: more centralised and militarized, the new rules bid fair to address the question of law and order, and yet they also challenged liberal notions of popular spontaneity and the nation in arms.[42] Hence, of course, the opposition in the *cortes*. But the problem would not go away, and thus we see provincial juntas from time to time themselves attempting to tackle the issue, a good example in this respect being the ordinance issued for the control of the guerrillas by the Junta of Asturias in 1810.[43]

Curiously, the attempt to control the guerrillas was not all one-way. As the war went on, so some of the leaders of the more stable guerrilla bands realized the advantages of coming to some accommodation with civilian society, and in consequence set out to try to develop a normative framework for the guerrilla bands, which they both adopted for their own forces and sought to impose on others. By acting in this fashion they achieved a double purpose: on the one hand they obtained the practical benefits – above all, help and support from the local community – resulting from acting within a framework of legality; and on the other they found a moral justification for forcing other *partidas* that refused to comply with the rules to submit to their authority, thereby increasing their own power (in the case of refusal, they could pursue 'rebel' bands, destroy them and add any survivors to the ranks of their own men). Thus, in March 1811, eight *cabecillas* in Castilla la Vieja, one of them the already famous D. Gerónimo Merino, met in Novares and published a proclamation whose preamble announced that they were 'intimately convinced of the need to establish...a system of government' that would put an end to the manner in which they had, however inadvertently, hitherto been 'harming their fellow citizens, offending justice and discrediting the most just and important cause that they defend'.[44]

We have here a lucid attempt to regulate the irregular, limiting a war based on a lack of fixed rules with sets of more or less precise norms. But as such efforts did not have any central coordination, they could themselves become a problem: by clashing with one another, rival codes of conduct were at the heart of many of the competence disputes that from the very beginning affected the relationship between the guerrillas and the civilian authorities. In this respect, one of the most frequent problems was that of fixing the boundaries of authority in every district or region. In October 1809, for example, some members of the Junta of Navarre registered a protest with the Junta Central Suprema against the fashion in which their province was being raided by some *partidas* 'that, not pertaining to any army, enter and act in it without any title other than one issued by the Junta of Arnedo, which is under the orders of the Junta of Molina de Aragón'.[45] Not only were these *partidas* imposing requisitions, harassing the civilian populace and employing violence, but in addition they lacked the sanction of the Junta of Navarre, although this was in fact the only body other than the Junta Central that had the right to authorise guerrilla activity in it. Not until the following year was the problem solved, and even than the solution was hardly to the Junta's liking: by a mixture of brutality and cunning, the famous leader, Francisco Espoz y Mina, succeeded in establishing a monopoly of force in the province that ended the problem of the free-lance activity of which the Junta had complained, but at the same time he also imposed such an iron hand on the Junta of Navarra that it was reduced to a mere group of puppets.

Was the case of the Junta of Navarre that has just been described in part an attempt to defend the local populace? In part, certainly: the ravages

indulged in by irregular bands whose activity hardly differed from that
engaged in by simple bandits were often very serious, whilst in a draft
of a letter of General Mahy to General Castañ n, for example, we read
the following:

> The Junta Superior of the Kingdom of León has complained to me of
> the devastating behaviour of the *partidas* that pretend to be at your
> orders. I am sure that you do not approve of such actions, but I am
> also certain of the truth of what has been reported to me, in con-
> sequence of which it is absolutely necessary that you summon
> the...leaders and make them understand, first, that they shall
> be undeserving of the name of patriots unless they change their
> conduct towards their ruined fellow countrymen, and, second, that
> anybody who undermines national security and well being – the
> main object of the armed forces that have been mobilized against
> the enemy who wants to destroy our beloved Fatherland – will be
> punished according to the laws.[46]

In this case the Junta's complaint does not derive from a conflict of
competence, but from the need to put a stop to plunder and speak up
for the local community. But at the same time it is difficult completely
to discard questions of power and influence: self-made men like El
Empecinado and Espoz y Mina were, after all, a serious threat to the
long-established oligarchies that almost invariably monopolized the
organs of both central and local government in Patriot Spain. Meanwhile, we might cite other instances where there is simply no possibility
of ambiguity. Here the struggle assumes a very different aspect: it is a
political confrontation. What is at stake is who should have the
decision-making power, the power to organize military operations, to
administer justice, to allot resources. A typical instance of such a
conflict comes from La Rioja where the final months of 1809 saw the
outbreak of a ferocious dispute between the Junta of Logroño and a
guerrilla commander named the Marqués de Barriolucio who had been
granted control of the district by the distant Junta of Ciudad Rodrigo,
which *faute de mieux* had taken the place of a proper Junta of Old Castile.
Thus, moving into the area, the Marqués disarmed a number of *partidas*
that had been formed by the Junta of Logroño, either disbanding them
or adding their men to his own, seized large quantities of supplies,
munitions and confiscated goods, appointed men loyal to himself to
key positions of authority, assumed control of the various prisoners
languishing in custody on charges of disloyalty.[47] Such at least is the

version of events that was offered by the Junta of Logroño. If it is to be believed, what Barriolucio was doing was in effect engaging in a species of *coup dé tat* in order to secure a series of rights – and, beyond them, the cooperation of the local populace – to which he could have obtained access in no other way. In a word, indeed, he was bidding for control of the area.

In this case the guerrillas played an important role in a conflict between two corporate powers, whose prerogatives, very vaguely defined, overlapped in the same space. Such overlapping appears very clearly in a petition presented to the Junta Central in Seville by the representatives of Logroño:

> Five contiguous Juntas can be observed to be operational in [Logroño]: that of Soto de Cameros [NB: the Junta of Logroño itself], that of Barriolucio in Navarre, that of Arnedo, that of Menciso and that of Covaleda. Each is operating in the towns and villages that recognize them, so that there are continuous conflicts between them, and this obviously produces... such confusion and disillusionment that the interests of not just the whole province but also the entire nation are severely affected. This evil has spread to the *partidas*... and, to our great shame and distress, the important services that they have been performing... may have sometimes been... undermined because of the dissension and conflict which they have experienced, this having sometimes reached such a pitch that the stronger bands have disarmed their weaker fellows.[48]

Because of this competition, guerrilla warfare acquired a new dimension. In brief, the guerrilla band can be seen to have become not just a means of fighting the French, but also a tool in the power struggle that raged between the different factions born from the political chaos of 1808. And in this fashion the *partidas* – at least those big enough to achieve a measure of influence and independence – joined with the generals, the central government, the juntas and, in the end, the *cortes* of Cádiz in helping to shape the future of Spain.

With matters in this state the *partidas* made hay. Feeding on the political struggles between diverse local power élites, they started to entertain an extravagant idea of their own importance, acting outside any principle of operational unity and without any concerted plan. For a very lucid and pitiless diagnosis of this phenomenon, we might turn to a letter written to the Junta Central by the Junta of Nájera – a local committee of government established by the Marqués de Barriolucio in La Rioja that should probably be added to the five authorities listed above, though it is just possible that it is the otherwise rather mysterious Navarrese body mentioned in connection with the marquess – as part of his attempt to take over the area. Thus:

> The main cause of all of this, Señor, is undoubtedly the fact that all these troops do not recognize a central authority, or rather, perhaps, that no authority has the strength to get them under control. All of them want to be independent leaders; all dispose of the property of the nation, the *pueblos* and the citizenry alike as if they were sovereigns. And, still worse, with unbelievable impudence, they frequently make use of the infamous word 'traitor' to satisfy their greed at the cost of the honour and survival of many unfortunates, who find themselves despoiled and stripped of everything, before being heard and judged.[49]

A further issue that needs to be touched on here is that of provincialism. This is a feature common to all states lacking a strong central power, whilst it is likely to be especially pronounced in time of war, and especially, invasion. In Spain, certainly, between 1808 and 1813 every province thought of itself as the key to the entire war and the central bastion of Spanish resistance. The guerrilla bands, obviously, could not escape this problem, even if their answer was never going to be homogeneous. Both Martín Javier Mina y Larrea and his distant relative, Francisco Espoz y Mina, for instance, had a strong sense of territoriality, and would not allow any kind of meddling in Navarre. Already in November of 1809 we have a proof of this in a letter written by José Antonio Colmenares, an agent of the Junta Central who established himself in the area of Molina de Aragón and from there sought to exercise general authority over a broad region embracing the modern provinces of Soria, Guadalajara, Cuenca, Logroño and Teruel. Although Mina was not yet famous and his band still very small, he was evidently still a force to be reckoned with. Thus, in an attempt to extend his authority into southern Navarre, Colmenares dispatched an army officer named Juan Garcés de los Fayos to Viana. No sooner had he got there, however, than his mission came to an abrupt end, Colmenares complaining that 'in that town [he] was captured by a guerrilla commander...called Don Francisco Mina [*sic*: in reality this must be a reference to 'El Mozo': at this time Espoz y Mina was not an independent commander, whilst he did not adopt the name 'Mina' until the following year] who took away from him his commission, papers and baggage'.[50] This habit, meanwhile, was perpetuated by Espoz y Mina after he emerged as the new leader of Navarrese resistance in the wake of the capture of 'El Mozo' in March 1810, as witness the fact that any other *partida* that entered the province from beyond its frontiers was either disarmed by him or integrated into his own forces.

This does not mean that the Navarrese leaders were provincialists, at least not in the strict sense of the word. Francisco Espoz y Mina was not shy of fighting outside Navarre, as is shown by the action that he launched in western Aragón in 1811 in order to lure Suchet away from the attack he was planning on Valencia. Meanwhile, he also exploited a commission issued by the Junta of Aragón as a means of consolidating his authority in Navarre in the early days of his command.[51] Yet, for all that, provincialism was certainly present, it being this force that was the underlying reason for perhaps the most well-known conflict that took place between a guerrilla leader and a junta in the course of the war. We come here to the clash between Juan Martín 'El Empecinado' and the Junta of Guadalajara. On the surface this was motivated by issues of competence, and, in particular, the question of who should have the command of military operations in the district, but beneath this was the issue of *patria chica* versus *patria*.[52] To put this still more simply, which should take preference: Guadalajara or Spain? In so far as the Junta was concerned, there was no question here as to what the answer should be, and it therefore did everything that it could to obstruct any moves on the part of El Empecinado that were not exclusively devoted to the protection of the province and its rulers. For this, the justification was quite simple. So far as the Junta was concerned, as it had raised many of the famous guerrilla commander's men, it ought also to have the exclusive use of them, and all the more so, or so it claimed, as it was forced to rely entirely on its own resources. Thus:

> Although intended for the defence of the province that supplies, arms, uniforms and pays it, this small division has not always operated within its boundaries...but the frank and generous conduct which this exemplifies has never received its just reward: no matter what the dangers have been in which it has found itself, it has never been supported by the different corps of the neighbouring provinces.[53]

Juan Martín's answer was very sharp. The Junta's attitude, he thundered, contradicted all the principles of good government, all the maxims of the ancients, and all the lessons of Spain's current misfortunes. And at the same time it was spreading 'the spirit of provincialism' and could persuade the soldiers to look 'with indifference and even contempt on the troubles of other provinces, and cause them to become unwilling to obey the orders of a general, who wisely and at the right moment calls them somewhere else'.[54]

This difference of opinion is very striking. Contrary to what one might have initially suspected, it is the uneducated peasant, the individual with an experience of life limited more or less to the boundaries of his district, who rejects the idea that the province is the key to the life of the nation, and who understands that victory depends on the union of every community in the country, and, by extension, the extirpation of every localism. By contrast, it is the members of the Junta, men who stem from the dominant élites and who, as traditional holders of public offices in such institutions as the Ministry of Finance and the Post Office may be considered to be representatives of the state, defend at all cost a localist spirit that is detrimental to the war effort. In the end the Consejo de Regencia was to come down in favour of El Empecinado in this dispute, and therefore to make a stand for a national concept of the war, but the incident brings us to a very important point that might serve as the conclusion for this chapter. Thus, the idea of Spain as a nation, interpreted according to the bourgeois construction of the term, cannot be associated with all the élites. In the same way it is not possible to exclude the idea that the populace possessed a certain political flair, at least in some of their representatives.[55] Obviously this sophistication did not extend to all the *guerrilleros*, nor the peasants from which they sprang. On the contrary, the majority of the documents suggest that most of the common people identified primarily with their home districts and had a strong preference for staying there, and that these preferences were not overcome by serving in the *partidas* or the regular armies. At this point in Spanish history, then, the chief emotional bond was with the local community, just as the chief instinct of the populace was to protect the economic activities which permitted not just their survival but that of their families. In this respect, El Empecinado therefore stands out as an even more remarkable individual: a man who truly transcended his background. And, to return to the question of regulating the irregulars, it can be seen that the process should not just be interpreted in terms of the reconstruction of the state or the expansion of its power. In reality, moves to control the guerrillas could just as easily be the work of local oligarchies who were frantic to safeguard their own interests, in which respect it is interesting to note that, as the nineteenth century wore on, the guerrilla was to be associated not with the liberal state, but rather the Carlism that was its antithesis.

Notes

1. Cf. V. Scotti-Douglas, 'Spagna 1808: la genesi della guerriglia moderna (1): guerra irregolare, *petite guerre, guerrilla*', *Spagna Contemporanea*, no. 18 (Autumn, 2000), pp. 9–31.
2. S. de Covarrubias Orozco, *Tesoro de la Lengua Castellana, o Española*, F. Maldonado (ed.) (Madrid, 1995), p. 613. Lit. 'Cuando entre particulares hay pendencia y enemistad formada, que acuden unos a una parte y otros a otra; pero éstas castigan los príncipes de las repúblicas severamente.'
3. Real Academía Española, *Diccionario de la lengua Castellana en que se explica el verdadero sentido de las voces, su naturaleza y calidad, con las phrases ò modos de hablar, los proverbios ò refranes y otras cosas convenientes al uso de la lengua* (Madrid, 1726–39), IV, p. 93. Lit. 'Encuentro ligéro de armas, ò contrariedad de dictámenes de poca entidad.'
4. *Ibid*. The game was played according to a version of the well-known 'Beat Jack out of Doors', and it may be that there are some subconscious echoes of the realities of the civilian population's experience of war in the 'horse and musket' period here: the game is a species of 'beggar thy neighbour' in which two players compete for all the cards in the pack and the inference is that soldiers – 'jacks' in common parlance – quartered on the populace had to be 'beaten outside doors' before they ate them out of house and home. Curiously enough, then, we can even see links with popular resistance to the military. I owe this insight to my friend and colleague, Dr Charles Esdaile, of the University of Liverpool.
5. Setting aside Grandmaison, a short list of French treatises on *petite guerre* includes J. de Jeney, *Le partisan ou l'art de faire la petite guerre* (Den Haag, 1749); J. de la Croix, *Traité de la petite guerre pour les compagnies franches, dans lequel on voit leur utilité, la différence de leur service d'avec celui des autres corps, la manière la plus avantageuse de les conduire, de les équiper, de les commander et de les discipliner, et les ruses de guerre qui leur sont propres* (Paris, 1752); and J.L. Lecointe, *La science des postes militaires, ou traité de fortifications de campagne* (Paris, 1759).
6. After the first French edition in 1756, the book was translated into German in 1758 and into Spanish in 1780, whilst it appeared in both languages in a variety of different editions.
7. Published in Valencia, the book was translated by Captain Víctor Caballero, who added to it many personal observations on the use of light troops in war: cf. M. García Hurtado, *Traduciendo la guerra: influencias extranjeras y recepción de las obras militares francesas en la España del siglo XVIII* (La Coruña, 1999), pp. 103–4. For a general discussion of the assimilation of French military thought in Spain, cf. V. Scotti-Douglas, 'La guerra "alla francese" nel XVIII secolo e la sua fortuna in Spagna', *Spagna Contemporanea*, no. 17 (Spring, 2000), pp. 161–3.
8. Further information about the history and evolution of the term 'partisan' may be found in the article cited in n. 1.
9. Cf. J. Gómez de Arteche, *Guerra de la Independencia: historia militar de España de 1808 a 1814* (Madrid, 1866–1903), II, pp. 692–6.

10. Anon. *Apuntes de la vida y hechos militares del Brigadier Don Juan Martín Díez El Empecinado por un admirador de ellos* (Madrid, 1814), p. 6.
11. As in N. Rivas Santiago (ed.), *El alcalde de Otívar, héroe en la Guerra de la Independencia* (Madrid, 1940), pp. 28, 30. *Partida de guerrilla* in the sense of light infantry detachment may be found in F. Casamayor, *Diario de los sitios de Zaragoza*, H. Lafoz Rabaza (ed.) (Zaragoza, 2000), pp. 49, 65.
12. The first known use of the term in English comes in a letter written by the then Sir Arthur Wellesley in the summer of 1809.
13. G. García de la Cuesta to Junta of León, 29 May 1808, Archivo Histórico Nacional, Sección de Estado (hereafter A.H.N., Estado) 68-D, no. 167.
14. Proclamation of the Junta of Seville, 6 June 1808, Instituto de Historia y Cultura Militar (Madrid), Colección Documental del Fraile (hereafter IHCM. CDF. DCCCLXIV, p. 50.
15. Cf., for instance, the dramatic description of popular wrath given by José María Blanco y Crespo – better known as Blanco White – in his *Letters from Spain* (London, 1822), p. 431: "' We wish, Sir, to kill somebody," said the spokesman of the insurgents. "Someone has been killed at Trujillo; one or two others at Badajoz, another at Merida, and we will not be behind our neighbours. Sir, we will kill a traitor."
16. Proclamation of the Junta Central, 26 October 1808, A. Dérozier, *Manuel Josef Quintana et la naissance du libéralisme en Espagne* (Paris, 1970), II, pp. 165–74.
17. *Ibid.*, p. 167.
18. For a recent version of the text of this document, cf. F. Díaz Plaja, *La historia de España en sus documentos: el siglo XIX* (Madrid, 1954), pp. 73–6.
19. Lit. 'La España abunda en sugetos dotados de un valor extraordinario, que aprovechandose de las grandes ventajas que les proporciona el conocimiento del pais, y el odio implacable de toda la nacion contra el tirano que intenta subyugarla por los medios mas iniquos, son capaces de introducir el terror y la consternacion en sus ejércitos. Para facilitarles el modo de conseguir tan noble objeto, y proporcionarles los medios de enriquecerse honrosamente con el botin del enemigo, é inmortalizar sus nombres con hechos heroicos dignos de eterna fama, se ha dignado S.M. crear una milicia de nueva especie, con las denominaciones de partidas, y quadrillas.'
20. Lit. 'Atendiendo á que muchos sugetos de distinguido valor é intrepidez, por falta de un objeto en que desplegar dignamente los talentos militares . . . se han dedicado al contrabando . . . á fin de proporcionarles la carrera gloriosa y utilisima al Estado que les presentan las circunstancias actuales, se les indultará para emplearlos en otra especie de partidas que se denominarán cuadrillas.' The term *cuadrilla* was most probably employed on account of its association with the ancient organization of the Santa Hermandad, though it had also been employed as a military term for a subdivision of a larger unit since the fifteenth century.
21. Lit. 'se le tomarán y pagarán á un precio en que encuentre moderada ganancia'.
22. Lit. 'Todos los que bajo las expresadas reglas deseen alistarse y formar estas cuadrillas, se presentarán desde luego a la junta provincial de su respéctivo distrito, ó al Capitán General de la provincia: y aún al general en jefe del ejército de campaña que se halle en ella, para su admisión, destino, y servicio. Y verificada la formación de cada partida y cuadrilla, se les mandará por los intendentes respéctivos abonar los sueldos que quedan señalados, precedida la

correspondiente revista de Comisario, y en defecto, de la Justicia mensualmente, con arreglo a ordenanza.'

23. For the text of the *Instrucción* and a variety of documents associated with it, cf. A.H.N. Estado, 51-A, nos. 3–6.

24. V. Alcalá Galiano to M. de Garay, 10 April, 1809. Lit. 'O me engaña mucho mi juicio, o este pensamiento ha de hacer impresion en el animo del Emperador, y ha de producir miedo y aun terror a los soldados franceses, luego que llegue à su noticia. Esta nacion dá siempre mucho valor y aprecio a todo lo nuevo, no medira con serenidad y sosiego sobre las cosas, y se figurarà inmediatamente llenos los campos de España de corsarios que los robarán y asesinarán al menor descuido.'

25. *Shorter Oxford English Dictionary* (Oxford, 1956), II, p. 1587.

26. 'Instrucción para el Corso Terrestre contra los Ejércitos Franceses', A.H.N. Estado, 51-A, no. 6. Lit.'Todos los habitantes de las provincias ocupadas por las tropas francesas que se hallen en estado de armarse están autorizados para hacerlo, hasta con armas prohibidas, para asaltar y despojar, siempre que hallen coyuntura favorable en particular y en común, a los soldados franceses, apoderarse de los viveres y efectos que se destinan á su subsistencia, y en suma para hacerles todo el mal y daño que sea posible en el concepto de que se considerará este servicio como hecho a la nación, y será recompensado á proporcion de su entidad y consecüencias.'

27. *Ibid.* Lit. 'Habiendo conseguido Napoleon por las artes mas bajas y viles destruir y desorganizar la fuerza militar de España, apoderarse de sus principales fortalezas, y cautivar á su Rey, ¿no es bien claro que es preciso que sean paisanos los que se reunan ahora para combatir sus huestes?'.

28. Javier Mina, 1789–1817, began waging guerrilla warfare in Navarra in the summer of 1809, and very rapidly became the most famous and feared guerrilla leader in the region. Captured fortuitously in March 1810 and taken to France, he regained his liberty in April 1814. In 1816 he went to Mexico to aid the local insurgents in their fight for freedom and independence, but was captured and shot in November of the following year. For a recent biography, cf. M. Ortuño Martínez, *Xavier Mina: guerrillero, liberal, insurgente* (Pamplona, 2000).

29. For a discussion of these schemes, cf. P. Pascual, *Curas y frailes guerrilleras en la Guerra de la Independencia* (Zaragoza, 1999), pp. 71–81.

30. 'Reglamento según el que podrán erigirse las Cruzadas, si S.M. lo tuviese a bien', 30 December 1809, A.H.N. Estado, leg. 41-A, no. 5^2.

31. The bibliography on Cura Merino is neither very rich, nor of sure historiographical value. The two most recent works, however, are E. de Ontañón, *El Cura Merino, su vida en folletín* (Madrid, 1933), and J.M. Codón, *Biografía y Crónica del Cura Merino* (Burgos, 1986).

32. The text of General Lacy's *Reglamento* may be found in J.M. García-Rodríguez, *Guerra de la Independencia: ensayo histórico-político de una epopeya española* (Barcelona, Caralt, 1945), II, pp. 292–3.

33. For the background to this force, cf. J. Fàbregas Roig, *La Guerra Gran, 1793–1795: el protagonisme de Girona i la mobilització dels Miquelets* (Lérida, 2000), and J. Fàbregas Roig, *Catalunya i la Guerra Gran: l'aportació dels corregiments meridionals* (Tarragona, 2000). As yet, however, the period 1808–14 is still awaiting its monograph.

34. García-Rodríguez, *Guerra de la Independencia*, II, p. 293. Lit. 'Uno de los principales objetos de las partidas será la persecución y captura de desertores, ladrones y mal entretenidos, que deberán conducir al comandante de la división de tropas más cercanas.'
35. *Reglamento para la partidas de guerrilla*, 11 July 1812, ICHM. Depósito de la Guerra, 1812/4; for the decree of 1814, cf. *Decretos del Rey Don Fernando VII* (Madrid, 1818–46), I, pp. 96–9.
36. Further remarks on the propaganda war may be found in V. Scotti-Douglas, 'Las "comisiones reservadas" de los confidentes de la Junta Central Suprema Gubernativa', in J.A. Armillas (ed.), *La Guerra de la Independencia: Estudios* (Zaragoza, 2001), I, pp. 165–90.
37. Lit. 'Cuando aprehendan a malos españoles, fuera de población, cuanto dinero, alhajas, ropas y efectos les encuentren será absolutamente suyo; pero deberá preceder una exacta justificación de ser malos.'
38. Lit. 'que servirán de recomendación a los comandantes, siempre que por separado no haya quejas fundadas de las mismas justicias que obren contra él'.
39. They are, in chronological order, *Reglamento para la reducción y reforma de las Juntas provinciales*, 1 January, 1809; a decree dated 28 February 1809 confirming a proclamation by the Junta Provincial de Valencia; a manifesto addressed by the Junta Central to the French high command in defence of the guerrillas; and a preliminary draft of the decree of July 1812.
40. E.g. N. Mahy to Ayuntamiento of Potes, 24 September 1810, IHCM, Colección Duque de Bailén (hereafter IHCM. CDB), 11/15/1.
41. Cf., for instance, 'Exposición al Congreso Nacional del Estado Militar por Don Luis de Landáburu y Villanueva, Ayudante de Estado Mayor', 19 July 1811, IHCM. 30/41/81.
42. For an interesting discussion of this debate, cf. J.R. Aymes, 'La guérrilla dans la lutte espagnole pour l'indépendance (1808–1814): amorce d'une théorie et avatars d'une pratique', in *Bulletin Hispanique*, LXVIII, nos. 3–4 (July–December 1976), pp. 337–8.
43. *Ordenanza que se ha de observar en el Principado de Asturias por todos los Comandantes de Partidas Sueltas*, 29 May 1810, IHCM. CDB. 19/23/81.
44. *Proclama de los Comandantes de Partidas de Patriotas de Castilla la Vieja*, 15 March 1811, IHCM. CDB. 26/36/34.
45. Petition of M. de Valenza and C. Ametria, 18 October 1809, AHN. Estado, 41-D, no. 78. Lit. 'que sin pertenecer á Exercito alguno, entran y obran en el sin mas título que el de una Junta de Arnedo, que se halla bajo las ordenes de la de Molina de Aragón'.
46. N. Mahy to F. Castañ n, 3 October 1810, IHCM. CDB. 13/17/29. Lit. 'La Junta Superior del Reino de León se me queja del porte devastador que observan las partidas de guerrilla que se dicen dependientes de V.S. Estoy seguro de que V.S. no es capaz de subscribir á semejantes procedimientos, como lo estoy tambien de que el relato que se me ha hecho es puntual, y de consiguiente es de toda necesidad que V.S. convoque a los que sean tenidos por jefes y se les haga entender que se harán indignos del nombre de patríotas sino mudan su conducta con sus arruinados conciudadanos, y que sera castigado con arreglo á las reales instrucciones cualquiera agresor contra la seguridad y protección que debe concederse al país con objeto principal de la fuerza armada contra el enemigo que aspira á la ruina de nuestra amada patria.'

47. E.g. 'Causa criminal formada por el Sr. Don Gorgonio Maximiano Ortiz de Córdoba, Comandante de Cruzada y individuo de la Real Junta de Soto, 8 November 1809, AHN. Estado, 41-E, no. 98.
48. Petition of P.J. del Canto and B. Bonifaz, 4 December 1809, AHN. 41-E, no. 127. Lit. 'Cinco juntas entre si inmediatas, se obserban en aquella provincia: la de Soto de Cameros, la del Marques de Barriolucio en Navarra, la de Arnedo, la de Menciso y la de Covaleda. Cada una obra en los pueblos que la reconocen: son continuas las Competencias que se suscitan entre ellas, y esto produce desde luego por primer fruto y consecuencia inmediata el entorpecimiento y disgusto que se dejan entender con gravísimo perjuicio del interés de toda la provincia y aún de la nación entera: este mal trasciende á las partidas de guerrilla y es lástima y sumamente doloroso que los importantes servicios que ellas han estado haciendo y deben esperarse cada vez mayores de este sistema tan conocidamente útil á la Patria cuanto perjudicial a los franceses, se haya obscurecido o debilitado alguna vez con los encuentros y disensiones que han tenido entre si hasta desarmar la mas fuerte á la que no lo era tanto.'
49. Junta of Nájera to Junta Central, 30 November 1809, AHN. Estado, 41-E, no. 124. Lit. 'La causa principal de todo es sin duda, Señor, el no reconocer todas estas tropas un centro de autoridad, apoyado con la fuerza correspond iente. Todos quieren ser jefes independientes, todos disponen como soberanos de los efectos de la nación, y aún lo que es mas de los pueblos y particulares valiendose frecuentemente del infame título de traidores para saciar su codicia a costa del honor y subsistencia de muchos miserables, que con un transtorno inaúdito, se ven saqueados, y privados de todo, antes de ser oidos y juzgados.'
50. J.A. Colmenares to P. de Rivero, 23 November 1809, AHN. 41-E, no. 122. Lit 'Habiendo enviado yo al Reino de Navarra en consecuencia de la Real Orden de 11 de agosto, que me autorizó para ello, â D. Juan Garcés de los Fayos, que por el Ministerio de Guerra aspira á que se le declare el grado de brigadier ..., iba este hombre a empezar en Viana su comisión y en dicha ciudad lo ha prendido un comandante de guerrilla de aquel reino llamado D. Francisco [*sic*] Mina, quitandole los titulos de su comisión, papeles y equipajes.'
51. Cf. J.L. Tone, *The Fatal Knot: the Guerrilla War in Navarre and the Defeat of Napoleon in Spain* (Chapel Hill, 1994), p. 94.
52. For a detailed description of this conflict, cf. A. Cassinello Pérez, *Juan Martín, 'El Empecinado', o el amor a la libertad* (Madrid, 1995), pp. 109–70.
53. Cf. *Representación que la Junta Superior de Guadalajara ha dirigido a S.A.S. el Supremo Consejo de Regencia contra el Brigadier Don Juan Martín el Empecinado*, 11 April 1811, AHN. Estado, 3010. Lit. 'Esta corta división, adscrita a la defensa de la provincia que la mantiene, arma, viste y paga, no siempre ha operado dentro de ella ... sin que su conducta franca y generosa haya tenido su retribución, pues sean cuales fueran los apuros en que se han visto, nunca ha sido sostenida por los varios cuerpos de las provincias inmediatas.'
54. J. Martín to Consejo de Regencia, 22 July 1811, AHN. Estado 3146, Lit. 'derrama el espíritu del provincialismo, tan contrario a los buenos principios, como reprobado por las cláusulas de los sabios y experiencia de resultados desastrosos, pudiendo contribuir esta máxima a que los ánimos de los soldados

miren con indiferencia, y acaso con desprecio las desgracias de otras provincias, y se hagan sordos a la voz de un general, que sabia y oportunamente les llama a otra parte.'

55. For the details of the Council of Regency's ruling, cf. Concejo de Regencia to Estado Mayor del Segundo Ejército, 7 April 1811, ICHM. CDB. 36/40/78.

8

The Pen and the Sword: Political Catechisms and Resistance to Napoleon

Emilie Delivré

Research on the important topic of the impact of Napoleon outside France is expanding, but not yet fully developed. In particular, our knowledge regarding the influence of resistance to Napoleon in Europe as a whole is still rather limited. For example, what factors could explain the diversity of European national reactions to the Napoleonic imperium? Does the answer lie in differences between the strategies that were adopted by the nations of Europe, or differences in the projects of Napoleon himself? Or is does it lie in pre-existing and deeply-rooted differences between the various national histories of Europe? And, if this last is the case, what importance should be attributed to such factors as revolution (or its absence), the Enlightenment, the dominant religious confession and national unity (or, again, its absence)? Can we expect to find a similar reaction to Napoleon in the cases of Germany, which was divided in terms of both politics and religion, Italy, which was divided in terms of politics but united in terms of religion, and Spain, which was united in terms of politics and religion alike?

In order to advance a tentative answer to these questions, this chapter focuses on a specific aspect of the reaction to Napoleonic rule in the form of the political catechism. Political catechisms appeared in various countries, and most of them both encouraged and expressed resistance to the emperor. They are extremely significant because they form part of an attempt to build national strategies: short texts that essentially consisted of questions and answers, they point to the desire of the élite to reach the people by means that were likely to be both familiar and accessible to them. By focusing on this aspect of resistance, this chapter will try to show the possible relevance of political catechisms as literary sources for a historical interpretation of the Napoleonic Wars.

The analysis of catechism as a genre is relevant for two reasons. Firstly, although the origins of the phenomenon are religious, in most European countries it gradually developed a more political form. At the same time, by the beginning of the nineteenth century catechism had become so widespread as a means of expression that it may be said to have become a pan-European phenomenon. Secondly, despite their rigid form and religious origins, political catechisms vary greatly. They embodied and communicated the ideals of opposing political parties, and they played a variety of different (albeit usually quite important) roles in the great upheavals of the period under investigation. And, thirdly, political catechism was thus a form of expression which both reflected the nuances of, and was adapted to the cultural reality of, diverse European entities. Studying this genre during the Napoleonic Wars is therefore a valuable lens for the investigation of different nations' modes of expressing their origins, their religion, and their hatred for their enemies.

Meanwhile, by studying political catechism on a European scale, and by cross-referencing such texts from different countries, we should be able to pose interesting questions that go beyond the fundamental question of identity. For example, given that the period under investigation is characterized by a growing desire on behalf of the élite to educate the common people, should catechisms be understood as a means of education rather than a tool of persuasion? And, if they were indeed means of education, what criteria were employed to decide on the limits that were to be placed on giving the uneducated masses access to knowledge? Other interesting questions relate to the image of the enemy. We should ask not only how the enemy is portrayed – often 'manicheistically' and as a caricature – but also how that image affects personal and collective memories. What became of distinctive national characteristics, given that catechisms were often legitimated by a religious origin that was held to be universal and timeless? Next we should enquire as to the identity of these texts? Were they part of the official apparatus of state propaganda? Were they journalists, or priests, or independent, and even marginal authors? What, too, of the question of readership? Were the texts widely circulated amongst thousands of commoners who were ready, in theory at least, for partisan war, or were they never really known outside a very limited group of intellectuals? And, finally, was the art of political catechism born in the context of a specific ideology and a specific enemy, and thereby condemned to remain a phenomenon of one specific moment in time, or was it rather a device of wider origins and applications that was in consequence promised a greater future?

In what follows, we shall first briefly review the literature on political catechism, discuss the history of this phenomenon and define the texts that are available for study in so far as the Napoleonic period is concerned. Moving on, we shall then examine the specific case of German political catechisms dating from the Napoleonic Wars in order to present and analyse the content of a sub-group of these writings that are particularly important and quite distinct, but have until now remained relatively unknown. And, last but not least, we shall towards the end examine the *raison dê tre* of political catechism during the Napoleonic Wars, and its relation with the concept of resistance. What, though, of the literature? Unfortunately, there is no historical research that deals with the overall question of political catechism. Nevertheless, there are a number of interesting articles that deal with the subject in the context of specific countries and specific periods. Most of these concern the French and Italian catechisms dating from the 1790s, but some works may also be found concerning the Spanish 'war of independence'.[1] In the Spanish context, one might also cite the comprehensive work of Manuel Morales Muñoz although this deals with the whole of the Spanish nineteenth century.[2] Beyond these monographs and articles, there is a limited body of comparative or semi-comparative works on the phenomenon of political catechisms whose chief protagonists are the Frenchman, Jean-René Aymes, the Italian, Luciano Guerci, the Mexican, Tancke de Estrada and the German, Michel (whose contribution is short but particularly engaging and influential).[3] In consequence, then, it is much to be hoped that this chapter will form a significant addition to the existing literature, and all the more so as it will bring in the German case, which has hitherto not been discussed in any great detail, and thereby develop a more generalizable interpretation of political catechism.

Initially little more than mere syntheses of prayers, catechisms first became prominent in the sixteenth century. This can be attributed to a number of reasons, including, not least, the use made of catechism by Reformation and Counter-Reformation in the sixteenth century. First, the term 'catechism' was redefined to dramatic effect by Martin Luther whose pioneering works – the so-called 'little' and 'big' catechisms – helped form the identity of the territorial protestant churches in the Holy Roman Empire. And then, in the wake of the Council of Trent, Catholicism, too, began to generate new catechisms. Nor is this surprising: due to their reliance on short question-and-answer couplets, catechisms allowed the reader to memorize simple versions of fundamental concepts very quickly. At the same time, because of their format, catechisms could be produced in the form of little books that were ideal for children or those unused to handling heavy tomes. Once established in the literary canon, meanwhile, catechisms proved too useful to be allowed to fade into the background and were instead made use of by successive generations and adapted to their own purposes. Thus, during the eighteenth century, in particular, catechisms began to be made use of for purposes other than religious ones. In both Protestant and Catholic countries (though more so in the former, thanks to the influence of Luther), for example, they increasingly became a means of practical instruction – a kind of taught course in practical ethics. Authors made use of examples drawn from religion – one of the few common denominators of society – to reach a non-sophisticated public.[4] Meanwhile, in Protestant countries, much more than in Catholic ones, catechism soon became a method to teach any matter, from agriculture to the art of midwives (during the eighteenth century, one finds numerous such textbooks). And at the same time catechism also acquired a political dimension. First of all, we see the philosophers of the French Enlightenment making use of catechisms in an attempt to popularize their rationalism and modern science. Given that they believed that they were preaching a message that was comparable in its dimensions with that of Christianity, such a move was all too logical, and all the more so as some of the more bitterly anti-clerical *philosophes* realised that the use of traditional Christian forms offered more means by which they could satirize and discredit the Catholic Church: hence the frequent appearance of catechisms in the work of Voltaire.[5] And, as with the Enlightenment, so with the Revolution, the leaders of the new France attempting to use catechisms to spread the ideas of liberty, equality and fraternity. In this sense, despite the new social and political elements, catechisms remained unchanged in that they usually aspired to timelessness and universality. However, as we shall see, from now on that aspiration was to become decreasingly frequent and all the more so given the new genre of political catechism that now began to appear in Europe.

Again, the new trend seems to have originated from France (note a few exceptions, such as seventeenth-century England, where one finds many political catechisms). As witness the work of Jean Hébrard, the Revolution saw the publication of numerous revolutionary catechisms at the hands of Mirabeau and other writers, all of which were designed to educate 'the people' with regard to their new rights and the means that had been adopted to protect them.[6] However, it is important to note that the phenomenon was not limited to France. In Italy, too, a wave of republican catechisms appeared, which Luciano Guerci has studied in 'Les catéchismes républicains en Italie, 1796–1799'.[7] And one isolated example may even be found in Germany where a revolutionary sympathizer named Hofman published a similar tract entitled *Aristokratenkatechismus*.[8] Of different national origins to their French predecessors, they yet mirrored them most strikingly, these catechisms once again being marked by their desire to cement the loyalty of populace to the new constitutions that they had been given. As time went on, however, so the Italian 'Jacobins' who had initially welcomed the French were in some instances alienated by what they perceived as Napoleon's betrayal of the ideals of the Revolution. In consequence, the Italian catechism split as a political phenomenon: whilst some remained slavishly loyal to France, others were at least implicitly anti-Napoleonic whilst yet remaining heavily influenced by French models and political ideas.

Thus far, then, we are talking about a phenomenon that was clearly directed against the *ancien regime* (in this respect it should be noted that the Italian Jacobins who opposed Napoleon can clearly still be regarded as revolutionaries). However, catechism could also be made use in a context that was clearly counter-revolutionary or, at least, anti-French. This was first revealed south of the Pyrenees. Thrown into confusion by the *motín de Aranjuez*, the ambuscade of Bayonne and the Dos de Mayo, Spain rose in revolt against Napoleon in 1808, and no sooner had she done so than a series of catechisms appeared that mirrored the pre-occupations of the period. Clearly visible, then, are anger against Napoleon, Murat and Godoy; calls to take up arms and engage in guerrilla warfare; veneration of Ferdinand VII; loyalty to the church; and the depiction of an idealized nation. Still notorious today, these catechisms have been discussed by many different works. As examples we might mention, Jean-René Aymes' article, 'Du catéchisme religieux au catéchisme politique';[9] Alfonso Capitán Díaz's *Catecismos políticos en España, 1808–1822*[10] and 'Catecismos políticos en los inicios del siglo XIX español'.[11] Note also the article by José Mñ oz Pérez entitled 'Los catecismos políticos: de la ilustración al primer liberalismo español',[12] and finally Manuel Morales Mñ oz's 'Las enseñanzas de la virtud : reglas civico-morales en los catecismos del siglo XIX, Catecismos y la instrucción popular en la España del siglo XIX', and the fundamental *Catecismos en la España del siglo XIX*.[13] As an example of the sort of work commented on by these authors, meanwhile, we might cite the passionate *Catecismo civil y breve compendio de las obligaciones del español, conocimiento (práctico) de su libertad, y explicación de su enemigo, muy útil en las actuales circunstancias para la enseñanza de los niños ambos sexos, puesto en forma de diálogo*, the Junta

Central's own *Catecismo civil de España en preguntas y respuestas*, and, finally, the overtly clerical *Catecismo católico-político, que con motivo de las actuales novedades de la España, dirige y dedica a sus conciudadanos un sacerdote amante de la Religión, afecto a su patria y amigo de los hombres de 1808*, all of which date from the year 1808.[14]

These texts were all written to galvanize Spanish opinion, of course, but they also had a considerable impact on Germany. Thus, the blend of religious and civil ideas which they represented fell on fertile soil east of the Rhine. Thus, surrounded by large numbers of French troops as they were, many German intellectuals had been inspired by the Spanish example to call for a German insurrection against Napoleon. As such, they could not but be enthused by the manner in which the Spanish texts described the duties of the citizen *vis à vis* the nation and called him to take up arms against invasion. Along with proclamations calling for a German uprising, then, translated versions of the Spanish catechisms began to appear in print. For example, Joseph von Hormayr collected a few Spanish texts, some of which were catechisms, and had them translated and published in Vienna in the journal *Germanien*. Entitled the *Sammlung der Aktenstücke über die spanische Thronveränderung*, these were read by the poet Heinrich von Kleist. Particularly influenced by the *catecismo civil* mentioned above, in 1809 Kleist wrote his own *Katechismus der Deutschen, abgefasst nach dem Spanischen, zum Gebrauch für Kinder und Alte*. Intended, as the title suggests, for both children and adults, Kleist's work respected the standard question-and-answer form and consisted of a fictitious dialogue between a father and his young son, the latter answering the questions of the former. The dialogue was divided into seventeen chapters (the end of the tenth, the beginning of the eleventh and the whole of the twelfth chapters have been lost). Written towards the end of April and the beginning of May 1809 in Dresden, this particular catechism was never published during the life of its author. The reason for this was quite simple. Kleist's language was violent in the extreme – so much so, in fact, that when it appeared in 1862, even the notorious 'ultra', Heinrich von Treitschke, professed to be shocked by its tone – and there was simply no chance that such a document could have been permitted to circulate in the Germany of 1809. Thus, the 'Catechism of the Germans' glorified the notion of fatherland's love, celebrated German identity and national unity, demonized Napoleon and called on the author's fellow Germans to take up arms against the French, Von Kleist having been much impressed by the example of the Spanish guerrillas. What Von Kleist hoped, indeed, was to encourage the Germans who 'collaborated' with Napoleon to choose instead the cause of action and fight alongside the rest of the nation for the return of the Holy Roman Empire. And, when he saw that no such crusade was forthcoming – even the 'War of Liberation of 1813' was not the affair of the people of patriotic German legend – he slid into a depression that, complicated by serious personal problems, led him to commit suicide in 1814, and thereby to miss out on the fall of his great enemy, Napoleon.[15]

Nor was Kleist alone, his fellow patriot, Ernst Moritz Arndt, writing two further anti-Napoleonic catechisms.[16] These emerged in the context of the War of 1812. Having fled to Russia and taken service with Tsar Alexander I, the erstwhile leader of the Prussian reform movement, Freiherr vom Stein, decided to launch an attack on Napoleon's rear. The obvious theatre of operations for this strategy was Germany, this being the emperor's chief base for the attack on Russia, but Stein was not just motivated by military considerations: a convinced German nationalist, he also hoped to liberate the German states for their own sake and awaken the peoples of Germany to a sense of their identity. To this end, Stein sent for Ernst Moritz Arndt, a nationalist writer who was already very popular in literary circles. Obligingly, Arndt went to Russia, where he stayed for more than eighteen months as Stein's secretary, whilst in the process boosting his reputation as a writer to fresh heights (in Russia, of course, he was free of Napoleon's censors and possessed of resources and channels of distribution that far surpassed anything he had enjoyed in Germany). And, amongst many other things, Arndt published two catechisms. First to appear was the *Kurzer Katechismus für deutsche Soldaten* [Short catechism for German soldiers] which was published anonymously in Saint Petersburg at the end of October 1812. It was composed of fifteen chapters of equal length and was designed to be the bible of the so-called 'Russo-German Legion', which was a force created in Russia in the wake of the French invasion on the basis of German deserters and prisoners of war who could be induced to fight Napoleon (it should be noted that less than half the *grande armée* of 1812 was even notionally French). Conceived as a protypical army of the Geman nation – as, indeed, a precursor of the people's army that Von Kleist, Arndt and their fellows dreamed of as one day liberating Germany from the French yoke – it was supposed to be the bearer of 'national hope', and was originally officered by a number of Prussian officers who had refused to cooperate with the alliance between the German states, including, not least, Prussia, and Napoleon, and had in consequence emigrated to Russia.

The *Kurzer Katechismus* disappeared for a century and was rediscovered in 1905 by the historian, Max Lehmann. Nor is this long period of oblivion surprising. On the one hand, the Russo-German Legion proved a most disappointing failure. Recruited from men driven not by nationalist fervour but the desire to escape Russian imprisonment, it never became the nucleus of a new German army, nor, still less, a German people's war, and was eventually absorbed into the Prussian forces as an ordinary infantry regiment, and one, moreover, that – strange symbol of national unity! – was arrayed not in Prussian dark blue but in Russian green. On the other, as in the case of Kleist's efforts, there were practical difficulties that stood in the way of the Kurzer Katechismus becoming anything other than a piece of ephemera. Thus, Arndt's original catechism was anti-absolutist and promoted the same reformist ideas about the army as those of the Prussian reformers, such as Clausewitz, Scharnhorst or Gneisenau. In particular, Arndt proposed norms for German soldiers that moved away from the traditional scheme of an army dominated by the nobility. Still worse, by advocating a national army, Arndt parted with centuries of feudalism, whilst, like Kleist, he strongly criticized those German princes who had entered into alliances with Napoleon. In so far as those German soldiers who continued to fight in the ranks of the *grande armée* were concerned, the message was clear, what Arndt advocated being a mass rejection of military discipline and traditional loyalty. But even this was not an end to it: even if they came out against Napoleon, the German princes were still potentially anti-patriotic. Thus, as a nationalist, Arndt rejected dynasty-related notions of legitimacy and proclaimed the absolute supremacy of the nation: what was divine was not the prince, but the Fatherland. Hence, of course, the document's *de facto* suppression after 1814, Arndt's message being completely unacceptable in the context of the Germany created by the Congress of Vienna.

With Arndt convinced that the German nation should be united and not divided by the princes, the *Kurzer Katechismus* posed plenty of problems even before 1814. Thus, calling for desertion, mutiny and a German insurrection was all very well whilst the princes continued to support Napoleon as it was a good means of persuading them to think of changing sides, but once they had started to come over to the Allies then Arndt's rhetoric became redundant and even dangerous. New print-runs of his catechism were therefore blocked, and he was formally invited to show more respect towards royalty. Left with little choice in the matter, Arndt therefore decided to rephrase and reformulate his catechism under the name of *Katechismus für den deustchen Kriegs- und Wehrmann, worin gelehrt wird, wie ein christlicher Wehrmann sein und mit Gott in den Streit gehen soll* [Catechism for the German soldier, in which it is taught how Christian soldiers should behave and fight, with the help of God].

This second catechism appeared in August 1813 in Silesia. The fierce reaction of the authorities to the first version was due to the content of the first seven chapters, these being the parts in which Arndt invited the soldiers to disobey the orders of their 'traitor' princes, and condemned the officers who refused to believe in a united Germany. In consequence, Arndt had to eliminate those parts. This self-imposed silence, however, was less unbearable than it would have been before: in March 1813 Prussia had joined the war against Napoleon with an army reorganized along the lines advocated by the reformers, whilst it was possible to believe that an unstoppable national revolt had begun; in consequence, the necessity for extreme nationalist rhetoric was not as pressing as before. Thus, in the new catechism, the language used by Arndt was much more composed and restrained. In place of the 'dissident' sections mentioned above, there now appeared a long historical prologue and several new chapters, all this material being much more politically neutral than before, whilst even those chapters that were retained from the original version were heavily edited. As for the catechism, it now became less of a text for German soldiers than a text for soldiers in general, and, for that matter, less an exposition of a patriotic ethic than an exposition of a Christian one. Indeed, in line with the tradition of the north German states of Prussia and Mecklenburg – then the only German states fighting for the Allies – Lutheran influences became much more evident, especially in the annex, which was composed of patriotic songs that were mostly based on religious melodies. Not surprisingly, then, this second catechism met with more approval, and, by extension, success. So acceptable was it to the German princes, indeed, that when Napoleon returned to France in 1815 a third version appeared that was slightly different from its predecessor of 1813 but possessed of the same title.

Finally, to return to the case of Spain, by the time that Arndt was penning his soldiers' texts, the wheel had come full circle. In France and, later, Italy, the period from 1789 to 1799 had seen catechisms used to promote the cause of revolution. Thereafter in Spain, Austria and Germany they had been used as the cause of counter-revolution or, at least, resistance to France. In the German case this had at least potentially threatened political upheaval, but in Spain we are now presented with a mirror image of the situation in France in the years of the Revolution. Thus, in 1810 the Spanish uprising against Napoleon had become something very different. Seizing the opportunity afforded them by the convocation of a national assembly in Cádiz, a progressive faction known as the 'liberals' had seized power and forced through the famous constitution of 1812. To defend and enshrine their new creation, they found no better means than the catechism, and thus it is that the period 1812–14 saw the publication of many *catecismos* expounding the work of the *cortes* of Cádiz.

   Political catechisms, then, appeared in large numbers in Revolutionary and Napoleonic Europe, but they did so in the context of different societies, different cultures and different political situations, and therefore assumed many different forms. As a genre, indeed, they can be highly contradictory. But in so far as the subject of resistance to Napoleón is concerned, this is all to the good as it enriches our understanding of the subject and provides us with an alternative approach to its study. Above all, it helps us to understand that, to the extent that there was a European anti-Napoleonic rebellion at all, one should not overlook its diversity. Not only did insurgent movements take very different forms, but they were also expressed in different ways, and, significantly, appeared for quite different reasons. For example, in Italy anti-Napoleonic catechisms appeared on the surface to accept the canons of Napoleonic rule – there does not, in fact, seem to have been a single case that was directly critical of the emperor – and rather expressed their resistance by continuing to evince support for the principles of 1789, whereas in Germany the opposition's catechisms were both anti-Napoleonic and anti-French. Meanwhile, intranational differences are also quite telling. For example, the Spanish constitutional catechisms of 1812 were the products of a violent resistance movement against Napoleon, but they were as much concerned with building a new Spain as with fighting the emperor and are in fact only rarely explicitly directed against him, whereas their forebears of 1808–1809 essentially look to the defence of an old Spain and fill their pages with his demonization. And, last but not least, it is clear that the resistance espoused in the catechisms was by no means necessarily the same as the resistance espoused by the established order: in Germany, as we have seen, Von Kleist never secured official sponsorship at all, whilst Arndt was only able to retain it by dint of bending quite dramatically to the pressure placed on him by his political superiors; meanwhile, in Austria if Hormayr was permitted in 1809 to publish German translations of Spanish catechisms that could be read in the German context as putting duty to the nation before duty to the sovereign, it was only because the new war that was impending with France gave Vienna a strong interest in destabilizing such French satellites as Baden and Bavaria.

   To return to the question of the catechisms themselves, however, the German case in particular invites a series of additional questions. In those other areas of Europe where these publications appeared, they were as we have seen, fairly numerous. In the case of Spain, for example, Manuel Morales Muñoz has shown that one quarter of the eighty Spanish political catechisms written in the nineteenth century belonged to the years 1808–1814.[17] In Italy and France, too, there is a similar accumulation of such texts. Yet in so far as Germany is concerned, the vast majority of the political catechisms that appeared in the nineteenth century appeared in the context of the revolution of 1848, rather than the Napoleonic period. Indeed, throughout the period 1799–1815 the only catechisms to be found are the three mentioned above, whilst the example offered by the earlier tract of 1793 is even more isolated. We are, then, immediately faced by the task of trying to decide on the reasons for this great difference. On top of that, meanwhile, there is the issue of the link between levels of resistance and the publication of political catechisms though it is obvious that in this last respect a direct causal relationship between the one and the other should immediately be set aside (in the 'War of Liberation' of 1813–14, it seems certain that a far higher proportion of the German population was conscripted, or otherwise induced, to take up arms than was ever the case in the Peninsular War). In the rest of this chapter, we shall examine these issues, and in the process open up the debate to some additional questions, on the basis of some initial findings of a much broader research project on political catechisms.

As a general rule, in terms of their form the political catechisms that we have examined are not very different from one another. Thus, they all propagate a corpus of ideas, whilst at the same time explaining their meaning; they all enjoin action (if only intellectual); and they all employ dialogue to get over their message. Their content, of course, is another matter – to repeat the obvious, some catechisms are clearly reactionary, while others, inspired by enlightened and/or liberal doctrines, endeavour to transmit to the less educated masses new concepts and definitions – but the French or Spanish catechism was not distinct enough from the German catechism to suggest that we shall find the answer to the questions that we have posed in this sort of area. In so far as Germany is concerned, then, the following questions arise. Does the low number of German catechisms during the Napoleonic wars signify less political effervescence and lower levels of resistance than in Spain or Italy, or is it rather the fruit of a less religious society in which religious catechisms had ceased to have much relevance? Is it simply that German society was less open to the traditional form of question and answer? And what do we mean by Germany? Can we also find variations between different German states (the result, for example, of different confessional influences, or different degrees of Napoleonic influence)? And, lastly, could it be that, in divided Germany, the phenomenon of political catechism was unlikely to acquire much prominence simply because the very concept of a single catechism seemed to presuppose national unity?

None of these alternative hypotheses seems totally satisfying, however. There seems to be no general theory that is both valid for most cases and capable of explaining the presence (or absence) of political catechism and the differences in its nature. Yet one or two general points do stand out. Thus, the emergence of specific forms of catechisms (progressive or reactionary) may be said to depend, first, on the specific relationship between religion and politics in a particular country, and, second, the extent to which that relationship was affected by the experience of the Napoleonic Wars. Variables affecting the relationship between religion and politics include confessional identity, historical experience (in particular, the presence or otherwise of revolution, enlightenment and industrialization), social development (we here think particularly of the emergence of a bourgeois social class) and geographical location (it will be noted here that both Germany and Spain lay on the borders of France). Hence, at least, some of the differences between Spain and Germany: in the former, political catechism emerged in the light of a powerful Catholic Church directly threatened by – as it saw it – revolution, whereas in Protestant Germany – the zone of the country that produced both Arndt and Von Kleist – religion was both weaker in institutional terms and less threatened by changes in government with the result that the production of catechisms was more influenced by important intellectual debates about, for example, pedagogy.

One way of investigating the key relation between religion and the state is by studying the standard form of religious catechism at the end of the eighteenth century, and the changes that the Napoleonic experience brought. The form of religious catechisms before the wars often reflected the tension between liberal and reactionary forces both inside and outside the dominant Church about the educational value of catechism, and the role of the dominant confessions in the education of the masses.[18] Meanwhile, the way in which both the substantive content and the specific pedagogical form of such texts was perceived in a given country, or by a specific confession, directly influenced the development of political catechism. It seems that some evolutions of the genre (as the consequence of the relation between religion and the state) permitted the 'secularisation' of catechisms, and others not. And in some countries, the Napoleonic Wars were an important factor that favoured this evolution, creating the need for a familiar form of expression that could adapt itself to the exigencies of the situation and save the day in the emergency that now threatened.

The question of whether or not catechism could be made use of for political purposes, or, to put it another way, this process of adaption, was soon placed at the centre of theological debate in even (and perhaps mostly) the most religious of countries. For some members of the clergy, catechisms were first and foremost sacral texts from which it followed that they should never be drawn into the temporal sphere. Yet for others catechisms were transferable objects that could on occasion be made use of for other purposes, one such being moments when the Church needed a means of answering practical, every-day questions that were relevant to the faithful at a time of great difficulty. To the extent that the Napoleonic invasions represented such times, for such men it followed that it was necessary to guide the masses in precisely this fashion. Not surprisingly, such divisions were particularly noticeable in Spain, where the use of catechism by the French 'constitutional' Church to justify its position in the 1790s had caused particular offence, and where many of the clergy continued to oppose the politicization of catechism under any circumstances. However, the case of Germany, where the tradition of practical catechism was longer, differs. Here the debate was dominated not by the clergy but rather by the intelligentsia and, in particular, its Romantic elements. In respect to these elements, it was earlier asked whether there was less nationalist fervour in Germany than in other European states. Setting aside the masses – an entirely separate question – we see that this was not so: in the university world, in particular, anti-French feeling was widespread and the discussion of nationalist ideas commonplace. But that did not in itself mean that the concept of *katechismus* automatically came to the fore. On the contrary, for many German intellectuals, the experience of the Enlightenment – a period that was already identified with French cultural imperialism – made catechism the weapon of the enemy, of Napoleon – the false roman emperor – and of the proponents of cold reason. For more conservative figures, meanwhile, the use of such texts had also been one of the factors which transformed the revolution into a bloody terror. Many nationalist writers therefore refused to see in the new unity of religion, ethics and politics, in their organic conception of society, any place for the teaching method of catechism. In this, of course, Arndt and Von Kleist differed from their fellows, but it would not be going too far to suggest that this prejudice may well be a key to the relative absence of catechism from the armoury of German intellectual resistance to Napoleon. Indeed, in his own catechism even Von Kleist referred to the empty philosophical verbalism of the enemy, and apologized for his own use of the catechetical genre. As his hypothetical father says to his equally hypothetical child, 'Don't you find that, by offering you a catechism, your father errs in the same way as that which you are describing?'[19] Nor were matters aided by the fact that the most prominent pedagogues of the time (such as Pestalozzi) were strongly against the teaching method of catechism, which seemed to them archaic. At the same time, Fichte, who proclaimed the necessity of teaching the nation, also disliked catechism. And, last but not least, the sort of revolutionary message propounded by German nationalists may well simply have sounded incongruous in the context of the Lutheran forms so closely associated with dynasties such as those of Prussia and Saxony. In consequence, only Arndt and Von Kleist chose this genre, whilst we should here again note the former's efforts to conciliate his message with that of Lutheran tradition. Arndt's second catechism thus adopted strong religious tones, even though religion was obviously instrumentalized for the benefit of the nationalist cause, in which respect it differed from Spanish political catechisms with religious tones, where the opposite was invariably true (i.e. political concepts were made use of to advance the cause of organized religion rather than the other way about). This may have been much against his will: Arndt himself acknowledged that he preferred the unity of the nation to the supremacy of any particular confession, and avowed that he had only given his catechism a religious aspect as a means of injecting it with a mystical accent capable of impressing the simple soldier. But all the evidence suggests that without such a change there was simply no means of proceeding with the tactic: Von Kleist, after all, had not managed to get his work off the ground at all.

The weakness of anti-Napoleonic catechism is Germany is an interesting point that provokes further reflection. Despite frequent use by thinkers of the Enlightenment and the French Revolution of the genre of catechism as a means of spreading new universal religions based on the laws of 'nature' or the rights of man, this means of propaganda was at its most comfortable as an instrument of reaction, and, above all, Catholic reaction, and that despite the disputes outlined above. Unlike Lutheranism, for centuries the Catholic Church had been evangelizing new groups of potential converts, which also naturally meant adapting itself to new civilizations. For a living model of this, we have only to turn to the Jesuit missionaries of the seventeenth and eighteenth centuries. As Carlo Ginzburg writes, 'In order to spread the faith of Christ they consciously decided to accommodate themselves to all kinds of customs, from the caste system in India to the cult of ancestors in China.'[20] In the words of a Jesuit missionary quoted by the same author, 'One must be barbarous with the barbarians and polished with civilized people . . . In this way the uniform and unchanging gospel will be more easily insinuated into the spirits'.[21] In consequence, the principle of adapting the principle of catechism to a particular circumstance was well understood. In the crisis represented by the Revolutionary and Napoleonic era, meanwhile, catechisms presented unique advantages as a form of discourse. Inherent in the very concept of 'resistance' is that of an enemy, or, to put it another way, an 'other'. And how better to define this concept than through catechism? Thus, on the one hand this could be used systematically to set out the rival position, and on the other it could be used just as systematically to rubbish it. In this fashion, the old technique of sequencing questions and answers acquired a new relevance and efficacy, for it provided a means of, first, neutralizing the words of the enemy by placing them within the meaning of one's own ideology, and, second, proving the opposite of what the enemy claimed. The enemy was thus disqualifying himself by the mere fact of speaking.

Yet even here there were problems. For example, in Catholic Italy only one example of an anti-Napoleonic catechism specifically related to the cause of armed resistance to the French has ever been discovered (as opposed to catechisms that are secretly anti-Napoleonic, but which are yet 'jacobinical' in their outlook).[22] In the Catholic parts of Germany there was no use of catechism to stimulate resistance. And in Spain, as Aymes shows, with one exception no counter-revolutionary catechism appeared until 1808.[23] For much of the period in question this need not surprise us: the Spanish government was from 1795 to 1808 allied to France, whilst internal political debate was dominated by the hated figure of the royal favourite, Manuel de Godoy, from whose supposed clutches it came generally to be hoped that Napoleon would actually rescue Spain. Yet this leaves us with the issue of the period 1789–92. In these early days of the Revolutionary era, the regime of Carlos IV was deeply frightened by events in Paris and might therefore have been expected to welcome any means that could be devised of persuading the Spanish people to steer clear of the ideas that reigned across the Pyrenees. At the same time, too, the Spanish Church was ever more aware of the travails of its French cousin: aside from anything else, many non-juring clergy fled to Spain and took refuge in such provinces as Navarre and Catalonia. Yet counter-revolutionary catechisms came there none, and the inference is quite clearly that for Catholics there were deep inhibitions in this respect – that the Catholic Church, in short, was clearly opposed to an instrumentalization of catechism. As Cabarrus noted in the early 1790s, indeed, 'Political catechism has yet to appear among us.'[24] What, then, broke the log-jam? In brief, the answer is the coming of war, there being no coincidence in the discovery that the one exception to the rule – the catechism of the future liberal *cortes* deputy, Joaquín Lorenzo Villanueva – appeared at precisely the moment when armed conflict finally broke out between Bourbon Spain and Revolutionary France.[25]

From all this we may make a general point. Such were the difficulties involved in the secularization of catechism as a tool of counter-revolution that with the one unpublished exception of Von Kleist, it was only made use of when war against Napoleon had already broken out. In Spain, then, it appeared in 1793, and then did not surface again until 1808, whilst Arndt did not put pen to paper until Napoleon had gone to war against Russia in 1812. The distinction is a little blurred – the original version of Arndt's catechism called for both widespread desertion amongst the armies of the German states and revolution in the Fatherland, whilst the Spanish *catecismos* sought to stimulate resistance to the French throughout Spain rather than just in the areas that remained under the control of the Patriots – but it is therefore clear that on the whole catechisms were seen as a means of facilitating wars not of the people but of the state. To put it another way, the people were to take up arms more in accordance with norms and instructions received from above than in accordance with their own practices, experiences and instincts. And in this it must be said that they were a failure. Despite the long tradition accepting without question that Napoleon was faced by a great popular crusade in Spain and Portugal, the most recent research has shown that this was all but a myth. As Charles Esdaile has shown in a variety of works, voluntary enlistment was limited, conscription deeply unpopular and even the Spanish guerrillas an extremely complex phenomenon that defies many of the assumptions that have commonly been made about them. Nor, meanwhile, was the situation much better in Germany. Just as the Russo-German Legion was composed not of enthusiastic patriots, but men who had joined its ranks rather than starve to death in some Russian prison camp, so the German people did not rush to answer the cause in 1813. Prussia, true, hastily raised a mass army in March 1813, whilst her example was copied by many of the others states after they had changed sides in the course of the following autumn, but in the end the populace had to be forced to take up arms onwards, served but unwillingly and all too often did not let the figure of Arndt's Christian warrior get in the way of the business of pillage and rapine.

In reality, then, in so far as it was used as a weapon against Napoleon, catechism was a failure. It was not used very often, whilst its impact seems to have been very limited. To reinforce this point, it has only to be observed that its future lay not with the cause of reaction but that of revolution. Isolated though they were, one cannot fail to notice the fact that the three German anti-napoleonic catechisms we have discussed announced the evolution of German thinking and mentality: from this point onwards the genre of political catechism gradually became institutionalized, the production of these works reaching its climax in the revolution of 1848. In the same way, in Spain the development of catechisms that sought to defend the constitution of 1812 was proved to be a phenomenon that was repeated many times over in the *trienio liberal* of 1820–23. Nor is this surprising: apart from anything else the first half of the nineteenth century was an age in which the concepts of religion were losing their grip and becoming increasingly secularized. With hindsight, it is possible to argue that political catechism could never really succeed as a tactic of resistance. In trying to overcome the enemy, the resistance unconsciously incorporated in its argumentation some of the ideas that that same enemy stands for and therefore imperceptibly propagated some aspects of the new modernity. Also, for thinkers associated with the *ancien regime*, catechism was a double-edged sword in that it both called the people to arms but urged them to think for themselves and, in certain circumstances, act accordingly. But for men of the new age, there could be no such doubts, for getting the people to take up arms on their own account was the very heart of what they were about. At the same time, meanwhile, the concept of political catechism had originated amongst progressive thinkers. Amongst such groups, then, political catechism was perpetuated: indeed, the final authors of such texts would be socialists and communists – men who were the prophets of a new religion and the carriers of another kind of resistance.[26]

Notes

1. For the period of the French Revolution, cf. B. Durruty, 'Les auteurs de catéchismes révolutionnaires (1789–1799)', *Annales Historiques de la Révolution française*, no. 283 (January, 1991), pp. 1–18; J. Hébrard, 'La Révolution expliquée aux enfants : les catéchismes de l'an II', in M.F. Levy (ed.) *L'Enfant, la Famille et la Révolution Française* (Paris, 1990), pp. 171–92; J. Hébrard, 'Les catéchismes de la première Révolution et répertoire bibliographique des catéchismes révolutionnaires' in L. Andriès (ed.), *Colporter la Révolution : Lumières et Almanachs Populaires* (Montreuil, 1989), pp. 53–81; R. Texier, 'Les catéchismes du citoyen à la Révolution', *Impacts*, nos. 1–2 (June 1990), pp. 35–52. For the Spanish

case, cf. J.R. Aymes, 'Du catéchisme religieux au catéchisme politique (fin du XVIIIe siècle – début du XIXe)', in J.R. Aymes, E.M. Fell, and J.L. Guereña (eds), *Ecole et Eglise – en Espagne et Amérique Latine: Aspects Idéologiques et Institutionnels* (Tours, 1988), pp. 17–32; A. Capitán Díaz, *Los catecismos políticos en España. 1808–1822* (Granada, 1978); A. Capitán Díaz, 'Los catecismos políticos en los inicios del siglo XIX español : un intento de formación política y social del pueblo', in G. Ossenbach Santer *et al.* (eds) *La Révolución francesa y su influencia en la educación en España* (Madrid, 1992), pp. 437–49; M. Morales Muñoz, 'Los catecismos y la instrucción popular en la España del siglo XIX' in Aymes *et al.*, *Ecole et Eglise*, pp. 33–46; M. Morales Muñoz, 'Las enseñanzas de la virtud: reglas civico-morales en los catecismos del siglo XIX', in R. Duroux (ed.), *Les Traités de Savoir-Vivre en Espagne et au Portugal du Moyen-Âge à nos Jours* (Clermont-Ferrand, 1995), pp. 277–86; J. Muñoz Perez, 'Los catecismos politicos: de la ilustración al primer liberalismo español, 1808–1822', *Gades*, XVI (1987), pp. 209–10; M.A. Ruiz de Azúa (ed.), *Catecismos políticos españoles* (Madrid, 1989). For the Italian case, cf. L. Guerci, 'Les catéchismes républicains en Italie (1796–1799)', in M. Vovelle, *L'Image de la Révolution Française* (Paris, 1989), I, pp. 359–68; L. Guerci, *Mente, cuore, coraggio, virtu repubblicane: educare il popolo nell? Italia in rivoluzione, 1796–1799* (Turini, 1992).

2. M. Morales Muñoz, *Los catecismos en la España del siglo XIX* (Malaga, 1990).

3. Cf. J.R. Aymes, 'Catecismos franceses de la Révolución y catecismos españoles de la Guerra de la Independencia : esbozo de comparación' in Ossenbach Santer, *La Révolución francesa y su influencia en la educación en España*, pp. 407–36; Guerci, 'Mente, cuore, coraggio, virtu repubblicane'; D. Tanck de Estrada 'Los catecismos políticos: de la Révolución Francesa a México independiente', in S. Alberro *et al.* (eds) *La Révolución Francesa en México* (Mexico, 1992), pp. 491–506; M. Michel, *Politische Katechismen: Volney, Kleist, Heß* (Frankfurt am Main, 1966).

4. For a discussion of these issues, cf. J.-C. Dhotel, *Les origines du catéchisme moderne d'après les premiers manuels imprimés en France* (Paris, 1967), and J.R. Armogathe, 'Les catéchismes et l'enseignement populaire en France au dix-huitième siècle', in A. Colin (ed.) *Images du peuple au XVIIIe siècle* (Aix, 1973), pp. 103–22.

5. Voltaire's catechisms include *Le catéchisme de l'honnête homme* (1763); *Catéchisme chinois ou entretiens de Cu-Su, disciple de Confutzee, avec le Prince Kou, fils de Low, tributaire de l'empereur chinois Gnenvan, 417 ans avant notre ère vulgaire* (1764); *Catéchisme du jardinier ou entretien du Bacha Tuctan et du jardinier Karpos* (1765); *Catéchisme du curé* (n.d.); *Catéchisme du japonais* (n.d.).

6. Hébrard, 'Les catéchismes de la première Révolution'.

7. Guerci, 'Les catéchismes républicains en Italie'.

8. A.J. Hofman, *Der Aristokratenkatechismus: ein wunderschoenes Buechlein, gar erbaulich zu lesen fuer Junge und Alte* (Mainz, 1792).

9. Aymes, 'Du catéchisme religieux au catéchisme politique'.

10. Capitán Díaz, *Los catecismos políticos en España. 1808–1822*.

11. Capitán Díaz, 'Los catecismos políticos en los inicios del siglo XIX español'.

12. J. Mñ oz Pérez, 'Los catecismos politicos : de la ilustración al primer liberalismo español, 1808–1822'.

13. Morales Mñ oz, 'Enseñanzas de la virtud'; M. Morales Muñoz, *Los catecismos en la España del siglo XIX*.

14. Anon., *Catecismo civil y breve compendio de los obligaciones del español, conocimiento (practico) de su libertad, y explicatión de su enemigo, muy ùtil en las actuales circunstancias para la enseñenza de los niños de ambos sexos, puesto en forma de diálogo* (Madrid, 1808); Anon., 'Catecismo civil de España en preguntas y respuestas, mandado imprimir de orden de la Junta Suprema, por la viuda de hidalgo y sobrino' (Sevilla, 1808), in Morales Muñoz, *Catecismos políticos del siglo XIX*, pp. 22–5; Anon., 'Catecismo católico-político, que con motivo de las actuales novedades de la España, dirige y dedica a sus Conciudadanos un sacerdote amante de le Religión, afecto a su patria y amigo de los hombres (Madrid, 1808), in *ibid.*, pp. 28–62.

15. H. v. Kleist, 'Katechismus der Deutschen, abgefasst nach dem Spanischen, zum Gebrauch für Kinder und Alte', in H. v. Kleist, *Politische Schriften und andere Nachträge zu seinen Werke*, ed. R. Koepke (Berlin, 1862). The Spanish *catecismo civil* appeared in German as 'Bürger-Katechismus und kurzer Inbegriff der Pflichten eines Spaniers, nebst praktischer Kenntnis seiner Freiheit und Beschreibung seines Feindes. Von großem Nutzen bey den gegenwärtigen Angelegenheiten. Gedruckt zu Sevillia und für die Schulen der Provinzen vertheilt'.

16. E.M. Arndt, *Katechismus für den deutschen Kriegs und Wehrmann* (Leipzig, 1813), and Kurzer Katechismus für deutsche Soldaten' (1812) in R. Weber, *Drei Flugschriften* (Berlin, 1988), pp. 1–33.

17. Morales Muñoz, *Los catecismos en la España del siglo XIX*, pp. 79–94.

18. For a discussion of these issues, cf. W. Harle *et al.* (eds), *Theologische Realenzyklopaedie* (Berlin, 1988–98), XVII, pp. 686–710; *ibid.*, XXIX, pp. 33–49.

19. Von Kleist, *Katechismus der Deutschen*, chapter 8.

20. C. Ginzburg, *History, Rhetoric and Proof* (Hanover, 1999), p. 77.

21. *Ibid.*, p. 78.

22. P. de Felice, *Catechismo Reale, ossia istruzione ove per via di domande e risposte si propongono i dritti de' re e gli obblighi de' sudditi, per uso della diocesi di Sessa* (Napoli, 1799).

23. For a discussion of these issues, cf. J.-R. Aymes: 'Catecismos franceses de la Révolución y catecismos españoles de la Guerra de la Independencia : Esbozo de comparación'.

24. Aymes: 'Catecismos franceses de la Révolución y catecismos españoles de la Guerra de la Independencia', p. 424. The Spanish original, which is somewhat ambiguous, reads, 'El catecismo político esta por hacer.'

25. J.L. Villanueva, *Catecismo del Estado segun los principios de la Religion, por el doctor D. Joaquin Lorenzo Villanueva, Presbitero, calificador del Santo oficio y Capellan Doctoral de S. M. en la Real Capilla de la Encarnacion* (Madrid, 1793).

26. For just two prominent examples, cf. L. Blanc, *Catéchisme des socialistes* (Paris, 1849), and R. Owen, *The Catechism of the New Moral World* (Leeds, 1838).

This page intentionally left blank

9
The Patriotism of the Russian Army in the 'Patriotic' or 'Fatherland' War of 1812

Janet Hartley

In general, it is probably fair to say that the term 'popular resistance' conjures up visions of the reaction of populaces to invasion and occupation. But in the Napoleonic Wars – a period, after all, of mass armies – the peoples of Europe were conscripted for military service in immense numbers, thereby providing us with an alternative focus for the study of popular resistance. What justification is there for the study of the Russian army as opposed to the Russian people in 1812? The military performance of the Russian army in 1812 has been examined extensively but the 'mood', if you can call it that, of the army has not been the subject of the same level of investigation. Scholarship has focused on the so-called 'people's war' (in Russian, the *narodnaia voina*); that is, the resistance by ordinary people, by which is meant essentially the peasants, or, in fact, the serfs, to the invaders and the contribution that this made to the defeat of the Napoleonic forces.[1] The extent to which this popular resistance can be seen as 'patriotic' or 'nationalistic' has been the subject of extensive debate.[2] On the whole, Western historians have dated the emergence of modern forms of Russian nationalism to the later nineteenth century and have characterized peasant resistance during the Napoleonic invasion as 'xenophobic' rather than 'nationalistic' but, nevertheless, the events of 1812 are regarded as an important stage in this development.

The trauma and consequences of the invasion of 1812 have, inevitably, been a source of fascination to Russian scholars, and not only to Russian scholars of course. The Russian scholarly journals of the second half of the nineteenth century include a large number of memoirs, contemporary accounts and correspondence relating to the invasion. Tolstoi's *War and Peace*, published in 1866–69, reinforced the fascination with the participation of individuals in the great events of history. But the greatest stimulus to Russian scholarship on 1812 came one hundred years later, with the jubilee publications of 1912. These include the seven volumes entitled *The Fatherland War and Russian Society*, which brought together many of the most distinguished prerevolutionary Russian historians, including, just to mention two, Semevskii, whose two-volume study of peasants in the reign of Catherine II remains the great classic work on the subject, and Tugan-Baronovskii, who wrote an influential, if rather provocative, account of the development of the factory in Russia.[3] Local historical journals and archives were very active in publications of contemporary materials in the jubilee year and have provided the basis for much of my own study of 1812.[4] It has to remembered that the tsarist regime was vulnerable in 1912, almost as vulnerable as Alexander I had been in 1812. The defeat in the Russo-Japanese War in 1905–06 and the uneasy constitutional arrangements after 1906 had damaged the reputation of the tsar, and it is hardly surprising that the jubilee of a heroic Russian victory (followed by the 300-year celebration of the foundation of the Romanov dynasty in 1913) was welcomed as an opportunity to demonstrate how one hundred years earlier all members of society had pulled together, under the leadership of the tsar, and had triumphed together. This probably explains the publication in this year of such simplistic and nationalistic books as *The Fatherland War of 1812 and Russian Jews* and *Heroic Women in 1812*.[5]

The prospect and then reality of a German invasion of Russia after 1939 revived an interest in popular and patriotic resistance in 1812. A study was published in 1940 of the 'people's war' in Smolensk, which made much of peasant resistance, although the unfortunate timing of the publication meant that the author was unable, as later authors, to equate the Russian military retreat in 1812 with the identical and skilful tactics of Stalin.[6] That book provided invaluable local material on events in 1812, but was marred by a crude interpretation. It took another jubilee, however, to provoke a further outpouring of scholarship on 1812 – this time in 1962, on the occasion of the 150th anniversary of the 1812 invasion. This year saw a similar pattern to that of 1912 in that eminent Soviet scholars produced both individual and collective works on the invasion, and further collections of documents.[7] The emphasis, in this rather crude period of Cold War history, changed so that the role of the 'feudal élites' (nobles and clergy) was diminished while that of the 'people' was elevated to such an extent that they were now depicted as the only and the true 'patriots'. The 'people's war' was now also seen as an integral part of the class struggle against the feudal system. Nationalism was, of course, assumed to be part of the superstructure, an artificial creation of the bourgeois state intended deliberately to distract the proletariat from forming their natural class bonds across the boundaries of the nation state. But the Soviet state did not want to dismiss the significance of the role patriotism played in victory in the war of 1941–45, a struggle which is always referred to as the 'Great Patriotic War'. The patriotic support was interpreted as support for the Soviet régime and then was translated backwards to 1812, as, indeed, it was in other states, although with different ideological overtones.[8]

The fall of the Soviet Union has led to a revival of interest in 1812. The new popular historical journals which have emerged recount heroic events of 1812, whilst there is an interest in restoring tsarist monuments to 1812 and groups which re-enact battle scenes of that year. Much of this activity is not very scholarly, but, to the extent that there is an underlying theme, it is more a return to the all-encompassing view of the patriotism and heroism of Russian society portrayed in 1912 than to the divisions in society highlighted by Soviet scholars.

The emphasis by Russian and Soviet scholarship on the significance of popular resistance, has centred very firmly on the 'people's war'. This does not mean that the army has been totally neglected, but the treatment of this subject has been coloured by its association with the 'people's war'. I will start by discussing two aspects of the army which have been analysed in terms of patriotism, namely 'partisan' warfare and militias. I will then look at two areas which have been less studied, that is the extent to which a sense of patriotism can be detected in the *mentalités* of ordinary soldiers and of the officer corps in 1812.

'Partisan warfare' (*partizanskaia voina*) was seen by both contemporaries and Tsarist and Soviet historians as an important feature of the struggle against Napoleon's forces. I am not concerned here with primarily the effectiveness of partisans in the harassment of small groups of men which had become detached from the main body of the French troops. It is clear that General Kutuzov and General Bagration did have some doubts about the military effectiveness of partisan warfare and limited the number of regular troops released to perform this activity.[9] Napoleon was seemingly contemptuous at the time about the effectiveness of Russian, or Cossack, partisan units (as he was at the time about Spanish guerrillas). Both Russian and Soviet historians have described the success of Russian forces in the provinces of western Russia and have given accounts of encounters where numbers of Napoleonic troops were killed or taken prisoner.

My interest in partisans is not in their military activities *per se* but in the extent to which they can be portrayed as 'patriotic'. Part of the issue here is semantics. The word *partizan* was used in Russian in 1812 to describe the use of small detachments of troops to attack French stragglers, and which were released by the regular army for this purpose; it is the Russian word for 'guerrilla' and *partizanskaia voina* is translated as 'guerrilla war' or 'little war'. Many historians date the emergence of guerrilla warfare from the campaign in Spain in 1808, even though irregular fighting had occurred in other parts of the world before this time.[10] The significance of the Napoleonic period is that 'guerrilla war', in Spain, Russia or the Tyrol, was conducted not simply by detachments of regular troops but also involved the 'people' rising against the invader, with or without regular military support. Contemporary theorists, such as Clausewitz, who had analysed warfare in both Spain and Russia, stressed the role and significance of regular army units in this warfare. Denis Davydov, the prominent leader of partisan detachments in 1812, also contributed to the military theories of partisan warfare from the perspective of an army officer. It is within this tradition, we shall see, that Russian historians discussed the role of partisans in their publications of 1912.

Soviet historians received minimal guidance in this matter from the writings of Marx and Engels as these figures gave relatively little attention to guerrilla warfare and were generally sceptical about its potential effectiveness, at least in Europe. It was the experience of World War II that elevated the role of the partisan in Soviet eyes and led to the equating of partisan warfare with 'the people's war' in 1812. The definition of 'partisan war in 1812' in the *Soviet Historical Encyclopedia* makes it clear which element is perceived to be the most important: 'Warfare waged by the people of Russia, *especially the peasantry* [my emphasis], and by detachments of the Russian army in the rear and along lines of communication of the Napoleonic army in Russia in 1812.'[11] But the twentieth-century understanding of the word also has other implications which were not necessarily present in 1812, namely that partisans operate in occupied territory (and it is hard to call the French presence in western Russia a formal occupation), that this includes acts of sabotage against the invader (not really relevant in 1812), and that the partisans are local armed inhabitants, who may or may not include members of the regular army. In 1812, peasants were armed by the regular army. Kochetkov, writing in 1962 and on whose analysis I have drawn for the Soviet view of partisans, stated that for this reason it would be a mistake to make the analogy between partisan activity in 1812 and 1941.[12]

The issue of patriotism is, however, relevant to the composition and leadership of the partisan groups. In 1912 the Russian publications stressed the heroism and bravery of individual partisan leaders such as Lieutenant-Colonel (later General) D.V. Davydov, Captain A.S. Figner and Captain A.N. Seslavin, all, of course, officers in the regular army. The Soviet historian Kochetkov criticized so-called 'gentry' historians for emphasizing the role of nobles in the organization of the 'people's war'.[13] This is symptomatic of the Soviet approach to the whole question of popular resistance in 1812 where partisan warfare is inextricably linked to other aspects of the 'people's war' and to the attacks by peasants on the feudal order to the extent that distinctions between these various forms of activity are blurred, making it almost impossible to establish the composition of specifically partisan groups, as opposed, for example, to peasant bands armed with pitchforks and axes who were simply defending their homes against soldiers. As part of the deliberate attempt to downplay the role of the élites in the defeat of Napoleon, Soviet analyses stressed the role of 'non-nobles' in organizing armed groups of peasants, including retired soldiers and members of the lower urban classes. Russian historians, in contrast, emphasized the role played by local nobles and officials in forming partisan groups (although the role of a certain V.G. Ragozin, a sexton, that is, a member of the lower clergy, was particularly commended by Kniaz'khov).[14]

Peasant participation in partisan groups is particularly commended by Soviet historians. To Kochetkov, volunteering was a sign of patriotism (although he could offer no concrete evidence for this), albeit 'not the patriotism called for in tsarist manifestos' as 'the struggle with the invaders did not extinguish the struggle against serfdom'.[15] Kniaz'khov also praised the 'unknown heroes' including peasant partisan volunteers, and noted that Davydov promised Bagration that he would attract peasant volunteers by going into villages and asserting that the partisans would defend their priests and churches, this being a tactic that suggested a direct appeal to the most basic Russian national feeling (one sees here, of course, the symbiosis of Russian indentity with the Orthodox faith, to which matter I shall return later).[16] Our problem, of course, is that these peasants were precisely 'unknown heroes' and left no record of their reasons for joining the partisans. All the evidence that I have found of the 'people's war' suggests that peasants fought to defend their land, goods and families from the invader and that broader motives may be found in a gut, xenophobic, reaction against the 'Godless' and foreign invader. Beyond this, however, it is hard to go, and this is particularly true of the issue of a broader anti-feudal protest, all that can be said in this respect being that disorder in the countryside, which had been made more acute in western Russia by the virtual disappearance of law and order in the wake of the invasion, gave additional opportunities for violence.[17]

A further complication in the interpretation of the partisans as 'patriotic' is the leading role of Cossacks in these armed detachments. Cossacks had traditionally been used by the imperial army for skirmishes and irregular activities. They were particularly suited to this role as they were primarily horsemen rather than footsoldiers. The renowned ferocity and bravery of the Cossacks, coupled with their reputation for indiscipline, also accounted for their use in this way. But the characterization of this activity as specifically Russian 'patriotism' is problematic. Cossacks are not a separate ethnic group (although they were designated as such in the Soviet period); they comprise mainly Russian and Ukrainian peasants and fugitives who had fled to the southern borderlands. They nevertheless regarded themselves as a separate group within the Russian empire, with a separate institutional and social structure, who owed a loyalty to their Cossack host as well as to the Russian tsar. The eighteenth and the early nineteenth century saw the transformation of Cossack communities from active resistors to central tsarist authority to loyal servitors of the state,[18] but this did not mean that they had lost their sense of separate identity or their distrust of Russians officials and grandees. Cossacks were Orthodox Christians, but many were Old Believers (that is, they rejected the reforms made to the Orthodox Church by the state in the mid-seventeenth century). Nor did the local population of western Russia always treat Cossacks as fellow 'patriots'. Indeed, peasant resistance to Cossack marauders could be just as fierce as resistance to Napoleonic troops; one contemporary account notes that Cossacks were regarded by peasants as 'worse than the enemy'.[19]

The final word on partisan activity should lie with Tolstoi's account in *War and Peace*. It sees the young Petia, an eager and excited schoolboy 'with rosy cheeks and bright eyes', accompanying the Cossack A.K. Denisov, leader of a partisan group comprising men of the regular army, Cossacks and hussars, but guided by an elderly peasant, against some French stragglers who were holding some Russian prisoners (including Pierre, one of the leading characters in the novel):

> Petia went closer, and his eyes fell on the pale face of a terrified Frenchmen, clinging with both hands to the shaft of a lance that was pointed at his breast. 'Hurrah boys!' shouted Petia, spurring his foaming horse, and riding up the street.... By the time Petia rode up,

he was overmastered. 'Too late again!' thought Petia. He made his way to where the fighting was briskest ... A volley hit the air, the bullets whistled round. Petia was still tearing round the courtyard; but instead of holding the bridle, he was waving both arms wildly in the air, and leaning heavily over on one side. His horse ... stopped short and Petia fell heavily. For a moment his hands and feet moved, his head was rigid. A bullet had entered his brain.... 'Done for!' repeated Dologhow, as if he found a particular pleasure in using those words; and he went back to the prisoners who were crowding round the Cossacks.... [Denissov] lifted Petia's head with trembling hands, and was looking at the poor, bloody and mud-stained face. 'I am fond of sweet things – these are capital raisins – take them all...' The words [spoken by Petia to an imprisoned French drummer boy the day before] irresistibly recurred in his mind; and the Cossacks looked on in amazement as they heard the short, hard breathing, almost like a dog's bark, that broke from Denissov's oppressed chest. He suddenly turned away and clutched convulsively at the railings.[20]

Thus Tolstoi depicted the 'heroism' of partisan warfare.

The clearest links which have been drawn between 'patriotism' and the army, by both Russian and Soviet historians, but from very different perspectives, are the temporary militias that were established in 1812. Much has been written on the militias, but, as with the partisans, much of what has been written serves to obscure more than it does to clarify the composition and role of the militias.[21] To non-Communist Russian historians, and especially those of the Tsarist era, the militias are particularly indicative of the patriotism of the nobles, who volunteered to form the officer corps of the militias, and who donated foodstuffs. But to Soviet historians, the true patriotism was shown by the peasants, many of whom wished to join the militias, whereas nobles were sometimes condemned as 'anti-patriotic'.

Militias were not unique to the year 1812, and had been levied in 1806 during the war of 1805–07. In 1812 a special levy for the temporary militia was made (in addition to the regular levies of that year) which raised over 200 000 men in Russia and over 74 000 in the Ukraine.[22] They were intended to be temporary units, and indeed they were disbanded at the end of the campaign in 1814. The 'temporary nature' of the militias was marked symbolically by the fact that soldiers in the militia retained their beards, unlike ordinary conscripts who were shaved once they had been accepted as recruits, as a sign that they now left the peasant estate and had become soldiers. When rumours reached him that militia conscripts were in fact being integrated with regular units of the army, Alexander I decreed that this was not to be allowed.[23] Militias were raised in sixteen provinces, including the provinces closest to the invasion route. That seems to imply that the primary task of militias would be confined to local defence, although in fact militia units fought at the battle of Borodino and some fought outside the borders of the country in the campaigns of 1813 and 1814. A record of the officers rewarded for their service noted 13 officers from the Nizhnii Novgorod militia and ten from the Kazan' militia who fought at the battle of Dresden.[24]

The most problematic aspect of the militias, and the one which has most exercised Russian scholars of all shades of opinion is their composition, and, in particular, the extent to which they comprised volunteers. The manifesto calling for the raising of militias in 1812 was directed to nobles with the intention that nobles should volunteer to serve as officers. As nobles had been freed from compulsory service to the state in 1762, they could not, of course, be forced to serve, and there is evidence both that young nobles volunteered and that older nobles left retirement to join the militias. Later a veteran of the Decembrist uprising, V.I. Shteingel', for example, had retired from active naval service in 1810 because of ill health, but re-enlisted in 1812 and served in the St Petersburg and Novgorod militias from 1812 to 1814.[25] Nobles also supplied the militias at their own expense and gave their serfs as conscripts.[26]

Some nobles may indeed have been motivated by patriotic feelings. Others, however, may have seen enlistment in the militias as a career opportunity that would otherwise be denied to them, a factor which has been ignored by both Russian and Soviet historians. To most young nobles, service in the army was far more desirable than in the civil service, and in particular service in local government institutions, but many lacked the social connections to gain a commission in a regiment. Once accepted in a local militia, however, it seems that it was easier for these nobles to transfer to a regular regiment. M.M. Spiridov, for example, who had been educated at home rather than at a prestigious cadet corps or noble boarding school in Moscow or St Petersburg, joined the Vladimir militia in 1812, aged probably sixteen, and then moved to a grenadier regiment in the following year.[27] More striking is the case of A.A. Kriukov, who originally entered service in 1805 as an actuary. He joined the Nizhnii Novgorod militia in 1812 as a cornet, and then transferred to a more prestigious hussar regiment in 1815.[28]

Soviet historians have not examined the various reasons why nobles enlisted in the militias; rather they have castigated nobles for being 'unpatriotic' as they were reluctant to serve in the militias and put forward, in the words of one historian, 'every excuse to avoid service'.[29] This was indeed true of particular individuals, and was acknowledged at the time and by Russian historians. In Moscow, Governor Fedor Rostopchin noted that several nobles opposed the formation of the militia.[30] Nobles, of course, were being asked to do more than volunteer their own services; they were also being asked to supply their 'human capital', serfs, in order to serve in the militias, and also to supply the soldiers with arms, uniforms, horses and provisions. It is hardly surprising, then, that it proved impossible to supply the militias in full. In Smolensk province the shortfall was in the region of 7000 men and in Kaluga province it was almost 5000 men, but these provinces were in the path of the Napoleonic armies; other provinces, including Moscow, eventually conscripted more men than had been requested.[31] Militias suffered from shortages of clothing, provisions and arms.[32] The Nizhnii Novgorod militia 'had not a single doctor' in October 1812. In March of the following year, the militia was still short of uniform and supplies.[33] A recent, post-Soviet, study stated that the Khar'kov militia apparently never formed properly and challenges Soviet figures for the militia of that province.[34] It is difficult, however, to portray these shortages as 'anti-patriotic'. The majority of nobles in Russia were not wealthy, and in consequence they were simply unable to provide the human and material resources required. It was estimated in the 1760s that 32 per cent of nobles owned fewer than ten serfs; in 1797, 83.5 per cent owned fewer than 100 serfs.[35] Russian regiments were also regularly under strength as the full complement of recruits rarely reached the recruiting station without losses through death, disease and desertion and regular regiments also suffered shortages of supplies.

The militias also included non-noble volunteers. Kabanov mentions volunteers for the militia who were teachers at national schools, university students and seminarists.[36] One student in Khar'kov seemingly accompanied his request for enlistment in the militia with the words 'I am a son of Russia and also love my fatherland'.[37] But while some of these may have been motivated by patriotism as Kabanov suggests, they, even more than nobles, may well have also seen the militia an opportunity. Sons of clerics (Orthodox parish clergy had to marry) were obliged to attend seminaries and the most able sought careers elsewhere. Teachers in national schools were usually the sons of clerics; salaries were poor and irregularly paid and many young and physically able teachers would welcome the opportunity to escape their posts. Universities lost many of their students during the Napoleonic Wars as it became easier for them to get commissions in this period.[38] Minor officials also enlisted; Karl Hoffman, a collegiate registrar, requested a testimonial to join the Novgorod militia.[39]

Some volunteers, then, may have been hoping to get commissions as officers in the militias, though it should be noted that two of the groups with the greatest interest in securing this goal – seminarists and sacristans – were in theory only allowed to join the ranks.[40] Soviet writers, however, lay special emphasis on volunteers from non-privileged members of society who enlisted as ordinary soldiers in the militias. According to the Soviet historian, Babkin, it was peasants and the ordinary (unprivileged) townspeople who were 'patriotic'. He cited a peasant who enlisted his three sons, addressing them with the words, 'We shall not let the miscreants drink our Orthodox blood; we will leave only bones; let the insatiable foe gnaw them'.[41] He also noted volunteers who were house serfs, peasants on crown land, coachmen (who are in effect state peasants in this period), and townspeople. Babkin goes as far as to claim that the 'patriotic spirit' of the peasants was such that they disguised serious illnesses and injuries so that they could enlist in the militias, one Nikifor Evstefeev even trying to hide the fact that his left leg was incapacitated by an old wound![42]

There are problems, however, with Babkin's assertions, not least in the fact that it is not always clear from the records what social estate some of his 'volunteers' came from. One of his main examples of patriotism, for example, is an elderly woman who brought her two grandsons to be enlisted with the words: 'Only return to me when there is no enemy left on Russian soil', which is all very well until one realizes that it is not clear from his source whether or not she was a peasant.[43] There is indeed an archival record of 13 coachmen in Moscow province volunteering out of 'zeal and love of the fatherland',[44] but this request had to be approved by Governor Rostopchin himself, which suggests that it was rather unusual. Serfs, of course, could not volunteer without permission from their masters, whilst state peasants (which includes coachmen) could not do so without permission from the state.[45] Babkin, inevitably, castigated the nobility for not allowing their serfs to volunteer for the army and claimed that serfs fled their estates in order to enlist ('thus the serf régime mocked true patriots').[46] But in fact there is little evidence that serfs or peasants wished to join the army, whether on a permanent or a temporary basis. Sergeant Bourgogne recounted meeting some Polish peasants who 'made us understand that they had to go to Minsk to join the Russian army, as they belonged to the militia; they had been forced to march against us by blows from the knout, and the Cossacks were stationed in the villages to drive them out'.[47] Military service, as we shall see, was an obligation and not a privilege for these poor unfortunates.

While Russian and Soviet historians have lauded the patriotism of peasants and other 'non-privileged' volunteers for the militias and partisan groups, they have made little attempt to penetrate the mind of the ordinary soldier, conscripted from the same social groups. One simple reason for this is simply the dearth of material on the subject, although it has to be said that lack of concrete evidence has not deterred these historians from asserting that feelings of patriotism and anti-feudalism motivated members of the militias and partisan groups. The vast majority of Russian soldiers were illiterate. There are no letters home from soldiers, whilst there is only one memoir by a ordinary soldier of which I am aware, and this gives no indication of patriotism or even the mindset of an ordinary soldier.[48] We have no evidence of the common soldier's experience of battle. There are no accounts of the attitude of Russian soldiers towards the lands and peoples through which they passed in 1813–14 or of their experience as an army of occupation in France from 1815 to 1818. We simply do not know what the Russian soldier thought.

The Russian army was, of course, a very different force from that of French Revolutionary of Napoleonic armies. This was a premodern army, and had more in common with the armies of the Austrian empire than with those of France, or with Prussia after the military reforms. The Russian army was a conscript army, and the mechanism of recruitment had not changed fundamentally from the time of Peter I. It was theoretically possible for peasants to volunteer to enlist if they had the permission of their noble landowners or the state peasant commune, but this was rare (although I suspect about as rare as peasants volunteering to join the militia). Furthermore, service in the Russian army was not a temporary obligation, as it was in France or Prussia. Peter had established that service was for life; this was later reduced to 25 years in 1793 but in most cases this in effect meant for life. Once a soldier was conscripted, he was in practice – as symbolised by the loss of his beard – separated forever from village, family and peasant society, and, in effect, regarded as dead. Most Russian veterans ended up in garrison regiments or were cared for by monasteries, as an obligation imposed on them by the state. The few who returned to their village were generally old, sick or maimed, and found themselves outcasts, who were unwanted, unwelcomed and unable to contribute to the economic life of the village.

The dispatch of recruits from the villages demonstrates the true nature of the Russian army. There was no place here for the type of ceremonies which took place at the time of the *levée en masse* in France where recruits were reminded of their patriotic and civic duty to the nation. The departure of Russian conscripts, in contrast, was like the departure from life of a loved one. The songs accompanying the conscripts were laments rather than assertions of patriotic fervour. Robert Lyall, a British traveller in early nineteenth-century Russia described the scene in terms which could equally apply to a funeral:

> I have seen recruits upon *télegas* and sledges, drawn at a solemn pace, and surrounded by their relations and friends who bewailed their fate in the most lamentable manner; while they, dejected and absorbed in grief, sat like statues, or lay extended like corpses.[49]

The recruit was typically the man (not always young and not always unmarried) who was the least valued member of the community – often a drunkard, idle or a trouble maker – or a member of an impoverished family that was unable to afford to buy a substitute to go in his place (and substitutes became far more expensive in 1812).[50] Service in the Russian army, far from being a patriotic duty, was universally seen as the worst fate that could befall an individual.

Does this mean that it is impossible to give any indication of the *mentalité* of the Russian soldier? Contemporary commentators – French as well as Russian – commented on the bravery and stoicism of Russian troops under fire. But this might arise from fear of their commanders, not to mention the practice of training canon on the backsides of the infantry. There is no evidence that Russian soldiers fought any less bravely outside Russia where the 'fatherland' was less directly in danger. Russian rates of desertion on campaign may have been lower than for some other European armies, although the statistics are not accurate enough to be certain. This may anyway have been not so much due to 'patriotism' as to the fact that the Russian passport system and mechanisms of social control made it almost impossible for a recruit to merge unnoticed into urban society and thereby forced deserters into a life of brigandage on the edges of society. It could also have been partly due to the ferocious punishments inflicted on deserters who were caught. Despite these disincentives, desertion rates of new recruits between the village and the recruiting post were extremely high, and this suggests that when the opportunity arose the Russian soldier was as at least as eager to abandon his military duty as his fellow soldiers in other European armies of the time.[51]

There are soldiers' songs and folk songs which commemorate heroic victories against the enemy, brave Russian commanders and the defence of the country. This is, however, difficult evidence to use. It is not clear who wrote the songs, and when they were written; many were collected as folk songs by ethnographers in the late nineteenth century. Nor do we know how popular these songs were, the extent to which they genuinely reflected soldiers' sentiments, or indeed if they were sung more by peasants than soldiers. But there are nevertheless a few popular songs which celebrate Russian victories over the French with words that are clearly contemporary. For example:

> Remember, remember, Russians...
> The French fled from Moscow;
> Russian soldiers saw them off.

Or again:

> In the year eighteen twelve
> The French declared war
> On mother Moscow made of stone,
> On the whole of our Russia.[52]

The themes of saving Russia, and of 'stone Moscow' recur in other contemporary songs.[53] Ordinary soldiers were depicted sympathetically in Russian dramas, as loyal, honest but simple folk, but their attitude towards their country was not explored or considered in this medium.[54] After the end of war, monuments were raised to the heroic defenders of the country, but soldiers were rarely depicted realistically and were more often portrayed in classical style or as Russian medieval knights.[55]

A modern sense of patriotism cannot, therefore, be proved for the ordinary Russian soldier. There some, rather tentative evidence, however, the Russia soldiers did have a religious identity and that defence of Orthodoxy could become equated with defence of Russia (which may perhaps explain the reluctance of Soviet historians to explore the question of soldiers' loyalties). The association of Orthodoxy, or Christianity, with the defence of the fatherland had roots not in the French Revolutionary Wars, but in the conflicts between Russia and the Ottoman Empire in the second half of the eighteenth century, and was deliberately fostered in Russian celebratory odes and in state ceremonials marking victory over the infidel.[56] Russian soldiers took holy icons into battle up to the First World War;[57] whilst troops were blessed by priests before battle. The religious element was of particular significance in the Napoleonic Wars as Napoleon had been anathematized by the Orthodox

Church in 1806 and was popularly regarded as the anti-Christ. Priests in the provinces through which the Napoleonic armies passed deliberately whipped up popular feeling against the 'Godless' invader,[58] and there is no reason to think that ordinary Russian soldiers were immune from this. But even this religious patriotism has to be treated with caution. A sizeable proportion of the Russian army was neither Orthodox nor Christian, and there is no evidence that Lutheran Balts, Catholic Lithuanians or Muslim Kalmyks fought less bravely than Orthodox soldiers. Ferocious attacks on enemy soldiers, and at times civilians, were not just confined to Muslim opponents. Russian troops had acted with great ferocity in the attack on Warsaw in 1794; over 100 000 Poles entered Russia with the Napoleonic armies and there is some evidence to suggest that traditional hostility to these neighbours was more evident than against the 'Godless' French.[59]

The patriotism of the officer corps, in contrast, has been more clearly documented. Russian and Soviet histories and contemporary documents cite nobles entering, or re-entering, military service, and the donations of noble assemblies as evidence of patriotism.[60] Pushkin was 13 and a schoolboy in 1812 but recalled later in poetry his envy of boys who were slightly older and who had enlisted:

> You'll recollect: the wars soon swept us by,
> We bade farewell to all our elder brothers.
> And went back to our desks with all the others,
> In envy of all those who had gone to die
> Without us.[61]

Both Soviet and non-Soviet historians have, however, struggled with the patriotism of the Russian officer corps. The reason for that, it seems to me, lies not so much with the activities of the officers in 1812 but with events in 1825, when army officers, many of whom had served during the period 1812–14, led their men in an abortive rising known as the Decembrist Revolt in an attempt to force a constitution on Russia in the interregnum between the death of Alexander I and the accession of his brother, Nicholas I. This rebellion sits uneasily with the historiography of 1812. To the Russian historians of 1912, it must have been potentially embarrassing to acknowledge that some of the 'heroes' of 1812 (and a significant number of the Decembrists fought at the battle of Borodino and were rewarded for bravery at this or other battles) later became rebels and traitors. This was particularly the case in 1912 as Nicholas II's difficult relationship with the recently formed state duma made reference to an earlier, unsuccessful, armed attempt to introduce a constitution potentially provocative. The problem for Soviet historians was rather different. The Decembrists were portrayed favourably, albeit as rather romantic and confused individuals, not only because they physically opposed the tsar, and by extension the feudal order, but also because some of the political and social ideas of the more radical Southern Society could be directly related to Bolshevism. The result is that the Soviet period led to extensive scholarship on the Decembrists, including the publication of many of the papers of the investigating commission of 1826 and many memoirs, all of which provide invaluable source material for the historian. But the Decembrist movement has been treated by Soviet scholars quite separately from the studies of 1812 and the links between the two have not been explored.

There is no doubt, in fact, about the patriotism of the Decembrists. Nikita Murav'ev ended his studies at Moscow university in 1812 aged 16 and enlisted as he 'had no thought other than ardent love for the fatherland'.[62] The experience of 1812 was a formative one. Baron Andrei Rozen (a Baltic German and not an Orthodox Russian) commented that 'the extraordinary events of 1812 had also brought about a powerful feeling of the people's strength, and a sense of patriotism of which no one had before a conception.'[63] M.I. Murav'ev-Apostol' recalled in 1826 that his 'love for the fatherland which we saved from the Napoleonic yoke inspired me'.[64] S.P. Trubestskoi stated that:

> The invasion of Russia by Napoleon in the year 1812 aroused in Russians a love for the Fatherland in the highest degree; the happy conclusion to this war found all Russians proud of their names and everyone was happy to have participated in these sublime deeds which attested that each of them was useful to their Fatherland.[65]

The difficulty for the Russian government was that this form of patriotism was potentially dangerous, not only to the régime but also to the whole political and social order. Officers, and soldiers, had seen how people lived outside Russia: 'By comparison, the question naturally arose, why isn't it like that here?' asked Aleksandr Bestuzhev.[66] Patriotic officers now demanded that Russians should have at least as much as the European peoples who they saved (made more galling by the fact that the defeated powers of France and Poland had been granted constitutions, the former with Alexander's agreement and the latter by his expressed desire). 'The Poles received a constitution' noted A.M. Murav'ev bitterly, while 'Russians as a reward for their heroic exertions in the year 1812 got – military colonies!'.[67] The opening words of the constitution of the Northern Society were: 'All the European nations are attaining constitutions and freedom. The Russian nation, more than any of them, deserves one as well as the other'.[68] This meant not only a European, Napoleonic-style constitution but also posed a threat to serfdom, not least because some of the Decembrists had become particularly aware of the sufferings of the peasants in 1812. N.I. Turgenev went so far as to state that the peasant role in partisan warfare 'gave them the right to freedom'.[69] And ultimately, at least some of the Decembrists drew the logical conclusion from their experience in Europe, not just in the campaigns but also by witnessing events in Spain in 1820, that rulers could never be trusted to implement constitutional and social change without force; 'there is no compact with kings' stated P.D. Kakhovskii.[70]

The experience of the Napoleonic invasion of Russia demonstrated that if 'patriotism' could be an asset for the state, it could also be a danger. It was an asset when it led to enlistment in the regular army and the militias, when it resulted in donations of money, goods, horses and, in the case of nobles, serfs for the struggle and when it encouraged peasants to resist the invaders. But patriotism could be a danger when it led to demands for fundamental change to the political and social order as a 'reward' for the sacrifices made by the Russian people in freeing Europe from Napoleonic tyranny. Patriotism had be controlled and tied firmly to conservative values, such as tsardom and Orthodoxy, which also implied loyalty to the current political and social order, and to a vague sense of 'Russianness' that in turn was linked to Russian Orthodoxy and to the Russian tsar. It was this form of patriotism that was deliberately cultivated in the reign of Nicholas I and that was embodied in the expression 'Autocracy, Orthodoxy and Nationality' by the Minister of Education, Count S.S. Uvarov. The problems with this definition are all too obvious. Although the Russian Empire was predominantly Christian, not all Christians were Russian Orthodox (and the Orthodox included the Old Believers). By the late eighteenth century the ethnically Russian population had fallen to under 50 per cent; by 1833 it was estimated to be 45.32 per cent.[71] This only left tsardom, and by implication, the social and political order associated with tsardom, as a binding force for the empire. This did not prove to be either a stable basis for Russian patriotism or for the state in the following decades.

Notes

1. Some of the extensive scholarship is summarized in my 'Russia and Napoleon: state, society and the nation', in M. Rowe (ed.), *Collaboration and Popular*

Resistance to Napoleon (Basingstoke, 2003), pp. 186–202. For typical Russian (pre-1917) and Soviet analyses of the 'people's war', see V.P. Alekseev, 'Narodnaia voina' in A.K. Dzhivelegov, S.M. Mel'gunov, V.I. Pichet (eds), *Otechestvennaia voina i russkoe obshchestvo* (St Petersburg, 1912), IV, pp. 227–37, and L.G. Beskrovnyi, *Otechestvennaia voina 1812 goda* (Moscow, 1962), pp. 337–48.

2. Hartley, 'Russia and Napoleon', pp. 191–6; W.C. Fuller, *Strategy and Power in Russia* (New York, 1992), pp. 207–18.

3. V.I. Semevskii, 'Volneniia krest'ian v 1812 g. i sviazannyia s Otechestvennoi voinoi', in Dzhivelegov *et al.*, *Otechestvennaia voina*, V, pp. 74–113 and M.I. Tugan-Baranovskii, 'Voina 1812 g. i promyshlennoe razvitie Rossii', in *ibid.*, VII, pp. 105–12. A full version of the latter's work later appeared in English as M.I. Tugan-Baronovsky, *The Russian Factory in the Nineteenth Century* (Chicago, 1970).

4. In particular my articles: 'Russia in 1812, part I: the French Presence in the *Gubernii* of Smolensk and Mogilev', *Jahrbücher für Geschichte Osteuropas*, XXXVIII (1990), pp. 178–98, and 'Russia in 1812, part II: the Russian administration of Kaluga *gubernija*', *ibid.*, XXXIX (1990), pp. 399–416.

5. S.M. Ginzburg, *Otechestvennaia voina 1812 goda i russkie evrei* (St Petersburg, 1912); A.E. Zarin, *Zhenshchina geroini v 1812* (Moscow, 1913).

6. P. Andreev, *Narodnaia voina v Smolenskoi gubernii v 1812 godu* (Smolensk, 1940).

7. Beskrovnyi's work on 1812, cited in note 1, was published in 1962, as a collection of articles: *1812 god. K stopiatidesiatiletiiu Otechestvennoi voiny. Sbornik statei* (Moscow, 1962) (hereafter *1812 god*).

8. See, for example, J. Werner, *We Laughed at Boney (or, We've been through it all before)* (London, 1943), which equates the British patriotic resistance to Napoleon with resistance to Hitler.

9. A.N. Kochetkov, 'Partizanskaia voina' in *1812 god*, p. 174; S.A. Kniaz'kov, 'Partizany i partizanskaia voina v 1812-m godu', in Dzhivelegov *et al.*, *Otechestvennaia voina*, IV, p. 209.

10. For a concise summary of the practice and theories of guerrilla warfare, see W. Laqueur, 'The origins of guerrilla doctrine', *Journal of Contemporary History*, X, no. 2 (April, 1975), pp. 341–82. The Bulavin revolt in the reign of Peter the Great has been characterized as an earlier example of guerrilla war: cf. C.W. Ingrao, 'Guerrilla warfare in early-modern Europe: the Kuruc War (1703–11)' in B.K. Király and G.E. Rothenburg (eds), *War and Society in East Central Europe*, (New York, 1979), I, p. 62.

11. Entry by L.N. Bychkov in *Sovetskaia istoricheskaia entsiklopediia* (Moscow, 1967), X, p. 886; translated in S.L. Wieczynski (ed.), *The Modern Encyclopedia of Russian and Soviet History* (Gulf Breeze, 1982), XXVII, p. 22.

12. Kochetkov, 'Partizanskaia voina', p. 167.

13. *Ibid.*, p. 167.

14. Slezsinskii commented that activity in Smolensk province depended on the availability of nobles and officials to form these groups: cf. A. Slezsinskii, 'Smolenskie partizany v 1812 godu', *Russkaia starina*, CIII, no. 9 (September, 1900), p. 663; Kochetkov, 'Partizanskaia voina', pp. 167, 172–7; 'Kniaz'kov, 'Partizany', p. 215.

15. Kochetkov, 'Partizanskaia voina', p. 166.

16. Kniaz'kov, 'Partizany', pp. 210, 214.
17. Hartley, 'Napoleon in Russia, part I', pp. 192–8.
18. See P. Longworth, 'Transformations in cossackdom, 1650–1850' in Király et al., *War and Society in East Central Europe*, pp. 393–407.
19. I.I. Prokhostsov, *Riazanskaia guberniia v 1812 godu preimushchestvenno s bytovoi storony: materialy dlia istorii Otechestvennoi voiny* (Riazan', 1912), II, p. 4.
20. Tolstoi, *War and Peace* (Everyman edn, London, 1958), III, pp. 295–6.
21. For a non-Communist account, cf. A.K. Kabanova, 'Opolcheniia 1812 goda' in Dzhivelegov et al., *Otechestvennaia voina*, V, pp. 43–74. The Soviet scholar who has most thoroughly studied the militias is V.I. Babkin in two publications of the same date: 'Organizatsiia i voennye deistviia narodnogo opolcheniia v Otechestvennoi voine 1812 g', in *1812 god*, pp. 134–63; *Narodnoe opolchenie v Otechestvennoi voine 1812 goda* (Moscow, 1962). His views are echoed by Beskrovnyi, *Otechestvennaia voina*, pp. 456–64.
22. Beskrovnyi, *Otechestvenaia voina*, pp. 461–2.
23. Alexander I to L. Wittgenstein, 29 December 1812 Old Style, in L.G. Beskrovnyi (ed.), *Narodnoe opolchenie v Otechestvennoi voine 1812 goda* (Moscow, 1962), pp. 26–7.
24. List of officers in the militia who fought at the battle of Dresden, Russkii gosudarstvennyi voenno-istoricheskii arkhiv, Moscow (hereafter RGVIA), *fond* 846, *opis'* 16, *delo* 3395, f. 2.
25. A.A. Pokrovskii et al. (eds.) *Vosstanie Dekabristov: Materialy i Dokumenty. Dela Verhovnogo Ugolovnogo Suda i Sledstvennoi Komissii* (Moscow, 1925–2001), XIV, pp. 148–9.
26. Kabanov, 'Opolchenie', pp. 46–7.
27. *Vosstanie Dekabristov*, V, p. 106.
28. *Ibid.*, XII, p. 134.
29. Babkin, 'Organisatsiia', p. 143.
30. Kabanov, 'Opolchenie', pp. 47–8.
31. Beskrovnyi, *Otechestvennaia voina*, p. 459.
32. Report from the Moscow militia, 14 August 1812 Old Style, in Beskrovnyi, *Narodnoe opolchenie*, p. 60.
33. Papers on the St Petersburg and Novgorod militias in 1812, RGVIA, *fond* 846, *opis'* 16, *delo* 3447, ff. 46, 119.
34. S.V Potrashev, 'Uchastie Slobodsko-Ukrainskoi gubernii v Otechestvennoi voine 1812 g.', in *Otechestvennaia voina 1812 goda: Istochniki, Pamiatniki, Problemy* (Borodino, 1998), pp. 139–41.
35. J.M. Hartley, *A Social History of the Russian Empire, 1650–1825* (London, 1999), pp. 39–40.
36. Kabanov, 'Opolchenie', pp. 60–1.
37. S. Khrapov, 'Russkaia intelligentsia v Otechestvennoi voine 1812', *Istoricheskii Zhurnal*, 1943, no. 2, p. 73.
38. J.T. Flynn, *The University Reforms of Alexander I 1802–1835* (Washington, 1988), pp. 33, 62.
39. O. Kozadevlev to A.I. Gorchakov, 29 October 1812 Old Style, RGVIA, *fond* 846, *opis'* 16, *delo* 3447, f. 65.
40. G.L. Freeze, *The Parish Clergy in Nineteenth-Century Russia: Crisis, Reform, Counter-Reform* (Princeton, 1983), p. 167.
41. Babkin, 'Organisatsiia', p. 137; Babkin, *Narodnoe opolchenie*, pp. 33–4.

42. Babkin, *Narodnoe opolchenie*, p. 37.
43. Babkin, 'Organisatsiia', p. 137, Babkin, *Narodnoe opolchenie*, p. 33. The source for this quotation is an account by Count Rostopchin, which may not be totally reliable as he was deliberately trying to foster a Russian, patriotic, resistance to the invader.
44. A request by coachmen from Moscow in the name of Rostopchin, 5 August 1812 Old Style, Beskrovnyi, *Narodnoe opolchenie*, p. 55.
45. A recent English historical account of 1812 misses this point and states that 'On 1812, 190 000 serfs joined the militia, thousands more the partisans': N. Nicolson, *Napoleon in 1812* (London, 1985), p. 67. I have in fact come across 'volunteers' in the course of my research for my forthcoming book on war, state and society in Russia 1762–1825, but the evidence suggests that this was a purely financial arrangement and that substitute recruits were in effect bought by richer peasants.
46. Babkin, *Narodnoe opolchenie*, pp. 39–40.
47. P. Cottin and M. Hénault (eds), *The Memoirs of Sergeant Bourgogne* (London, 1975), p. 165.
48. 'Zapiski soldata Pamfilova Nazarova, v inochestve Mitrofana, 1792–1839 gg', *Russkaia starina*, XXII, no. 8 (August, 1878), pp. 529–56.
49. R. Lyall, *Travels in Russia, the Krimea, the Caucasus and Georgia* (London, 1825), I, p. 141.
50. See J.M. Hartley, 'The Russian recruit' in J. Klein, S. Dixon and M. Fraanje (eds), *Reflections on Russia in the Eighteenth Century* (Cologne, Weimar, Vienna, 2001), pp. 32–42.
51. *Ibid.*, p. 42.
52. A.V. Buganov, *Russkaia istoriia v pamiati krest'ian XIX veka i natsional'noe samosoznanie* (Moscow, 1992), pp. 159–60.
53. V.V. Kalash, 'Otechestvennaia voina v russkoi narodnoi poezii', in Dzhivelegov *et al.*, *Otechestvennaia voina*, V, pp. 175–6.
54. E.K. Wirtschafter, 'The common soldier in eighteenth-century Russian drama', in Klein *et al.*, *Reflections on Russia*, pp. 367–76.
55. M.A. Nekrasov and S.M. Zemtsov, *Otechestvennaia voina 1812 goda i russkoe iskusstvo* (Moscow, 1969).
56. A. Zorin, *Kormia dvuglavogo orla . . . Literatura i gosudarstvennaia ideologiia v Rossii v poslednei treti XVIII – pervoi treti XIX veka* (Moscow, 2001), pp. 65–122.
57. Cf. W. Ryan, 'Magic and the military in Russia', in Klein *et al.*, *Reflections on Russia*, p. 85.
58. For more details, see J.M. Hartley, 'Napoleon – saviour or antichrist?', *History Today*, XLI, no. 1 (January 1991), pp. 28–34.
59. Hartley, 'Napoleon in Russia, part I', pp. 180–1.
60. See, for example, the patriotic activities of the Kaluga nobles in Hartley 'Napoleon in Russia, part II', pp. 408–9, and Beskrovnyi, *Otechestvennaia voina*, p. 463.
61. O. Figes, *Natasha's Dance: a Cultural History of Russia* (Penguin, 2002), p. 82.
62. *Vosstanie Dekabristov*, I, p. 294.
63. G. Barratt, *Rebel on the Bridge: a Life of the Decembrist Baron Andrey Rozen, 1800–84* (London, 1975), p. 37.
64. *Vosstanie Dekabristov*, IX, p. 217.
65. L. Ia. Pavlova, *Dekabristy – uchastniki voin 1805–1814 gg* (Moscow, 1979), p. 94.

66. V.I. Semevskii, *Politicheskiia i obshchestvennyia idei Dekabristov* (St Petersburg, 1909), p. 207.
67. V.A. Fedorov, *Memuary Dekabristov: severnoe obshchestvo* (Moscow, 1981), p. 124.
68. A.G. Mazour, *The First Russian Revolution, 1825* (Stanford, 1961), p. 91.
69. Pavlova, *Dekabristy*, p. 94.
70. I. de Madariaga, 'Spain and the Decembrists', *European Studies Review*, III, no. 2 (April, 1973), p. 149.
71. Hartley, *Social History*, pp. 10, 15.

10
Popular Resistance in Napoleonic Europe: Issues and Perspectives

Charles J. Esdaile

Popular resistance is a subject that must inevitably lie at the heart of any discussion of the Napoleonic empire. In the first place, as the French themselves recognized, it was inevitable. As Napoleon told his brother, Joseph, in 1806, 'Two weeks earlier or later you will have an uprising. It always happens in a conquered country.'[1] On one level the reason was obvious, for occupation by the imperial armies was generally an experience that was as ruinous as it was unpleasant. But in addition to this there was also the issue of reform. To quote Michael Broers, 'The consolidation of Napoleonic rule was a turbulent process, and the initial response it met with among the vast majority of people was resistance.'[2] Resistance, then, was something that was always there, and, furthermore, something that the French themselves had every expectation of having to deal with as soon as they made a new conquest. That said, however, it was not just part of the general backdrop to the history of Napoleon's Europe. Thus, its extent was one of the chief factors that determined whether a given state or region should be considered part of – in Broers' parlance – the 'inner' or the 'outer' empires, and, by the same token, of the extent to which the reforms associated with Napoleonic rule took root. At the simplest level collaboration was – on one reading of the situation, at least – less likely in areas where the local élites on whom the French and their allies inevitably depended for the implantation of their policies were likely to find themselves the victims of murder or mutilation. And at the same time the very policies of Napoleonic rule could not take effect against a background of violence that precluded the rule of law and drained away resources that might have funded, say, new systems of state education. End that violence, however, and it was a different matter. To quote Broers again, 'Perhaps an essential defining characteristic of the lands which became the "inner empire" ... was that the balance slowly – and usually grudgingly – tipped away from resistance towards collaboration.'[3]

Beyond all this, there is also the issue of the role of guerrilla warfare in the fall of the Napoleonic empire. On the surface popular insurgency made the takeover of various parts of Europe a costly affair, and plunged the French into protracted military campaigns that in a variety of ways seriously destabilized the imperial war machine. Up until 1808, it is said, the emperor's conquests paid for themselves, whereas the Spanish guerrillas thereafter ensured that war was a drain on the treasury. By the same token, French casualties up until 1808 could be made up without pushing the French people further than they would stand on the conscription front, whereas after 1808 the daily blood-letting that was the cost of the war in Spain ensured that the army's demands for manpower rose steeply. Grumbling on the home front at the steady rise in taxation and conscription, meanwhile, was matched by grumbling in the army. Faced in Calabria and Spain by seemingly endless struggles that entailed a great deal of danger but precious little glory, the once loyal soldiers of the emperor grew cynical and resentful, with the result that their willingness to sacrifice their lives fell off dramatically. Still worse, perhaps, frightened, harassed and frustrated, the troops became increasingly undisciplined and engaged in acts of revenge or casual brutality that served only to augment the numbers of their opponents and discredit the cause of collaboration. Also problematic in this respect was an increase in desertion that provided the Allies with an important source of manpower whilst simultaneously augmenting the need for new conscripts: by 1813, for example, the Duke of Wellington had no fewer than three regiments of cavalry and seven battalions of infantry that were recruited in whole or in part from foreign deserters, whilst substantial numbers of deserters also appear to have been serving with the famous guerrilla commander, Francisco Espoz y Mina.[4]

Well might, then, Napoleon have referred to the Peninsular War as his Spanish ulcer. And this is not even the end of the story. Other instances of popular insurrection were less far-reaching in their effects, but they are nevertheless not to be discounted. In 1809, for example, the Tyrolean revolt and the amorphous series of peasant risings that gripped the Kingdom of Italy seriously hampered operations against Austria, whilst in 1812 and 1813 partisan bands – in part inspired by the Spanish example – considerably increased the scale of French defeat in both Russia and Germany. Not for nothing, then, did the Napoleonic Wars give us the very word 'guerrilla'. To quote George Rudé, 'A new element had crept into the situation: the protesting voices of the European peoples themselves.'[5]

In saying all this, of course, we must not go too far. It is, for example, important to note that popular resistance was not the only factor that defined the extent to which areas were 'napoleonized'. Where areas were only taken under French control after 1810, there was simply not the time to transform reformist principles into administrative and juridical realities. Also important were the attitudes of the satellite rulers appointed to rule the wider empire: placed on their thrones by French bayonets, Napoleon's siblings were frequently none too willing to restrict themselves to the role of marionettes, and in the case of both Joseph and Louis they sought very hard to mediate between Paris on the one hand and the local élites on the other. At the same time even collaboration might wear an independent hue: in Naples, for example, notables who were quite prepared to go along with some aspects of French policy proved extremely reluctant to go along with others. Moving on from this, we must also be careful what we mean by 'popular resistance'. In Calabria, the Tyrol, Spain and Portugal, there were bloody popular revolts against the French (or, at least, their surrogates), whilst there was also certainly a limited amount of popular involvement in the campaigns of 1812 and 1813 in Russia and Germany. But these examples are exceptions rather than the rule: whilst popular resistance of various sorts was widespread, it on the whole took forms that did not involve resort to the force of arms. At the head of the list probably comes draft evasion, but also important were such areas as smuggling and simple non-compliance, most notably with respect to French-approved forms of religious observance. And, last but not least, neither popular revolt nor guerrilla warfare was a new phenomenon in European history. Spain, for example, had seen the Catalans rise in rebellion in the 1640s; Britain had experienced the Monmouth rising of 1685 and the Jacobite risings of 1689, 1715 and 1745–46; and Genoa had to cope with an insurrection in Corsica that began in 1729 and was only brought to an end by cession of the island to France in 1768. As for guerrilla warfare, not only was it a feature of several of these revolts, but the War of the Spanish Succession had seen the appearance of numerous bands of irregulars in Spain; at the same time, wherever armies waged war in the course of the eighteenth century, desperate peasants fought to defend their homes against marauding bands of soldiers, or took their revenge for the numerous injuries done to them by murdering stragglers from the armies or attacking supply columns or convoys of wounded. To drive home the point still further, meanwhile, it is also worth pointing out that even in the Napoleonic period guerrilla warfare was not a phenomenon that was solely linked to French occupation: in Finland, for example, the Russian invasion of 1808–09 sparked off a bitter partisan struggle that foreshadowed the 'winter war' of 1939–40, whilst in Serbia the national insurrection in opposition to Turkish rule that exploded in 1804 was headed by irregular bands known as *hajduks*. In the end, however, all that is by-the-by, for it is difficult to find a commentator on the Napoleonic Wars who has not underlined either the significance of the armed people in the struggle or the supposedly ubiquitous nature of the phenomenon. This, for example, is the opinion of Geoffrey Best: 'Most peoples whom the French dominated...sooner or later offered armed resistance in one mode or another.'[6] In much the same vein, we have the views of Jeremy Black, 'Uprisings were not new, but they were more important in the period, in part because the French destroyed or took over existing power structures, leaving rebellion as the only way to express discontent.'[7] And lastly, if only to show that the idea is well established, we might cite Herbert Fisher: 'The Spanish rising was the first example of a long series of popular and national movements which ultimately shattered the Napoleonic empire.'[8]

There is, then, a general assumption that popular resistance was an important issue in so far as Napoleonic Europe is concerned. From this it might be expected that the subject ought to have generated a substantial historiography, but, with respect to the English language at least, this is simply not the case. No general study exists of the role played by the people-in-arms in the Napoleonic Wars, and it is significant that not one of the speakers at a recent conference that was based on the theme of responses to the experience of Napoleonic rule chose to concentrate on guerrilla warfare.[9] Also interesting here is the treatment accorded to popular resistance in several recent monographs on the Napoleonic empire. Let us take, for example, Broers' excellent *Europe under Napoleon*. In this we have a long section – twenty-four pages, no less – headed 'resistance', whilst the subject also figures in other places, such as the author's separate discussion of the Peninsular War. Yet throughout the focus is overwhelmingly political and cultural rather than military, and the reader is left with little clue as to who joined the guerrillas or, except in the most general terms, the forces that produced their enlistment. At the same time, too, the general impression created is that, even in the context of Spain and Portugal, in the end guerrilla warfare was not very important in a military sense.[10] This is all very well – Broers' views are not only entirely plausible, but backed up by the sources – but the fact is that the reader is entitled to rather more exposition of his views in this respect than he is prepared to give them. Moving on from Broers, we come to Stuart Woolf's seminal *Napoleon's Integration of Europe*. In this case, from the very beginning we are confronted by the perception – entirely correct, be it said – that armed insurrection was the exception rather than the norm. Thus: 'In practice, outbreaks of collective political opposition were rare and local...Apart from Spain, only two revolts seriously challenged French authority; the endemic war in Calabria and the Tyrol rising.'[11] Beyond that, however, discussion remains vague: Woolf tries hard to establish the conditions that produced revolt rather than other forms of resistance – for him the key factors appear to be Catholicism, rough terrain and the availability of outside aid – and makes a series of interesting connections, most notably with banditry, desertion, seasonal migration and the organization of agriculture, but all this is compressed into a mere seven pages, and the general effect is to pose more questions than it answers.[12] And, lest it appear that the author of the current paper is inclined to exempt himself from criticism, it should be noted that his own *Wars of Napoleon* suffers from exactly the same deficiencies: there is an attempt to explain the incidence of revolt – in addition to the factors noted by Woolf, attention is drawn to the importance of popular radicalization in response to reformist absolutisms in the period immediately preceding the coming of the French – not to mention a considerable amount of material on the various revolts, but at no point can it be said that the subject is ever addressed from the inside. Support for some of his arguments may be found in Broers' *Europe under Napoleon*, in that its author points out that resistance was likely to be fiercest in areas where enlightened absolutism had either made no progress whatsoever, or alternatively had only recently begun to make inroads on traditional society, but, some ten years on from when the passages in question were first written, the impression is one of flaccidity – even of superficiality. Perhaps this is over-harsh, for *The Wars of Napoleon* does adopt a genuinely critical approach to the subject. Thus: 'Though Europe experienced great suffering on account of the Napoleonic empire, only in certain areas did passive resentment and low-level unrest explode into active revolt. Where it did, moreover, it was fuelled by factors that were by no means always directly connected to French rule...As for the efficacy of popular resistance, it is all too clear that in itself it presented little threat to French domination.'[13] But assertion is one thing, and argument quite another: the case put forward by the author may well be plausible, but in the end it was not backed up by the necessary weight of evidence.

The reasons why the general historiography of the Napoleonic Wars is so lacking when it comes to the analysis of guerrilla warfare is not hard to establish. Such is the romantic appeal of the subject that many traditionalist and, perhaps more to the point, populist accounts do not delve beneath the surface at all but are rather absolutely unquestioning in their acceptance of the heroic version of events. Typical of this tendency is the British author, Corelli Barnett, whose account of the emperor's career can only be described as orthodox. For example:

There was nothing novel about the Spanish uprising in itself. On previous occasions, after all, Bonaparte had barged into deeply traditional societies and set about reconstructing them on the model of Bonapartian France ... And on those occasions, too, outraged peoples had taken up arms against him, with the result that the deceptively easy shortcut of conquest had proved to lead him only into a morass of political and social complication. The novelty about the Spanish revolt ... consisted in its order of magnitude.[14]

For academic historians interested primarily in political and social history, by contrast, the issue is not lack of critical thinking. That said, however, with the greatest respect it might be suggested that they wear blinkers of their own. Uninterested in military history – indeed, in some instances overtly hostile to it – it is difficult to suspect that they have not seized upon the relative paucity of armed popular resistance, not to mention the obvious questions that may be asked of its efficacy, as an excuse for skimming it with the lightest of brushes. Even for those historians who have wished to examine the subject in the context of a general study of Napoleonic Europe, there has been the problem of language and access to the archives: in the case of the present author, for example, his command of Spanish, French, Portuguese and Catalan is not matched by a similar command of German, Italian and Russian, just as the relatively generous research budget he has enjoyed in recent years has been barely sufficient to cover the costs of working in one country, let alone half a dozen. Ask interesting questions though they might, then, historians in the end cannot but be superficial once they stray beyond the frontiers of their own specialisms. And finally there is the issue of the immense complexity which compounds the problems facing the would-be historian of irregular warfare in the Napoleonic period. To quote Geoffrey Best, 'The main stream of military historical writing has understandably neglected [the guerrillas] ... because they are in fact difficult to categorise and assess.'[15]

As Best continues, we therefore have no 'adequate typology' of the guerrillas. All the more is the case given the deficiencies in the English-language historiography pertaining to the individual areas affected by armed resistance. Let us take, for example, the question of the Tyrol. Thus, the only modern works available in English on the war of 1809 consist of one book and one conference paper, and both of these are only 'modern' in terms of their year of publication, the dates concerned being 1986 and 1989. Largely composed of military narrative, they have little to tell us with regard to either the identities or the mentalities of the insurgents and are inclined to see the rebellions almost wholly in terms of loyalty to the Habsburgs, adumbrated though this may have been in terms of a desire to defend a favourable regional settlement that was threatened by foreign annexation. And, still more alarmingly, they in neither case seem to have made much use of the series of German-language works on the Tyrol that appeared in the early 1980s.[16] The level of analysis on which they rest, meanwhile, is exemplified by the following passage from Eyck:

> The Tyrolean uprising of 1809 – *anno neun* as some of it native chroniclers proudly and reverently have called it...took place in some of the most scenic mountain areas of Europe. The men...who took part in the rising struggled for their ancient and cherished liberties. They fought in their colourful costumes representing the various districts populated by a free, proud and conservative peasantry. Their war was directed at one and the same time against foreign occupiers...and toward reassociation with their beloved Habsburg dynasty.[17]

If the Tyrol is bad, meanwhile, Portugal is even worse, for there is no discreet study of her insurrection and guerrilla movement at all, the only information that we have coming from British accounts of the Peninsular War. Yet these are in reality all but useless: written by historians interested only in the doings of Wellington's army, their treatment of the subject is at best superficial. To take Oman, for example, all he does in this respect is to copy out various passages from the memoirs of French soldiers who fought in the successive invasion armies of Junot, Soult and Massena.[18] Depressingly enough, there is little more to be got from modern English-language histories of Portugal – the two most recent, indeed, do not discuss the matter at all – whilst even accounts of the campaigns of some pretension do little more than claim that in 1809 the French were 'constantly harassed by guerrillas' or that 'the partisan war ceaselessly sapped the strength of [Soult's] field army'.[19] Similarly, there is Jan Read, who tells us that in 1810 the 'stranglehold' exercised by the irregulars was 'so complete... that from 18 September to 15 November the garrisons at Almeida and Ciudad Rodrigo received no single message from Masséna... and Napoleon himself was dependent on what he read in the English newspapers'.[20] This, however, is not good enough. Setting aside the fact that we do not in any sense 'get inside' the resistance, relying on French memoirs as a source for the Portuguese insurrection is a risky step. Many of the works consulted – Pelet, Lemonnier-Delafosse, Barrès, Marbot – say little or nothing on the subject in the evident hope of glossing matters over, whilst those that do tell us little more than that a prominent part in events was played by the clergy. Let us take, for example, Maximilien Foy, an officer who served in the French army that first occupied Portugal in 1807:

> The inhabitants of Torre de Moncorvo... hung on the enemy's rear. Father José Joachim de l'Assomption [*sic*], a monk of the order of Black Friars, marched at the head of this multitude with his gown tucked up, firing a musket like the rest. Another monk, Father José Bernardo de Azevedo, went to Coimbra with... a crowd of peasants to slaughter some French soldiers who were in the hospital of that city... The priests perambulated the towns and hamlets, preaching the French crusade.[21]

Similar remarks, meanwhile, can be made with respect to Spain. Here, too, the memoirs of French veterans are not to be relied upon, or, at least, taken at face value. Thus, in the first place, emphasising the guerrilla war was a convenient way of explaining away French defeat in Iberia: the victors of Austerlitz, Jena and Friedland had only been worsted because they were confronted by an enemy who did not fight fair. To quote Joseph Bonaparte's close friend and confidant, Miot de Melito:

> By that time [i.e. the summer of 1809] the formidable guerrilla system had been adopted by the Junta. Spread throughout every corner of Spanish territory... the guerrillas did us more harm than its regular armies, intercepting all our communications and forcing us neither to send out a dispatch without an escort, nor to allow soldiers to travel the roads on their own... This petty war undermined us most gravely. We only possessed the ground actually occupied by our armies, and our power never extended any further. All administration ceased, and there was neither order, nor justice, nor finance.[22]

And, in the second, it also provided a roundabout means of legitimizing France's cause. When they were not motivated by a desire for plunder, the guerrillas, we are told, were the creation of a reactionary and superstitious clergy desperate to protect the power, privileges and possessions of the Catholic Church, whilst every French veteran was also keen to stress the appalling atrocities committed by their irregular opponents. And, if they were faced by reaction, supersitition and savagery, it followed that they themselves were apostles of enlightenment and civilization, and the emperor himself the liberator that he had always claimed to be (it will be recalled in this respect that on St. Helena he always attributed his defeat in the Peninsula not to force of arms, but rather to the fact that the inhabitants of Spain and Portugal were too backward, too primitive and too put upon to appreciate the benefits of his rule).[23] Typical, perhaps, are the remarks of the apothecary, Blaze. Thus:

> An enlightened government that would have overthrown the religious houses and rendered the enormous mass of priests and monks... who were making their fatherland groan beneath the weight of their tyranny... useful to state and society would never have suited [the clergy]. To avoid this danger they harnessed their own interests to those of Heaven. Through their efforts the struggle became a war of religion sullied by all the horrors that religious fanaticism could inspire... The clergy skillfully employed the influence which they still enjoyed over Spanish credulity... to inflame the populace... In this fashion they encouraged a naturally cruel and barbarous people to commit the most revolting crimes with a clear conscience. They accused us of being Jews, heretics, sorcerers... As a result, just to be a Frenchman became a crime in the eyes of the country.[24]

In this respect, of course, it did not help that Spain was in their eyes hopelessly backward. Let us here quote the hussar officer, Rocca:

> With regard to knowledge and the progress of social habits, Spain was at least a century behind the other nations of the continent. The... insular situation of the country and the severity of its religious institutions had prevented the Spaniards from taking part in the disputes and controversies which had agitated and enlightened Europe.[25]

When they were not being gulled by their priests, meanwhile, the common people were driven by greed. For the German officer, Von

Brandt, for example, their chief motivation was the 'hope of plunder', whilst for Joseph Bonaparte's *aide-de-camp*, Bigarré, 'Appetite for gain and not love of glory was the chief desire that inspired them.'[26] Meanwhile, according to the Frenchman, Fée:

> At that time one had to travel in Spain in the same way as one did in Arabia: woe be to he who strayed from the caravan. The Spaniards, in whose veins were still to be found some drops of African blood, became veritable Bedouins: motivated more by love of pillage than patriotic duty, they stalked their prey, threw themselves upon it, seized what they wanted and disappeared amongst the rocks to split up their booty and torture their prisoners.[27]

The distortion that we see with regard to Portugal is therefore mirrored in the case of Spain. Thus, from the beginning the most exaggerated accounts of the guerrilla war were circulating in British, French and Spanish accounts alike, and these have ever since been given the most widespread and general credence. Of this a good example is the famous claim by Bigarré. Thus:

> The guerrillas did much more harm to the French troops than the regular armies in the course of the Spanish war. It is recognized that they killed at least 100 men per day. In the space of five years, they therefore killed 180 000 Frenchmen without having lost more than 25 000 themselves.[28]

In other places, meanwhile, even more dramatic claims surfaced amongst French veterans of the Peninsular campaigns, the military theorist Jean le Mière de Corvey going so far, for example, as to put the death toll they inflicted at 80 000 men a year.[29] Whilst thousands of men may well have perished in minor combats rather than major battles and sieges, the constant repetition of such figures takes no account of the fact that many of the Allied participants in the 'little war' were not irregulars at all, but rather regular soldiers, and sometimes even members of either the British Royal Navy or even the Anglo-Portuguese army of the Duke of Wellington.[30] Notwithstanding such problems, however, author after author has been quite uncritical in their treatment of the subject. Let us begin, for example, with Sir Charles Oman, an author who is hardly noted for his generous treatment of the Spaniards. For example:

Old Castile, Navarre and the lands of the upper Ebro were kept in a constant turmoil by a score of guerrilla chiefs, of whom the elder Mina was the leading figure... On the whole, there were probably never more than 20 000 *guerrilleros* in arms at once in the whole region between the Sierra de Guadarrama and the... Bay of Biscay. They never succeeded in beating any French force more than two or three battalions strong, and were being continually hunted from corner to corner. Yet despite their weakness in the open field... they rendered good service... by pinning down... twice their own numbers of... French troops. Anyone who has read the dispatches of the commandants of Napoleon's 'military governments'... will recognize a remarkable likeness between the situation of affairs in northern Spain during 1810 and 1811 and that in South Africa during 1900 and 1901. Lightly moving guerrilla bands, unhampered by a base to defend or a train to weight them down, and well-served as to intelligence by the residents of the countryside, can paralyze the action of an infinitely larger number of regular troops.[31]

In so far as the world of the Anglo-Saxon historiography was concerned, Oman's magisterial conclusions set the seal of approval on the guerrillas, the eighty years that have passed since the publication of the last volume of his work having been accompanied by a veritable chorus of praise. On all sides the many populists who chose to write about the Peninsular War leapt to acknowledge the exploits of the guerrillas. To quote Longford, for example:

Spain was to be saved... not by grape-shot, greybeards and grandees, but by hardy guerrillas and the sudden flash of the knife. These peasants spontaneously organized themselves into small do-or-die bands... headed by folk-heroes, Juan Martín Díaz called 'El Empecinado'... Julián Sánchez... the Minas, elder and younger... One chieftain called Moreno killed or wounded nine Frenchmen with a single discharge from his enormous blunderbuss... Even the basic force of 200 000 veterans which Napoleon was compelled to keep, year after year, in Spain would never be safe from the noon-day ambush and things that went bump in the night.[32]

So enthusiastic were these writers that they were soon seeing the entire Spanish was effort in terms of the guerrillas, as witness the extraordinary account of the battle of Bailén – a wholly conventional field action fought entirely by regular troops of the old Bourbon army – that we must now quote from Richard Humble:

> As soon as Dupont put his demoralized troops on the march out of Andujar the Spaniards closed in and harried them. A running fight escalated into a full-scale engagement at Bailén ... against an enemy who did not bother to attack them when they formed square, but only when they were least ready.[33]

It was not just the writers of popular history who echoed the general refrain, however. Amongst historians of greater pretension Oman's theories have also been accepted without question and even pushed to fresh lengths. 'It was above all', wrote David Chandler, 'the interaction of Wellington's operations with those of the guerrilla bands that ... made the French problem wholly intractable ... Even with 320 000 men the marshals could not both contain the diffuse ... "war of the flea" and at the same time ... meet Wellington's latest foray deep into their territory.'[34] So enthusiastic, indeed, is Chandler that he sometimes makes it appear as if the guerrillas were among Wellington's first concerns. Thus:

> As for Wellington, he appreciated that he had to preserve England's only field army and at the same time give maximum possible assistance to Portuguese and Spanish resistance – especially the popular kind. Having established a safe base at Lisbon ... he conducted forays into enemy-held territory to divert French attention and thus ease the pressures on the guerrillas and partisans; then, in 1812 ... he began a systematic reconquest of Spain by conventional means.[35]

Nor have British historians been the only ones to pick up on the theme of the guerrillas. Since the 1960s, for example, a succession of American and Canadian historians have produced work that lays great stress on their contribution to the struggle.

> 'The War of Independence did not produce on the Spanish side great generals ... Nor did the conflict produce truly great political leaders ... The true giants ... must be sought elsewhere. They could be found ... in the craggy mountains, among the barren hills, in the forbidding gorges ... They were the leaders of those intrepid bands that almost from the very beginning made the war in Spain a nightmare for the Napoleonic armies. Swooping down from their mountainous hideouts ... they never let the invaders forget ... that Spain had not

given up the fight. It is not an exaggeration to say that these bands...made history. They carried on the war against Napoleon when there were few regular Spanish forces left to continue the struggle, and through their perseverance and the damage they inflicted on the enemy, as well as the incalculable help they rendered Wellington's...forces, they must be given a large, perhaps decisive share of the credit for the emperor's failure in the Peninsula.'[36]

In his detailed account of the 'little war' in Aragón – a study rendered the more valuable by the fact that it rests on detailed research in the French archives – Alexander argues that the 'combination of conventional resistance, galvanised by Wellington's army, and the irregular opposition of the *partidas* proved irresistible'; that 'the *partidas* could probably have sustained resistance indefinitely'; and even that 'the partisan leaders were able to forge from the spirit of opposition an army that managed to exploit French military difficulties and liberate Aragón'.[37] And, finally, for John Tone, whose study of the guerrillas of Navarre is by far the most detailed work that the English language boasts on the subject:

> Armed peasants made chaos of French communications and performed other tasks of value to both English and Spanish regular forces. Partisans scoured the countryside of French spies and sympathizers and brought a continuous stream of information to the Allies. The guerrillas also effected a kind of psychological warfare in which the French had to be constantly on the alert, while the Allied armies could rest securely in the midst of a vigilant peasantry. The guerrilla war was a long and demoralizing nightmare for France. In the regions of insurgency, where each peasant was a potential guerrilla, there could be no campaigning season, no safe havens, no truces. Everywhere and always there existed the possibility of a hostile encounter...In guerrilla country, the French governed only where they could actually have troops in place. When these troops were withdrawn, the territory reverted to the guerrillas, becoming valueless to the French, if not a positive drain on their resources. War in Spain did not pay Napoleon as it had in other parts of Europe. On the contrary, guerrilla action made the occupation of Spain a constant burden and made the Spanish war unwinnable.[38]

As has already been intimated, however, this chorus of praise (which is, albeit for different reasons, replicated in both the French and the Spanish sources) does not rest on secure foundations. Too much stress has been placed, for example, on the activities of a small number of 'heroic' individuals who are in reality quite unrepresentative of the guerrilla movement as a whole, whilst the quite exceptional case of northern Navarre – probably the only region in the whole of Spain where the rural populace was reasonably satisfied with social and economic conditions – has over and over again been cited as if it were representative of the Spanish struggle as a whole. On top of that there has been a general failure to engage with the Spanish archives: many of the authors whom we have cited have not done so at all, whilst those of which this is not true have only done so in a partial and selective fashion, and the result has been that the more reflective amongst them have found themselves confronting a series of contradictions that they have had considerable difficulty in laying to rest. Such problems as desertion, resistance to conscription and overtly unpatriotic behaviour – an example is the refusal of many guerrilla bands to serve outside their home regions despite the fact that their services were needed elsewhere – are therefore explained in terms of such half-reasons as 'localism' rather than occasioning the fundamental rethinking that they actually require.[39] As for the even thornier issue of banditry this is generally elided or shrugged off. To quote Gabriel Lovett, for example, 'There were undoubtedly rogue guerrillas preying on their countrymen almost as much as on their enemy...Yet the bad had to be accepted with the good, because the positive accomplishments of the irregulars...overwhelmingly outweighed the negative aspects of the guerrilla war.'[40]

This, however, is not good enough. If all elements of *la guerrilla* are taken into account, all well and good. But, if the word 'guerrilla' is taken to mean an irregular combatant fighting outside the apparatus of the state (which is in fact the definition that the writers whom we have cited invariably adopt), the number of 'rogue guerrillas' becomes so large that the positive accomplishments of the irregulars are not so much outweighed as totally eclipsed. On too many occasions, meanwhile, such awkward matters are not raised at all: Lovett, for example, at all times simply takes the fact of a great people's crusade against Napoleon as read, and that despite the fact that he has worked in archives which are literally bursting at the seams with evidence of a picture that is in reality much less flattering. About the only excuse that one can come up with for all this is that the Spanish historiography is not much better. Thanks in part to the experience of the Franco régime, military history in Spain is regarded with even greater prejudice than it is in Britain with the result that the guerrilla struggle has not received the attention that it merits. Astonishingly enough, until almost the very moment that this work was going to press there was no monograph on the subject as a whole, and but one article, even this being very general and written from first principles rather than based on archival research.[41] In so far as the author is aware, meanwhile, only two pieces of postgraduate work have appeared on the subject since the 1960s (if not before), and of these both are regional studies, whilst only one has resulted in publication.[42] Beyond this one can only turn to the various academic studies that have appeared of the experiences of one province or another in the Peninsular War, but these never have the subject as a their main theme and are frequently deficient in what they do say (as an example here one might cite not one but two recent studies of Huelva that failed to make any use of the very extensive papers of the Spanish general who headed the Patriot cause in the area following the appearance of the French in 1810).[43] Such as it is then, the historiography is dominated by the work of amateur historians who lack the formation necessary to produce anything other than more or less hagiographic biographies of one or other of the main guerrilla commanders or, alternatively, regional or thematic monographs that are generally as confused in their organization as they are antiquarian in their approach.[44] About the best that can be said about it, indeed, is that at least the subject does *have* a historiography: to return to Portugal for a moment, not a single Lusitanian historian appears ever to have investigated the issue of 'people's war' at all.

All this, of course, makes for a rather depressing story. However, with regard to two areas of Europe in particular, there are signs both of greater interest and the emergence of a more critical approach. Of these, the first is Italy. Here, too, the historiography was originally not very good. Aside from one very brief contribution to an early meeting of the annual conference known as the Consortium on Revolutionary Europe, for example, there is no general introduction to the subject.[45] Whilst it might be thought that the obvious focus for historians interested in popular resistance is Calabria, the material that this region has generated has, on the whole, been rather disappointing. Thus, practically the only works that we have on the subject in English are those of Milton Finley, an American military historian whose writing is not only resolutely narrative, but seemingly bereft of any knowledge of the Italian sources.[46] Working primarily from the memoirs and correspondence of French officers who served in Calabria, he is at the same time all too prone to falling prey to generalizations that could have flowed smoothly from the pen of any of Napoleon's generals. For example:

> Underlying the revolt was the religious fanaticism of the area... One of the most effective guerrillas in the early stages of the war (Papasodero) was a priest. Anti-French uprisings in Strongoli, Nicastro and

Castrovillari were led by local clergy. It was the priests who exhorted...Amantea not to surrender even when no hope was left...The many monasteries of Calabria offered guerrillas bases from which food and supplies could be obtained.[47]

In fairness, Finley does stress the importance of factors other than ideology in the causation of the revolt. Amongst the other issues that he mentions, indeed, are poverty, local traditions of brigandage, French pillaging and long-standing social and economic unrest, but this serves only to promote fresh neo-Napoleonic generalizations. Thus; 'The Calabrian guerrillas much preferred the short-term goal of loot to any thought of long-term reform.'[48] For an example of the way forward we must therefore turn to the works of Finley's fellow American, Alexander Grab. A specialist on the Kingdom of Italy, Grab has over the years produced with a series of articles and conference papers in which he has dissected popular resistance in his region of specialization and presented us with an archivally-based picture of affairs that can be regarded as being so close to reality as makes no difference. Thus, what we see is not a nationalist or even religious phenomenon but rather the expression of concrete social and economic grievances combined with the survival of pre-Napoleonic patterns of rural crime (or, to put it another way, responses to poverty). Popular resistance, then, was primarily a social phenomenon rather than an ideological one, and, what is more, one that was not called forth by Napoleon but rather only exacerbated by him. That there was a political dimension is undeniable, but in the end the watchword is ambiguity. 'Brigandage', writes Grab, 'constituted a violent response by the poor to their increasing destitution. Moreover, brigandage was also the most extreme reform of resistance of the Italian countryside to the growing power of the Napoleonic state, its increasing intrusiveness and mounting pressure, particularly in the realms of taxation and conscription.'[49] And war of liberation there was none: guerrilla warfare as such was absent from the Kingdom of Italy, whilst the brigands were indiscriminate in their depredations, plundering all and sundry without regard for nationality, social class or political persuasion; as for the peasant risings of 1809, these were essentially timeless in their form, the fact being that, give or take a few Habsburg flags, they could just as easily have taken place in 1509, 1609 or 1709.[50]

What makes Grab's work all the more interesting is that it ties in very neatly with the work of the current author. A specialist in the Peninsular War throughout his career, the latter was naturally well aware of the tendency of French authors to seek to maximize the contribution of the guerrillas to Napoleon's defeat in the Iberian Peninsula, whilst at the same time attributing their actions to a combination of greed, ignorance, fanaticism and the machinations of the clergy. These arguments, however, he was inclined to discount as the fruit of Napoleonic propaganda. And, whilst working on the Wellington Papers in Southampton in 1985, he came across a remarkable document that is so important that it is worth quoting from it at some length. Thus:

> It is very difficult to know what to say about the guerrillas. That some of them have been of eminent use during the progress of the war cannot be denied. They obliged the French to fortify themselves in every village and town in the country; they harassed the parties who were spread through the provinces either to subsist themselves or to procure supplies for the enemy's magazines; they murdered all stragglers and sometimes intercepted convoys of provisions and stores; they rendered the communications of the enemy very difficult and hazardous, and often cut them off for weeks together; and, finally, they assisted in keeping alive the spirit of resistance against the invaders. On the other hand, they doubled the calamities inflicted by the French. The inhabitants were compelled to feed the enemy with one hand and the guerrillas with the other. They plundered many towns with as little mercy as the French; and where the French preceded them they generally carried off all which the French left. Many of them under the pretence of patriotism and of serving against the enemy became regular freebooters and subsisted on the pillage of the country. It will probably become necessary one of these days to establish a new Santa Hermandad to clear Spain of these bands of robbers. They prevented the recruiting of the regular armies, for every Spanish peasant would naturally prefer rioting and plunder and living in free quarters with the guerrillas to being drilled and starved in the regular army. While some of them kept alive the spirit of resistance and the feeling of hatred against the French, others compelled the inhabitants to look to the French for protection, for the inhabitants would at length prefer the systematized pillage and regulated contributions of the enemy to the wasteful, capricious, uncertain and merciless plundering of their own countrymen. On the whole, therefore, it may be said that that the guerrillas did as much mischief to the country as they did to the French, but inasmuch as they certainly did considerable damage to the enemy, they were on the whole useful to the common cause.[51]

At the time that he first read these words, the current author was working on a study of Anglo-Spanish relations in the Peninsular War. Here, though, seemed to lie the basis of a whole new field of research, and over the years that followed a series of articles and conference papers were written that sought to examine the contradictions outlined in this document in the light of the ever-growing quantity of archival material that seemed to confirm the need for a revisionist approach.[52] Finally, in 2004 under the imprint of Yale University Press, there appeared *Fighting Napoleon: Guerrillas, Bandits and Adventurers in Spain, 1808–1814*, this being a full-scale monograph in which the problem is discussed at length.

The fruit of a substantial programme of archival research funded by the University of Liverpool and the Leverhulme Trust (whose generosity is in both cases gratefully acknowledged), this work poses the starkest of challenges to traditional views of popular resistance. Thus, what we see is a picture that is far removed from the normal image of a great 'people's crusade'. Indeed, almost every point of the usual canon is overthrown. The uprising of 1808, then, is seen not as an attack on the French invaders but rather an explosion of pent up social unrest that had strong echoes of the *grand peur* of 1789. Moving on, it is demonstrated that there was little popular interest in the war against Napoleon, and that the usual response to the conscription that was inevitably imposed once voluntary enlistment fell off, as it very quickly did, was draft evasion, riot and desertion. With desertion, however, came an increase in banditry and this was stimulated still further by the collapse in the economic life of the country brought about by the outbreak of war. Very soon, then, swarms of armed men were stalking the countryside of both the area occupied by the French and that which remained in the hands of their opponents – in the parlance of the day the Patriots – whilst they everywhere commingled with the bandits that had been so marked a feature of Spanish life for hundreds of years and were now once again in the ascendant on account of the economic misery that had gripped Spain in the reign of Carlos IV (1788–1808). From this milieu there emerged a variety of gangs – the original *partidas* – and these preyed on all and sundry: French, British, Portuguese and Spaniards; Patriots and *afrancesados*; soldiers and civilians; all suffered alike. Whilst continuing on occasion to kill the odd French courier, pounce on the odd French convoy, and sell the odd packet of dispatches to the Allied authorities, not to mention to assume the guise of *guerrilleros* when it suited them, many of these bands remained mere bandits: once the tide of French conquest receded in 1812–1813 leaders such as the Castillian *cabecillas*, Príncipe and Saornil, were revealed in all their criminality, for, rather than following up the retreating enemy they battened upon the civilian population and lived, as Sydenham put it, 'at free quarters'. From amongst these men, however, there emerged a number of more notable figures. Of relatively humble background, at heart they were mere adventurers – prospective bandits even – but they also possessed sufficient vision and common sense to realize that their survival and future prosperity depended on raising themselves above the common herd. In many cases genuinely exceptional individuals, they specifically associated themselves with the Patriot cause and struggled hard to turn their motley followers into disciplined and effective fighting forces. Acquiring military ranks, by the end of the war a number of them – the most prominent were Juan Martín (i.e. El Empecinado) and Francisco Espoz y Mina – were generals in the regular army, whilst their *partidas* had become brigades and divisions. From 1808 onwards, these men dedicated themselves to fighting the French, and in this they were joined by a large number of other *cabecillas* who had secured commissions from the civilian authorities, found themselves at the head of a *partida* by sheer accident, or been asked to take charge of specific guerrilla bands. Though they too contained their share of unscrupulous adventurers who aimed only at cutting a dash, feathering their own nests and ingratiating themselves with the authorities, this latter group were clearly of greater number and on the whole of greater repute, if at the same time generally of lesser calibre and enterprise: amongst their number were to be found students, government officials, army officers, ecclesiastics, and wealthy landowners, merchants and other proprietors. As such they had a stake in the system that provided them with a motive to fight the French that equalled the enlightened self-interest of self-made leaders such as El Empecinado – in some instances they may even genuinely deserve the term 'patriot' – whilst their exploits were on occasion no less impressive. But leaders are one thing, and rank and file quite another. Only in the very few areas of Spain where economic and conditions were such as to promote a genuine sense of contentment and well-being – the most obvious are the Basque provinces and northern Navarre – was *la guerrilla* genuinely a popular phenomenon in which men flocked to join the *partidas* out of a specific desire to fight the invaders. Whilst isolated cases can be found in the archives of men who came forward, or at least so they said, out of patriotism or a desire for revenge, beyond these areas such volunteers as the bands received seem to have come in as a result of desperation – one key to success was invariably the ability to pay a steady wage – of a desire to escape service in the regular army, or because for one reason or another they had no option: a favourite target of Espoz y Mina, for example, were the long columns of Spanish prisoners that regularly made their way from Madrid to the French frontier, whilst, as we have seen, many bands became a refuge for men who had had enough of fighting Napoleon's wars and could find no other means of survival (likewise bandits who found themselves in a tight spot and needed to find some way of escaping the noose). Nor is this surprising: in both the Tyrol and Calabria fears of conscription to the Bavarian and Neapolitan armies and, by extension, of being marched away to die in Napoleon's wars, played a major role in producing men for the fight, but in Spain King Joseph did not introduce compulsory military service. Meanwhile, an unknown number of the rank and file were men who were to all intents and purposes conscripts: in a number of cases, ploughboys and shepherds and the like seem literally to have been plucked from the fields, whilst in others guerrilla bands simply descended on one *pueblo* or another and rounded up all the men of military age at the point of a gun. Facing the point of a gun, too, were the many bandits and enemy prisoners who were given the choice of enlistment or execution. Still another form of compulsion was that based on economic dependence: where men of substance formed *partidas*, their first recruits seem often to have come from the ranks of their servants, journeymen, tenants or day labourers. Also made use of was deception: some men were brought in by simple trickery and others by false rumours that the French were indeed about to bring in conscription. Far from being a genuinely popular movement enthused by the determination to fight for God, king and fatherland, the guerrillas appear as a much more conventional phenomenon: men were not inspired to fight by the new force of patriotism, but rather driven to fight by the old ones of poverty, hunger, despair and the voice of authority.

From this motley crew were in some cases fashioned powerful fighting forces that were able to cause the French serious problems – one again thinks here of the bands of El Empecinado and Espoz y Mina, although there were other instances, such as men led in Cantabria and Asturias by Juan Díaz Porlier and those commanded in Soria by José Joaquín Durán. But even the most disciplined and militarized of the guerrillas could never free themselves of the fact that at root they were not a patriotic phenomenon. For reasons that ranged from a genuine sense of patriotism through an association with systems of privilege threatened by the French invasion to an opportunistic determination to make the most of a once-in-a-lifetime opportunity, many of their commanders were sincerely committed to the struggle against the French. However, for the rank and file it was a different matter. In so far as can be ascertained, few of the men who actually made up the *partidas* had any conscious interest in the struggle and it is clear that they deeply resented attempts to transform them into regular troops, whilst at the same time often being quite capable of either slipping off to become bandits on their own account or at the very least seizing upon such opportunities as they could to engage in looting and a variety of other excesses. Given the fact that, for all that they still killed many Frenchmen and their collaborators, large numbers of bands never rose above the level of banditry, it is in consequence clear that the French of the term 'brigands' for their irregular opponents is not so very inappropriate.

The task facing the historical community is therefore very clear. What is sauce for the Italian or Iberian goose is in all probability equally sauce for the Tyrolean gander, from which it follows that *anno neun* almost certainly needs to be revisited in the same manner (as, for that matter, Calabria). But beyond that stands a wider issue. In brief, we have a subject of great complexity that, for all its undoubted importance, has never been adequately studied in the context of the empire as a whole. If this is the case, meanwhile, it is in part because studies of the same subject on a national level have for the most part been inadequate. What is required therefore is more scholars who are prepared to set aside foolish prejudices, take the issue of popular resistance seriously and immerse themselves in the archives, both national and local, of Portugal, Spain, Italy, Germany and Austria. That said, however, the challenge is a difficult one. As the present author knows to his cost, a whole series of challenges await such historians. Not the least of these is the question of definition – who exactly are we referring to when we use the term 'guerrillas'? – but there are also serious problems of inter-pretation, whilst the sources are both extremely diffuse and extremely fragmentary. In the end what has emerged, at least in the case of the author's own work, is an artificial construct – a mosaic in which thousands of pieces of information have been pieced together to paint a picture of popular resistance that is highly revisionist. Inevitably, such a picture cannot but be open to challenge, but in this respect its creator would say three things. Thus, in the first place, it ties in very well with such serious research as has been done on popular resistance in other parts of Europe; in the second, it takes much better account of the numerous problems that are thrown up by the Spanish struggle than does the traditional version of events; and, in the third, it is no more artificial than the idea that the populace was motivated chiefly by issues of ideology.

And, finally, whatever may be said about the Esdaile construct, so to speak, it is quite clear that without more such research projects it will never be possible to arrive at an adequate typology of popular resistance in Napoleonic Europe as a whole.

Notes

1. Napoleon to Joseph Bonaparte, 2 March 1806, *Correspondance de Napoléon I publiée par Ordre de l'Empereur Napoléon III* (Paris, 1858–69), XII, p. 121.
2. M. Broers, *Europe under Napoleon, 1799–1815* (London, 1996), p. 101.
3. *Ibid.*
4. A full order of battle for Wellington's army in the summer of 1813 may be found in C. Oman, *A History of the Peninsular War* (Oxford, 1902–30), VI, pp. 750–3 (for the purposes of comparison, the full totals, excluding Portuguese, were eighteen regiments of cavalry, and fifty six battalions of infantry). For the presence of French deserters with the Spanish guerrillas, cf. C.J. Esdaile, *Fighting Napoleon: Guerrillas, Bandits and Adventurers in the Peninsular War, 1808–14* (London, 2004), pp. 114–17.
5. G. Rudé, *Revolutionary Europe, 1783–1815* (London, 1964), p. 114.
6. G. Best, *War and Society in Revolutionary Europe, 1770–1870* (London, 1982), p. 168.
7. J. Black, *Western Warfare, 1775–1882* (London, 2001), p. 55.
8. H. Fisher, *Napoleon* (London, 1912), p. 177.
9. For the proceedings of this conference, cf. M. Rowe (ed.), *Collaboration and Resistance in Napoleonic Europe: State-Formation in an Age of Upheaval* (London, 2003).
10. Cf. Broers, *Europe under Napoleon*, pp. 101–25, 169–73, 210–11.
11. S. Woolf, *Napoleon's Integration of Europe* (London, 1991), pp. 231–2.
12. Cf. *ibid.*, pp. 230–6 *passim*.
13. Cf. C.J. Esdaile, *The Wars of Napoleon* (London, 1995), pp. 140–1. For a more developed version of the passage from which this quote is taken, cf. C.J. Esdaile, 'Popular resistance to the Napoleonic empire', in P. Dwyer (ed.), *Napoleon and Europe* (London, 2001), pp. 136–52.
14. C. Barnett, *Bonaparte* (London, 1978), p. 145.
15. C. Best, *War and Society in Revolutionary Europe, 1770–1870* (London, 1982) p. 180.
16. The two works concerned are F.G. Eyck, *Loyal Rebels: Andreas Hofer and the Tyrolean Uprising of 1809* (New York, 1986), and L. Harford, 'Napoleon and the subjugation of the Tyrol', *Consortium on Revolutionary Proceedings*, XX (1980), pp. 704–11.
17. Eyck, *Loyal Rebels*, p. xi.
18. For an example, cf. c. Oman, *Peninsular War*, II (Oxford, 1902–1930) pp. 229–30.
19. D. Gates, *The Spanish Ulcer: a History of the Peninsular War* (London, 1986), pp. 139, 142.
20. J. Read, *War in the Peninsula* (London, 1977), p. 160.
21. M.S. Foy, *History of the War in the Peninsula under Napoleon* (London, 1827), pp. 443–5.
22. A. Miot de Melito. *Mémoires du Comte Miot de Melito, Ancien Ministre, Ambassadeur, Conseilleur dé tat et Membre d'Institut* (Paris, 1858), III, p. 568.

23. The attitude of French memoirs to the guerrillas is discussed in R. Farias, *Memorias de la Guerra de la Independencia Escritas por Soldados Franceses* (Madrid, 1919), pp. 317–20, and J.R. Aymes, 'La guerrilla en la literature testimonial francesa', in J.A. Armillas (ed.), *La Guerra de la Independencia: Estudios* (Zaragoza, 2001), pp. 23–4.

24. S. Blaze, *Mémoires d'un Apothécaire sur la Guerre d'Espagne pendant les Années 1808 à 1814* (Paris, 1828), I, pp. 69–70.

25. A.J.M. de Rocca, *Memoirs of the War of the French in Spain* (London, 1815), p. 21.

26. H. von Brandt, *The Two Minas and the Spanish Guerrillas* (London, 1825), p. 54; A. Bigarré, *Mémoires du Général Bigarré, Aide de Camp du Roi Joseph, 1775–1813* (Paris, 1903), p. 277.

27. A.L.A. Fée, *Souvenirs de la Guerre d'Espagne, dite de l'Independence* (Paris, 1856), p. 18.

28. Bigarré, *Mémoires*, p. 278.

29. Cf. G. Chaliand, *The Art of War in World History: from Antiquity to the Present Day* (Berkeley, California, 1994), p. 664.

30. For an analysis of the role played by regular soldiers in the 'little war', meanwhile, readers are referred to C.J. Esdaile, *Fighting Napoleon: Guerrillas, Bandits and Adventurers in Spain, 1808–14* (Yale University Press, 2004), pp. 27–60.

31. Oman, *Peninsular War*, III, pp. 488–92.

32. E. Longford, *Wellington: the Years of the Sword* (London, 1969), pp. 247–8.

33. R. Humble, *Wellington's Peninsular Marshals* (London, 1974), p. 70.

34. D. Chandler, 'Wellington at war: regular and irregular warfare', *International History Review*, XI, no. 1 (February, 1989), p. 9

35. *Times Literary Supplement*, 4 July 1986, p. 742.

36. G. Lovett, *Napoleon and the Birth of Modern Spain* (New York, 1965), II, pp. 665–7.

37. D. Alexander, *Rod of Iron: French Counter-Insurgency Policy in Aragón during the Peninsular War* (Wilmington, Delaware, 1985) pp. 239–41.

38. J. Tone, *The Fatal Knot: the Guerrilla War in Navarre and the Defeat of Napoleon* (Chapel Hill, North Carolina, 1994), p. 5.

39. E.g. J. Tone, 'The Peninsular War', in Dwyer, *Napoleon and Europe*, pp. 238–9.

40. Lovett, *Napoleon and the Birth of Modern Spain*, I, p. 679.

41. For the article, cf. M. Artola, 'La guerra de guerrillas', *Revista de Occidente*, X (1964), pp. 12–43. The monograph is Antonio Moliner Prada, *La Guerrilla en la Guerra de la Independencia* (Barcelona, 2004). This offers some fresh information, particularly on Catalonia, but does not develop its subject sufficiently.

42. The first of these studies is the unpublished Universidad Complutense de Madrid *tesina* of Antonio Carrasco Alvarez entitled 'La naturaleza de la guerra de guerrillas en Espana (1808–1814)', and the second the Universidad de Valladolid doctoral dissertation of Jorge Sánchez Fernández on *la guerrilla* in the area of Old Castile. Whilst not yet published in full, this has resulted in two useful studies, viz. *La Guerrilla Vallesoletana, 1808–1814* (Valladolid, 1997), and *Nos Invaden! Guerrilla y Represión en Valladolid durante la Guerra de la Independencia Española* (Valladolid, 2000).

43. For these two works, cf. M.A. Pena, *El Tiempo de los Franceses; la Guerra de la Independencia en el Suroeste Español* (Huelva, 2000), and D. González Cruz, *De la Revolución Francesa a la Guerra de la Independencia: Huelva a Fines de la Edad*

Moderna (Huelva, 2002). The general in question is Francisco Copons, whilst his papers – a veritable mine of information on the guerrillas – are held in the Real Academia de Historia in Madrid.

44. For some examples of the former, cf. R.G. de Barthèlemy, *El Marquesito: Juan Diáz Porlier, General que fue de los ejércitos nacionales, 1788–1815* (Santiago de Compostela, 1995), J. M Codón, *Biografía y Crónica del Cura Merino* (Burgos, 1968) and M. Ortuño, *Xavier* [*sic*] *Mina; Guerrillero, Liberal, Insurgente* (Pamplona, 2000). As for the latter, cf. R. Guirao, *Guerrilleros y Patriotas en el Alto Aragón, 1808–1814* (Huesca, 2000), and P. Pascual, *Curas y Frailes Guerrilleros en la Guerrade la Independencia* (Zaragoza, 2000).

45. For the paper concerned, cf. D. Koening, 'Banditry in Napoleonic Italy', *Consortium on Revolutionary Europe Proceedings*, V, (1975), pp. 72–9.

46. His most important contribution to the literature is M. Finley, *The Most Monstrous of Wars: the Napoleonic Guerrilla War in Southern Italy, 1806–1811* (Colombia, South Carolina, 1994).

47. *Ibid.*, pp. 134–5.

48. *Ibid.*, p. 137.

49. A. Grab, 'State power, brigandage and rural resistance in Napoleonic Italy', *European History Quarterly*, XXV, no. 1 (January, 1995), p. 40.

50. In addition to the above article, readers are also directed to A. Grab, 'Army, state and society: conscription and desertion in Napoleonic Italy, 1802–1814', *Journal of Modern History*, LXVII (March, 1995), pp. 25–54, and A. Grab, 'Popular risings in Napoleonic Italy', *Consortium on Revolutionary Europe Proceedings*, XX (1990), pp. 112–19.

51. T. Sydenham to H. Wellesley, 10 October 1812, University of Southampton, Wellington Papers, WP.1/361.

52. The most representative of these articles are C.J. Esdaile, 'Heroes or villains? The Spanish guerrillas and the Peninsular War, 1808–14', *History Today*, XXXVII, no. 4 (April, 1988), pp. 29–35; C.J. Esdaile, 'The problem of the Spanish guerrillas', in A. Berkeley (ed.), *New Lights on the Peninsular War* (Lisbon, 1991), pp. 191–200; C.J. Esdaile, '"Heroes or villains" revisited: further thoughts on the Spanish guerrillas', in E. Martínez Ruiz (ed.), *II semanario Internacional sobre la Guerra de la Independencia* (Madrid, 1996), pp. 191–210; and C.J. Esdaile, 'La guerrilla española, 1808–14: el gran malentendido de la Guerra de la Independencia', *Trienio*, no. 42 (November, 2003), pp. 55–76.

Index

Aachen 81
alarmas 7
Alberghini, Giovanni Battista 59–64
Alexander, Donald 213
Alexander I 19, 20, 167, 188, 194, 195
  army of 19, 20, 188
Alexander II, army of 19
almogovares 100
Alps, brigands in 29, 30, 33
Alvanés, Pedro Antonio 104
American wars and guerillas 138
Andalucía 11, 123
Aragón 136, 213
aristocrats and Bonapartism 79–80
  see also elites
Arndt, Ernst Moritz 16, 86, 170, 172
  catechisms 167, 168–9, 173, 174, 176, 177
Arquata Scrivia 59
Arzú 95
Astorga, Isidro 117
Asturias, Junta de 147, 148
atrocities *see* violence
Augereau, General 54, 55
Austria 202
  pillage by troops from 60
  political catechisms 169, 170
  War of Succession 138
Aymes, Jean-René 163, 165, 175

Babkin, V.I. 190
Baget, Joan 93, 95
Bagration, General 183, 185
Bailen, battle of 138, 140, 211–12
Balaguer, Teresa 93
Balkans 105
bande de Salembier 29
banditry 214
  deserters and 103–4, 218
  guerrillas as bandits 218–19, 221
  as heroic 26–7
  historically 26–7
  insurrection as 8–9, 22
  redistributing wealth 26

Rhineland 4
  see also brigandage
barbets 6, 7, 30, 31, 33
  operations against 47–8
Barcelona 95
  deserters from 102
Barnett, Corelli 206
Barres, M. 208
Barriolucio, Marqués de 150
Barrios, P. 100
Basa, Juan 104
Basque provinces, guerrillas 6, 219
Bavarian army in Tyrol 6
Becker, Nikolaus 70
Belcredi, Marchese 55, 56, 57, 58
Belgian brigands 37
Bellsolell, Antoni 102
Bennigsen, General L.L. 18
Bertran, Josep 99
Best, Geoffrey 204, 206, 207
Bestuzhev, Aleksandr 195
Bigarré, A. 210
billeting 29
  Rhineland 72, 73
Black, Jeremy 204
Blake, General Joaquín 99
Blanning, Tim 4, 79
Blaze, S. 209
Boadas, José 101
Boissé 41
Bologna 59
Bonaparte, Joseph 13, 201, 203, 208, 210
  anti-bandit tribunals 12
Bonaparte, Louis 203
Bonaparte, Napoleon 50, 208, 211, 215, 218
  on *barbets* 48
  and civil/military relations 76–80
  and collaboration 78
  Consulate 76–7
  cost of Spanish war 213
  customs court 83
  and Enlightenment propaganda 81–2
  ideological flexibility 79–80
  in Italy 7, 46–8

225